DisAppearing

DisAppearing

Encounters in Disability Studies

Edited by Tanya Titchkosky, Elaine Cagulada,
and Madeleine DeWelles, with Efrat Gold

CANADIAN
SCHOLARS

Toronto | Vancouver

DisAppearing: Encounters in Disability Studies
Edited by Tanya Titchkosky, Elaine Cagulada, Madeleine DeWelles with Efrat Gold

First published in 2022 by
Canadian Scholars, an imprint of CSP Books Inc.
425 Adelaide Street West, Suite 200
Toronto, Ontario
M5V 3C1

www.canadianscholars.ca

Library and Archives Canada Cataloguing in Publication

Title: DisAppearing : encounters in disability studies / edited by Tanya Titchkosky, Elaine
    Cagulada, and Madeleine DeWelles, with Efrat Gold.
Other titles: DisAppearing (2022)
Names: Titchkosky, Tanya, 1966- editor. | Cagulada, Elaine, editor. | DeWelles, Madeleine, editor. |
    Gold, Efrat, author.
Description: Includes bibliographical references and index.
Identifiers: Canadiana (print) 20220204527 | Canadiana (ebook) 20220204578 |
    ISBN 9781773383163(softcover) | ISBN 9781773383170 (PDF) |
    ISBN 9781773383187 (EPUB)
Subjects: LCSH: Disability studies. | LCSH: People with disabilities—Social conditions. |
    LCSH: Sociology of disability. | LCGFT: Textbooks.
Classification: LCC HV1568.2 .D57 2022 | DDC 305.9/08—dc23

Page layout: S4Carlisle Publishing Services
Cover design: Em Dash
Cover art: "Fleeting thoughts," Yvon Jolivet, 2019

21   22   23   24   25   5   4   3   2   1

Printed and bound in Ontario, Canada

Canadä

For those sparks of imagination that realize no lesser humans,
no disappeared, no others beneath thought

Contents

Alternative Thematic Table of Contents

- Can assist teachers of disability studies in engaging with this book through an alternative set of themes
- Can support student research by pointing toward relevant chapters
- Can help with undergraduate and college syllabus design

ENCOUNTERS IN

… ACCESSIBILITY AND BARRIERS

... EDUCATION K–12 (*SEE ALSO* UNIVERSITY)

... EVERYDAY LIFE

... MEDICINE

... MENTAL HEALTH/PSY COMPLEX

... POLICING/LAW/SOCIAL CONTROL

... YOUTH

Foreword

Rod Michalko

"What does it matter? What's your problem?"

He was surprised at the questions and even more surprised by the vehemence with which they were asked. At first, he thought that the guy might be putting on a show, a kind of tough love, but the guy seemed angry, really angry.

"Look," the guy continued, vehemence still flaming his words, "I don't have any problems with it. You're going to have to move on. It just doesn't matter."

He sat there trying to absorb the guy's words; the guy—fifteen minutes into it and he already forgot his name; right, he remembered—Jonathan, that's his name. "Jonathan," he began tentatively, "You're right, I know; I have to get beyond this. I know you say it doesn't matter and it's not a problem, but, I don't know, it seems huge to me, a real problem; it really matters."

"That's your problem, Rock."

Jonathan didn't forget my name, he thought. Then again, I wasn't yelling at him and I wasn't throwing words at him that could take an eye out, not that *that* would matter to him.

"You're letting it matter; that's your problem. You have to realize it doesn't make a difference. You have to take that step, otherwise you're going nowhere."

Rock wondered where they'd found this guy. They said Jonathan, a lawyer no less, was someone he should talk to and who could really help him. "He's quite inspirational," Rock remembered them saying, "He's been there, so he can help you get on the right track."

Rock didn't think that the track Jonathan was laying down for him was even possible let alone right. How is it not supposed to matter? His entire life was turned upside down and had stayed that way ever since … ever since that day. It took a little longer than a day, Rock knew, but it seemed quick and when they told him it was permanent—well, that was the day that he had in his mind, the day all this shit started, the shit that this goofy lawyer, Jonathan, was saying did not matter.

"Nearly every culture views disability as a problem in need of a solution."

Mitchell, David T., and Sharon L. Snyder. *Narrative Prosthesis: Disability and the Dependencies of Discourse*. Ann Arbor, MI: University of Michigan Press, 2000, p. 47.

"That's what I am saying; that's your problem. You think it's huge and it really matters, but it doesn't. You think I got to be a lawyer by thinking this stuff matters? You can't do anything if you think that way. It doesn't matter. It just happened; just happened to you; that's it; get over it."

Rock wondered what planet this guy was from. Just happened. It just happened. Of course, it just happened. Rock knew that, and he also knew it happened to him.

Rock managed to find his coffee cup. He had taken his hand off it as he was trying to duck all those sharp words flying at him from across the table. He reminded himself never to do that again—never take his hand off a coffee cup or anything else he was drinking.

Doesn't matter. Really? Who wants to be a lawyer anyway?

"Thing is, Jonathan, I think this thing changed me. I don't think I am the same anymore. There is something different now."

"There you go again," Jonathan said, adding disgust to the vehement shape of his words. "You've changed. You're different. That's bullshit, Rock. You're exactly the same guy you always were. This thing doesn't change you; it doesn't change anybody. It's just something that happened to you. That's it. It just doesn't matter. You're the same guy."

The same guy. That's bullshit, Rock thought. He didn't even recognize the guy, the guy he was, before this thing happened. He knew that guy was in him somewhere, but either he changed so much he couldn't recognize him anymore or—he was dead. More and more, Rock thought this; that guy, that guy before … is dead.

"You're probably right, Jonathan, but the thing is nothing feels the same. And, the other thing is I get mixed up a lot."

"Mixed up? About what?"

"This is going to sound weird. Sometimes, I think it matters, really matters— but sometimes I think it's something else too."

"Something else? Like what?"

"I still think it's a big problem; I am not saying it isn't. But, every once in a while, I feel … I feel that there is something more to it than that. Somehow, I feel that it matters to me; I mean, big time. It seems … it seems that it is not something that just happened. I know it happened, but it seems somehow different, like it matters more than that."

"Well," Jonathan spoke slowly this time, with something that seemed like pity in his words. "There is nothing I can do, nothing anybody can do to help you until you stop thinking like that. It just happened. You're a perfectly normal guy, just like you were before it happened."

Normal! That rocked him. Normal! There was no way on earth that he felt normal. How was it possible to even think that, let alone feel that? There was absolutely nothing normal about this thing.

And then, it hit him.

The guy actually thinks *he's* normal. Jonathan thinks he's normal; he really does.

"I sure don't feel normal," Rock said, trying his best to deflect the pity in Jonathan's words.

"It doesn't matter if you feel it or not. You're just a normal guy, just like anyone else."

"Really?" Rock said.

"Yes, really. It's just a nuisance; blindness is just a nuisance. You can do everything sighted people do, everything you used to do. The only thing is that you do them in a different way, that's the *only difference*. You're just as normal as everyone else. Forget about your blindness. It doesn't matter. You're normal; act like it."

Rock heard the words, but he didn't know what they were saying. Jonathan couldn't possibly believe he was normal; could he? What happened to the fact that he was blind? Did he really forget it? There was something disingenuous about Jonathan's words. Blindness did matter; it had to.

Rock's world was different now and not just his world, but *the* world. It was different too. There was something to this blindness.

Rock shut his eyes tightly. It didn't go away. His blindness stayed. It was right there, in front of him, in him. He had to do something with it, he knew that.

"I'll see what I can do," Rock said.

A version of this interaction did happen. It happened many years ago, and yet I remember it as though it were yesterday. Let me try to make sense of this interaction within the scope of this collection.

Disability matters and so, too, do matters of disability, matters such as medicine, rehabilitation, education (special and otherwise), and there is the matter of normalcy, something that matters to everything including disability. There are other matters as well, matters such as fear, shame, bewilderment, curiosity, and disgust. These matters surround disability, often veiling it, although disability also slips beneath the veil of fear, shame, and bewilderment. These matters, often understood as conceptions of disability, both define it and conceal the meaning of disability. And there are other matters of disability that attempt, sometimes successfully and sometimes not, to weave themselves into this veil, matters such as intrigue, pride, distinction, desire, and, at times, even love. As these matters attempt to weave themselves into the fabric that is disability, they reinforce the already veiled matter of disability. Yet another matter of disability is disability studies. Rather than attempting to weave itself into the veiled matter of disability, disability studies attempts to cut through this veil and to find a way into disability itself.

"It would appear that when Deaf people refuse to be identified as disabled, it is in response to the same medical model that critical disability activists and researchers also reject. And when Deaf people do embrace this label, it is not because they believe they have a lack or (hearing) loss, but because of the rich alliances they see with activist movements fighting for the rights of people with disability and to remove barriers to their social recognition and participation. Debates between disability studies/communities and their Deaf counterparts are complicated."

Leduc, Véro. "'It Fell on Deaf Ears': Deafhood through the Graphic Signed Novel as a Form of Activism." In *Mobilizing Metaphor: Art, Culture, and Disability Activism in Canada*, edited by Christine Kelly and Michael Orsini. Vancouver, BC: University of British Columbia Press, 2016, p. 126.

All of these matters have their ways, some similar to one another and some entirely different, of perceiving disability, of feeling it, and of understanding and experiencing (living) it. What matters most of all is that disability matters. This is what brings disability into appearance; this is what materializes it; this is what attributes meaning to disability, for, as Judith Butler (1993) says, "'to matter' means at once 'to materialize' and 'to mean'" (p. 32). How this materialization and appearance of disability is fashioned will influence the way disability is acted upon, treated, and experienced. In fashioning the appearance of disability, matters that do not matter to this fashioning are discarded. In so doing, this fashioning makes some matters of disability irrelevant and thus makes them disappear. Through a medical fashioning of the appearance of disability, for example, matters such as disability pride are disappeared. Ironically, the matters that are disappeared are merely forced under the cover of conventional conceptions of disability such as the one held by medicine.

This collection, *DisAppearing: Encounters in Disability Studies*, engages these matters of disability and the ways they create disability, fashion it, and materialize it into an appearance. *DisAppearing* is especially interested in revealing at least a little of the intrigue of how essential aspects of disability are concealed within its appearance by the creation process itself. This is no easy matter. Easy or not, though, each chapter in this volume begins with the unshakeable commitment to the premise that the disappearance of disability and the human acts of disappearing it must be revealed, even if only for a moment, if alternative ways of perceiving, understanding, and experiencing disability are to be made possible. Whether we are disabled or not, disability matters and the matters of disability appear and disappear right in front of us and, like so much of human life, go unnoticed. This collection attempts to bring such disability matters to attention and thus into appearance, and this is a crucial aspect of the matter of disability studies.

Disability studies not only matters to disability but is also one of the ways that disability is created, made to appear, and thus also one of the ways disability is disappeared. How disability is disappeared in the creation of its appearance is a phenomenon rarely noticed and almost never addressed. One thing that is recognized in disability studies, regardless of its particular form, is that disabled people, as Henri-Jacques Stiker (1999) implies, are "always other than what society made us and believes us to be" (p. 51). Disability studies may be read as a commitment to revealing this "more." The more of disability is not restricted to alternative versions of it; it also includes the more that society makes *itself* to be. Disability studies suggests that the more disability can be, the more society can be, and this is the radical gift of disability studies. Whether it presents us with this gift or even recognizes it is another matter altogether.

"Disability is a situation, caused by social conditions, which requires for its elimination, (a) that no one aspect such as incomes, mobility or institutions is treated in isolation, (b) that disabled people should, with the advice and help of others, assume control over their own lives, and (c) that professionals, experts and others who seek to help must be committed to promoting such control by disabled people....

"In our view, it is society which disables physically impaired people. Disability is something imposed on top of our impairments, by the way we are unnecessarily isolated and excluded from full participation in society. Disabled people are therefore an oppressed group in society."

Priestley, Mark, Vic Finkelstein, and Ken Davis. "Fundamental Principles of Disability." Disability Studies, Leeds. 1997. Accessed Jan. 15, 2022. https://disability-studies.leeds.ac.uk/wp-content/uploads/sites/40/library/UPIAS-fundamental-principles.pdf

Disability studies, like all matters of disability, creates disability in its own image. This disability imaginary—what it is, what it ought to be, its parameters, et cetera—creates the materiality, the matter, as background upon which the figure of disability appears. This human act of creativity and its resulting creation go largely unnoticed by those involved in these acts. Nonetheless, these imaginaries act to produce the appearance of their creativity and creation as though "natural." The naturalness of this background is achieved through disappearing the human activity that socially created it, thus preparing it for the appearance and materialization of all human life, including the life of disability. It is the taken-for-granted background of "normalcy" that provides for the appearance of disability in whatever form it takes, including disability studies. It fashions a version of disability that "fits" its understanding of the materiality of human life, a life that acts as background for the fashioned appearance of the figure of disability. In doing so, disability studies disappears all other imaginaries of disability not imagined through the parameters and perceptions of its borders.

What I have been metaphorically depicting as disability imaginaries, imagined territories, borders, and the like, are often depicted by invoking the metaphor of the "model." As there are many disability imaginaries, there are many models of disability; the social model springs immediately to mind, but there is, too, the charity model, the medical model, the tragedy model, the cultural model, the relational model, the affirmative model, and, I am sure, many others. The proliferation of disability imaginaries or models is restricted only by how we, all of us, understand disability, experience it, and are touched by it. The imagination as it is lived in and through culture is the richest and most fertile ground in which to nurture and upon which to create a multi-experiential life of disability.

The social creation of each disability imaginary and of each disability model necessarily involves the social act of disappearing disability. The appearance of disability simultaneously disappears imaginaries and/or models of disability that fundamentally depart from that appearance. The social model, for example, disappears the tragedy model of disability. How we come to understand disability and experience it, how we come to act upon it and think of it, how we come to feel it and be touched by it is grounded and shaped in how we imagine its appearance and in how we disappear disability as an implicit method for socially transforming the imaginary into the real. *DisAppearing: Encounters in*

Disability Studies immerses itself in the beauty and in the power of such social creation.

Rod Michalko
Toronto, 2021

REFERENCES

Butler, J. (1993). *Bodies that matter: On the discursive limits of "sex."* Routledge.

Stiker, H.-J. (1999). *A history of disability.* University of Michigan Press.

Introduction

Tanya Titchkosky, Elaine Cagulada, and Madeleine DeWelles

Disability is, of course, more than merely a thing gone wrong with one's body or mind or senses or emotions. As a complex blend of human experience, *disability* is woven into aspects of our identity, of how we know, and of the actions we take. Disability is infused within an entire universe of sentiments, expressed through experiences ranging from extreme difficulty to absolutely wondrous elation, from mundane tasks done differently to adventurous travels into the heart of struggles. Disability is also found within potent societal ideologies concerning the human spirit: overcoming, hard work, bad luck, super-senses, agile fortitude, and stick-to-it resolve. All this, and more, is disability. And yet, the complex universe of disability often disappears from view.

Hidden by the readily available sense that disability is simply an unwanted troubling problem in need of some sort of solution, other more complex and nuanced meanings of disability disappear from our lives. What is disability made to be, such that its complexity is often disappeared? For the complexity of disability to disappear, more dominant and expected versions of disability must appear. Appearing as calamity, loss, danger, and dysfunction, the cultural appearance of disability in everyday life is often negative. A central concern of ours is how disability is made to appear and disappear through interpretations of our bodies, minds, senses, and emotions reflective of the worlds from which they spring and into which disability dis/appears. Throughout this book, we use dis/appears not only because most screen readers will annunciate the slash but also because we want to foreground the important tensions between how we notice disability and how we do not.

This collection is dedicated to revealing the cultural values and assumptions that make these appearances possible while making other appearances of disability seem impossible. Can we imagine, for example, disability appearing as necessary, desirable, or not a problem? *DisAppearing: Encounters in Disability Studies* engages political, artistic, and philosophical provocations of the dis/appearing act of disability in our lives. The diversity of topics that the authors explore represents the singular aim of revealing what disability means while potentially remaking these meanings in more life-affirming ways.

The question of dis/appearance lies behind all the chapters of *DisAppearing: Encounters in Disability Studies*. It is this tension that is our key concern. Even though the complexity of disability as a creative and necessary space of interaction and knowledge creation is severely restricted, disability, nonetheless, appears in tension with how it is made to disappear. After all, disability appears as a go-to term for any sign or symptom that something is wrong—with anything. Economies become crippled, streetcars are disabled, workloads are insane, and arguments are lame (Mitchell, 2002). Its symbolic expression is also strewn throughout the physical environment with the blue and white wheelchair icon of access that suggests access is not a given and must be marked and sought out. Disabled people can be found on every margin of every group, political or otherwise, at the edges of all the goings-on of daily life, and on the borders of physical and social structures of education, work, transportation, governance, and pleasure.[1] *DisAppearing* is our way of emphasizing that all appearances of disability are related to a disappearing and that the reverse is true as well.

Faced with cultural powers organizing the disappearances and appearances of disability, disability studies theorists, artists, and activists express the belief that, in the words of Henri-Jacques Stiker (1999), "We are always other and more than society made us and believes us to be" (p. 51). Made and believed to be a limited and restricted condition, disability appears as such. Yet, as Rod Michalko's foreword suggests, disability is always more, and this can mix us up even as it provokes us to reconsider the meaning of disability. Herein resides our collective concern with appearance and disappearance—we are committed to revealing the "more."

The dis/appearance of disability is fleeting and difficult to engage. Disability is often recalled as a forgotten issue, part of the plans for next year's events, or perhaps the year after; a problem that other people or a different office are dealing with; disability appears as convenient grounds to dismiss others— "Oh no, they can't—they're disabled, you know." And, when things go wrong, disability is there at the ready as a sense-making device—"Well, that was crazy (or blind, or deaf, or lame, or ...)!" Disabled people appear often wrapped in technical tasks of accommodation, given another form to fill out, sent to yet another office for potential assistance, placed on a leave of absence, all of which balances disabled people (us) on the edge of being shown the way out. These disappearances are disturbing, in the ordinary ways they are thought of, spoken of, and enacted. This collection attempts to grapple with these disturbances by regarding them as moments for reflection, narration, and theorizing (Michalko, 2002).

THE INCEPTION OF *DISAPPEARING*

When this project was conceived, Tanya had been a disability studies professor at the Ontario Institute for Studies in Education (OISE) at the University of Toronto for more than a decade, and the other two editors, Madeleine and Elaine, had just begun working on their disability studies doctorates in the Department of Social Justice Education, also at OISE. Together, we experienced the question of the disappearance of disability. Disability was disappearing in many university locations—in meetings, in hallway conversations, in the planning of departmental events such as end-of-term parties and book launches, and in classrooms (even in the disability studies courses that Tanya was teaching and Elaine and Madeleine were enrolled in). In attempts to diversify the frames of analysis in these disability studies courses, through the pursuit of a seemingly intersectional[2] approach, disability not only moved from being a central concern to a marginal one but was sometimes dropped from discussions altogether. These disappearances were as startling as they were provocative. This book has come to be because we developed a shared interest in the many ways disability experiences and disabled people were made absent in our lives and work, including in our scholarly, artistic, political, and personal relations with disability.

We believe that our commitment to introducing disability studies can be realized through a focus on how disability disappears as an experience, interest, or concern in particular ways, ways that can be studied. Typically, disability studies interrogates how disability is conceptualized and made to appear in a variety of social contexts. A dominant trend within disability studies is to construct and apply a model to the understanding and examination of disability. Through rejecting the individualizing of disability within the medical and charity models, others have emerged: the social model, the human rights model, the capabilities model, the affirmation model, the cultural model, the critical disability studies model, the debility model, the political relational model, the transnational model.[3] While models are useful starting points for disrupting taken-for-granted understandings of disability as a natural lack, limit, or loss, there is no one dominant model to be found here. Instead, *DisAppearing* engages encounters with disability as they are enacted through interpretations in social contexts that make disability appear and disappear. Disability is thus examined *as* a feature of all our relations (Norris, 2014), and in this way disability studies becomes an occasion to better understand culture and ourselves. The chapters, for example, often start where other forms of inquiry might stop or where it appears that disability requires no further attention since inclusion or some other solution has been achieved.

Much of the work on *DisAppearing* coincided with the COVID-19 pandemic along with the long lockdown we all experienced in Toronto. In November 2019, Efrat Gold had joined the project, completing what would become our *DisAppearing* editorial team, a committed team of four animated by doing disability studies differently. As the COVID-19 global pandemic grew, by March 13, 2020, we no longer would be meeting face-to-face. We began meeting weekly electronically. Working on *DisAppearing* became a stable feature in our lives in the midst of pandemic upheaval. This experience became yet another way for us to notice disability disappearances and to hold on to them. For instance, during the pandemic, disabled people and people living in congregate settings were disappeared. News organizations, such as the BBC and Al Jazeera English (2021), have reported that disabled people have accounted for six out of ten deaths from COVID-19 worldwide and, in congregate settings, locked in their rooms without basic amenities. Knowledge of the difficulties and death experienced by disabled people during the pandemic made our work all the more pressing. And, of course, there is more. The chapters aim to make the complexity of disability more tangible by showing the assumptions used to keep the topic of disability confined, over-simplified, or even irrelevant to the everyday interests of programs, policies, interactions, and ways of knowing even within pandemic times and within critical forms of education. *DisAppearing: Encounters in Disability Studies* represents our shared interest in encountering disability at its supposed ends and certain solutions. Our interest is in getting to know disability's stories in new ways, ways that do not let the seal of certainty fasten a closure on meaning.

This book attempts to reveal the meaning of disability when it appears and also to ask what it means to downplay, cast into the background, or vanish disability as a concern altogether. In turn, the chapters address how dis/appearances of disability are made possible and produced and what this reveals about the ways that disability is understood. This relational orientation to disability demonstrates how disability appears and disappears and does so even within the field of disability studies, leading, we believe, to invigorating and unexpected encounters with ourselves and others while honouring our collective commitment to representing disability as always more and other than what society makes it and believes it to be.

There is yet another unique aspect to the inception of this book. In July of 2019, we hosted a day-long international conference called "Critical Disability Studies and Its Critical Influencers."[4] The event included scholars doing work in disability studies that was not only interdisciplinary but also engaged the intersections of related and influential forms of critical studies—Black, queer, and Indigenous studies, as well as feminist, Mad politics, and post-humanist studies.

Some of these scholars presented work, others were critical respondents; all have influenced the richness of this book. Starting from the pressing need to demonstrate that disability studies is influenced by, and can influence, a variety of critical studies, we invited participants to explore the risks and possibilities as well as methodological moves necessary to nurture the relations already foundational to disability studies. Given the critical commitments represented by participants at this conference, the reiteration of the critique that disability studies is white might serve to disappear the complex and intersectional work that *is* going on. Indeed, the need to expand the borders of disability studies[5] and to enhance what counts as disability studies, beyond whiteness, remained a powerful impetus for us and still does. How to work through and with divisions and differences, instead of merely reinforcing them, is a foundational interest—one that the reader will encounter throughout this collection.

FEATURES OF THE COLLECTION

We have placed boxed texts throughout that include the words of poets, activists, and scholars of critical fields, such as Black and critical Indigenous studies, queer and feminist studies, D/deaf studies, mad studies, and disability studies. Read alongside the chapter in which they appear or sequentially on their own, these boxed texts are ways for readers to orient themselves to the intersectional connections to and within disability studies. We include these short excerpts so as to offer anyone interested in the meaning of disability yet another way to develop relations to the cultural tensions that are often present when *we* are present with the dis/appearances of disability.

We intend these boxed texts as provocations to engage the aims and interests of disability studies, even though some of them do not make their relation to disability explicit. Searching for such relations will simultaneously reveal the ways in which disability studies intersects with other fields of cultural inquiry. Whether or not these boxed texts represent disability explicitly, disability remains present not only in these texts but in all our relations. The question now becomes "How?" How is disability present in all our social relations, including these boxed texts?

Another aspect of this collection is the editors' introduction to each of the parts that group the chapters together thematically, which draws out the significance of how disability becomes manifest, yet is made to disappear, only to reappear, often in unexpected ways. Each of the parts ends with a creative encounter, a poem, or a podcast, intended to represent the multiplicity of ways disability appears and disappears. We include, for example, a poem by Lynn Manning, *The*

Magic Wand, which we are thrilled to have permission to reproduce here in honour of his creative life that left us too soon. The editors' introductions serve to highlight existential themes of embodiment while simultaneously drawing out some of the theoretical and methodological moves of the authors. With essays, poetry, and incisive boxed texts, the various journeys into the meaning of cultural representations of disability are pathways into doing disability studies.

The pathways involve many different social settings and scenes. *DisAppearing* includes encounters with disability in educational settings, from elementary school to university, as well as encounters in novels and other textual representations, in hospitals and policing, as well as in the normative structure of everyday interaction, in dance, on the street, in community centres, and in considerations of injury and healing, life and death. The chapters in this collection invite readers into an analysis of cultural scenes of disability, scenes that are connected to a range of experiences—from race and racialization, to Indigeneity, to gender and sexuality, and to class and other important social locations—and historical coordinates that organize our imaginative lives (Bhabha, 1994; Bolt, 2021; Mitchell & Snyder, 2000). This is also why we include an alternative table of contents organized by scenes of encounters, such as accessibility, body, capitalism, etc. The alternative table of contents can be found after our more thematically organized one, discussed below. Readers are guided to engage with the marginality of disability in social thought and action, while exploring how to do disability studies. More than half the chapters are written by people who identify as disabled; there is work from people who are blind, deaf, have learning and intellectual differences, and who write from the perspective of autism. Even though an experiential perspective from a mobility disability is underrepresented in this collection, the feel of moving with disabilities, in their various manifestations, remains a critical feature throughout.

The issue of under- and over-representation of types of disability does not capture the relationship between the experience of disability and our relations with the social and political locations of its appearance. For example, in Chapter 4, Thomas Reid talks of running to catch an airplane while blind and with the help of a stranger as his sighted guide—here the issues of race, mobility, blindness, and transportation all coalesce to raise questions regarding when and how the freedom of movement arises in the movements of daily life. The question of mobility is found throughout, but not in its (stereo)typical form; instead it appears as disability intersects with space, time, interactions, and knowledge.

Disability experience and representation is the starting point, a way of opening culture to an analysis, one that explores rather than merely relies upon ableist frames and taken-for-granted norms of embodiment. This book represents the possibility for an engagement that will bring us closer to a more vibrant sense of humanity by weaving us into the stories of disability's dis/appearances in all of our lives.

The work here counters attempts to move closer to disability through more common forms of recognition, such as diagnoses, definitions, or programmatic treatments that more often than not result in distancing ourselves from the complexity of disability. Embracing an orientation that nurtures the need to question how meaning is made of disability, and the social and political consequences of doing so, is a way to loosen the power of medicine and science as the primary meaning-makers of our lives with disability. The chapters here are oriented toward the inescapable fact that we make disability meaningful through our interpretive relations with it in ways that require exploration. It is this exploration, this *more*—this sense that whatever else disability *is*, it is connected to, and thus flows through, all our relations—that this book dedicates itself to reflecting on. The political and personal positioning of readers and writers alike is a reflective one—what relations to disability are we called into? What relations call to us?

Another distinctive feature of this collection to discuss is *disability terminology*. Within disability studies there are concerns about how to articulate disability experience so as not to reify it as a natural problem. People-first terminology has been one way to signify this commitment. It suggests that by using the expression *people with disabilities* an emphasis will be placed on people rather than on disability. At the same time, however, there is identity-first terminology as well as language that centres the meaning and importance of disability as a form of oppression making disabled people an oppressed group, and the term *disability* is used by some as a critical space for critical inquiry. Disabled people and reclamations of terms such as "crip" are also used to express this commitment to a political and identity-based understanding of disability. Whatever position these debates on language use take, they all reflect the sense that terminology is powerful. Considerations of disability language use are part of the struggle to not only avoid but also examine the objectification and/or the degradation of disability and people who experience impairment.

No consistent disability terminology appears in this collection. How disability is expressed varies from one chapter to the next. What will be found throughout is a commitment to the understanding that terminology and the language choices we make is crucial in the struggle against disability degradation. *Disability*, *person with a disability*, *crip*, *debilitated*—all of these words bring us into relation with disability in ways that require examination.

A NOTE ON METHODS

"There is a story I know. It's about the earth and how it floats in space on the back of a turtle. I've heard this story many times, and each time someone tells the story, it changes. Sometimes the change is simply in the voice of the storyteller. Sometimes the change is in the details. Sometimes in the order of events. Other times it's the dialogue or the response of the audience. But in all the tellings of all the tellers, the world never leaves the turtle's back. And the turtle never swims away."

King, Thomas. *The Truth About Stories: A Native Narrative.* Toronto, ON: House of Anansi Press, 2003, p. 1.

The methodological premise behind this collection is that the appearance of anything—any action, person, place, or thing, as well as any thought or feeling—is made possible by the social context from which it springs and into which it appears. In this sense, whatever "presents itself in perceptual awareness is a candidate" for inquiry and, further, is an occasion to encounter its meaning more fully (Natanson, 1998, p. 22). The chapters in this collection not only uphold but also nurture this methodological premise by showing how disappearances of disability are intimately tied to the contexts of their appearances.

Disability comes to perceptual awareness all the time but usually with a twist, since it often seems as if it is about to disappear. As Frantz Fanon's (1967 [1952]) analysis of the white gaze—and its negation of Black bodies—reminds us, "All around the body reigns an atmosphere of certain uncertainty" (pp. 110–111). The white gaze asserts its power, negating Black bodily experience as viable and something in and of itself. Given the ableist, functionalist gaze, awareness of disabled people is surrounded by the certain uncertainty of Problem as this appears in our classrooms, policies, workplaces, social theory, and everyday lives. Disabled life appears wrapped in the certainty of Problem, if it appears at all. It takes work to release ourselves from the sense that we already know everything that needs to be known about disability as a problem.

Such work, which could be called interpretive disability studies, means enacting a pause—that is, hesitating before the dis/appearance of disability in order to wonder about what has been given to perceptual awareness and to ask after its orchestration (Al-Saji, 2014; Weiss, 2015). This hesitation can allow us to go back and ask: What might disability mean other than what we already know it to be? What values, institutional practices, policy demands, and political orientations make disability appear or disappear as it has—and what does this mean for our lives as disabled or currently non-disabled people? It is this commitment to the uncovering of something more than what we already know that serves as a resource to ramp up an encounter with disability that holds open the possibility of more fully understanding our lives together, perhaps "outside the confines of the scripts heretofore provided" but nonetheless "sutured" through all our connections and relations (Pickens, 2019, pp. 3, 19).

"One starting place might be accepting the partiality of knowledge. Its relational, alive, emergent nature means that as we come to know something, as we attempt to fix its meaning, we are always at risk of just missing something. If we accept the alive and ongoing nature of colonial relations, and the lived aspects of Indigeneity as critical to Indigenous ontologies, any attempts to fix Indigenous knowledge can only be partial. Reconfiguring ourselves as academics, geographers, or experts, could facilitate the creation of other kinds of hyphenations: expert/learner, geographer/settler, or academic/witness, for example.... As I suggest, for non-Indigenous people interested in engaging with Indigenous ontologies, this may involve becoming unhinged, uncomfortable, or stepping beyond the position of 'expert' in order to also be a witness or listener.... This might entail embracing the shifting relationality, complexity and circularity of Indigenous knowledge as productive and necessary. The situatedness and place-specific nature of Indigenous knowledge calls for the validation of new kinds of theorizing and new epistemologies that can account for situated, relational Indigenous knowledge and yet remain engaged with broader theoretical debates ... navigating among differing power relations at the scales of both the individual academic and the broader discipline."

Hunt, Sarah. "Ontologies of Indigeneity: The Politics of Embodying a Concept." *Cultural Geographies* 21, no. 1 (2014): 31.

At the crossroads of these appearances, edged as they are with potential disappearances, the authors in this collection aim to reveal the grounds that allow us to better encounter what makes disability dis/appear. Tanya has previously described such an approach as pursuing a politics of wonder (Titchkosky, 2011), and such a pursuit under contemporary bureaucratized governance is no easy matter. Wonder requires a "restless, reflexive return to how" disability and non-disability are ordinarily noticed as well as the context of that noticing to encounter it again by questioning the ways that disability appears as if potentially disappearing at every turn (Titchkosky, 2011, pp. 15–18). In sum, the methodological assumption that flows through this collection is that our interpretive relations with disability are complicated and hold meanings that trouble and may even transcend the everyday certainty that disability is a problem in need of a solution and further disturb the notion that disability is something that only individuals suffer (Ahmed, 2012; Goodley, 2021; Hartman, 2019; Hughes, 2019; Lowe, 2015; Slee, 2018).

One way we exemplify this methodological assumption is by organizing the chapters under five interrelated themes. These themes cluster chapters according to particular disappearances of disability through specific kinds of encounters. The themes of theory and practice, embodiment, drama, departures following diagnoses, and dreams not only are the context for our encounters with disability, in all of their complexity, but also serve as a way to frame how people notice what disability does and does not mean.

In the first part, "DisAppearing DisAbility: Demonstrations in Theory and Practice," disability is made to appear in the history of policy, personal experience, and political protest. The authors in this section are oriented by an understanding of disability studies that grapples, through theory and practice, with how disability is made meaningful.

"DisAppearing DisEmbodiment" marks the second theme of chapters, focusing on the ways in which the reality of our bodily existence is mediated by culture. Centring the experience of how embodiment appears and disappears, these chapters exemplify how disability studies can bring us nearer to our unique bodily integrity.

Part three, "DisAppearing Drama," represents disability studies work that is connected to performance studies, including theatre and dance. All chapters gathered in this part bring our focus onto the dramas of the appearances and disappearances of disability in scenes of everyday life.

Theme four is "DisAppearing Departures, Diagnoses, and Death." Diagnosis may feel like a departure—a leaving of one place to arrive at another, and sometimes to arrive at death. This can be scary, unsettling, and disturbing. But it may also leave us with a certain peace, such as the peace that follows leaving one way of knowing oneself for another, becoming, for example, a disabled person.

"DisAppearing Dreams" is the fifth and final part of this collection. It brings together chapters that illustrate how the meanings of disability may never be settled or certain. Disability might enter our dreams, allowing us to imagine disability in new ways, beautiful ways, or unsettling ways that first appear in our dreams, carrying us through our lives.

These themes attempt to capture the sense that disability is not a static entity but a way of being tied to all that we say and do. We would like to thank all the authors for their work in demonstrating the need for a disability studies that can attend to the complex nature of disability's dis/appearances.

"[Perceiving] disability as political, and therefore contested and contestable, entails departing from the social model's assumption that 'disabled' and 'nondisabled' are discrete, self-evident categories, choosing instead to explore the creation of such categories and the moments in which they fail to hold. Recognizing such moments of excess and failure is key to imagining disability, and disability futures, differently."

Kafer, Alison. *Feminist, Queer, Crip.* Bloomington, IN: Indiana University Press, 2013, p. 10.

NOTES

1. For recent related work, see Gold (2022), Schott (2021), and Walsh (2022).
2. Consider Crenshaw (1989) for how she introduced "intersectionality" within legal studies. See *Intersectionality* (2016) by Patricia Hill Collins and Sirma Bilge for how this term is used throughout academia.
3. We recognize that this list is not exhaustive but emphasize these few as examples of various disability models that reject the medical and charity models of disability.
4. A key question of this conference was "How are critical Indigenous studies, queer studies, and Black studies influencing CDS [critical disability studies] work today?" This conference was organized by Professor Tanya Titchkosky with organizational assistance from disability studies scholar Umit Aydogmus. The keynote speaker was Dr. Eman Ghaad, Dean of the Faculty of Education at the British University in Dubai. Graduate presenters included Elaine Cagulada, Maya Chacaby, Fiona Cheuk, Elizabeth Davis, Madeleine DeWelles, Dr. Maria Karmiris, Zoe Lee, and Nadine Violette. Respondents included Dr. Dan Goodley, Dr. rosalind hampton, Dr. Dai Kojima, Dr. Rebecca Lawthom, and Dr. Dolleen Tisawii'ashii Manning. Students for Barrier Free Access at the University of Toronto also presented and supported the event.

5.   For example, the work of Leroy Baker (2019), Christopher Bell (2011), Tsitsi Chataika (2019), Veena Das and Renu Addlakha (2007), Parin Dossa (2009), Nirmala Erevelles (2000, 2014), Anita Ghai (2015), Benedicte Ingstad and Susan Reynolds Whyte (1995), Devi Dee Mucina (2011; and in School for the Contemporary Arts, 2021), Pushpa Naidu Parekh (2006), Theri Pickens (2019), Sherene Razack (1998), Sami Schalk (2018), and James Wilson and Cynthia Lewiecki-Wilson (2001).

REFERENCES

Ahmed, S. (2012). *On being included: Racism and diversity in institutional life.* Duke University Press.

Al Jazeera English. (2021, February 2021). *COVID's disabled victims.* https://www. aljazeera.com/program/people-power/2021/2/4/covids-disabled-victims

Al-Saji, A. (2014). A phenomenology of hesitation: Interrupting racializing habits of seeing. In E. Lee (Ed.)., *Living alterities: Phenomenology, embodiment, and race* (pp. 133–172). State University of New York Press. https://philarchive.org/archive/ ALSAPO-3v1

Baker, L. (2019). *Normalizing marginality: A critical analysis of Blackness and disability in higher education.* Dissertation Abstracts International, *81,* 02(B). https:// librarysearch.library.utoronto.ca/permalink/01UTORONTO_INST/14bjeso/ alma991106685327706196

BBC. (2021, February 11). *Covid: Disabled people account for six in 10 deaths in England last year – ONS.* https://www.bbc.com/news/uk-56033813

Bell, C. (2011). *Blackness and disability: Critical examinations and cultural interventions.* Michigan University State Press.

Bhabha, H. K. (1994). *The location of culture.* Routledge.

Bolt, D. (2021). *Metanarratives of disability: Culture, assumed authority, and the normative social order.* Routledge.

Chataika, T. (2019). *The Routledge handbook of disability in Southern Africa.* Routledge. https://doi.org/10.4324/9781315278650

Crenshaw, K. (1989). Demarginalizing the intersection of race and sex: A Black feminist critique of antidiscrimination doctrine, feminist theory and antiracist politics. *University of Chicago Legal Forum, 1989*(8), 139–167. https://chicagounbound. uchicago.edu/uclf/vol1989/iss1/8/

Das, V., & Addlakha, R. (2007). Disability and domestic citizenship: Voice, gender, and making of the Subject. In B. Ingstad & S. R. Whyte (Eds.), *Disability in local and global worlds* (pp. 128–148). University of California Press.

Dossa, P. (2009). *Racialized bodies, disabling worlds: Storied lives of immigrant Muslim women*. University of Toronto Press.

Erevelles, N. (2000). Educating unruly bodies: Critical pedagogy, disability studies, and the politics of schooling. *Educational Theory, 50*(1), 25–47. https://doi. org/10.1111/j.1741-5446.2000.00025.x

Erevelles, N. (2014). Thinking with disability studies. *Disability Studies Quarterly, 34*(2). https://doi.org/10.18061/dsq.v34i2.4248

Fanon, F. (1967). *Black skin, white masks*. Grove Press. (Original work published 1952)

Ghai, A. (2015). *Rethinking disability in India*. Routledge.

Gold, E. (2022). *Tracing eugenics: The rise of totalizing psychiatric ideology in Canada*. [Doctoral dissertation, University of Toronto]. ProQuest Dissertation Publishing.

Goodley, D. (2021). *Disability and other human questions*. Emerald Publishing.

Hartman, S. V. (2019). *Wayward lives, beautiful experiments: Intimate histories of riotous Black girls, troublesome women, and Queer radicals*. W. W. Norton & Company.

Hill Collins, P., & Bilge, S. (2016). *Intersectionality*. Polity Press.

Hughes, B. (2019). The abject and the vulnerable: the twain shall meet: Reflections on disability in the moral economy. *The Sociological Review, 67*(4), 829–846. https://doi. org/10.1177/0038026119854259

Ingstad, B., & Whyte, S. R. (Eds.). (1995). *Disability and culture*. University of California Press.

Lowe, L. (2015). *The intimacies of four continents*. Duke University Press. https://doi .org/10.1215/9780822375647

Michalko, M. (2002). *The difference that disability makes*. Temple University Press.

Mitchell, D. T., (2002). Narrative prosthesis and the materiality of metaphor. In S. L. Snyder, B. J. Brueggemann, & R. Garland-Thomson (Eds.), *Disability studies: Enabling the humanities* (pp. 15–30). The Modern Languages Association of America.

Mitchell, D. T., & Snyder, S. L. (2000). *Narrative prosthesis: Disability and the dependencies of discourse*. University of Michigan Press.

Mucina, D. D. (2011). *Ubuntu: A regenerative philosophy for rupturing racist colonial stories of dispossession*. ProQuest Dissertations Publishing.

Natanson, M. (1998). *The erotic bird: Phenomenology in literature*. University of Princeton Press.

Norris, H. (2014). Colonialism and the rupturing of Indigenous worldviews of impairment and relational interdependence: A beginning dialogue towards reclamation and social transformation. *Critical Disability Discourse/Discours Critiques dans le Champ du Handicap, 6*, 53–79.

Parekh, N. P. (2006). Gender, disability, and the post-colonial nexus. *Wag.a.du: A Journal of Transnational Women and Gender Studies, 4*. http://colfax.cortland.edu/wagadu/Volume%204/Vol4pdfs/Chapter%2010.pdf

Pickens, T. A. (2019). *Black madness :: Mad blackness.* Duke University Press.

Razack, S. (1998). *Looking white people in the eye: Gender, race, and culture in courtrooms and classrooms.* University of Toronto Press.

Schalk, S. (2018). *Bodyminds reimagined: (Dis)ability, race, and gender in Black women's speculative fiction.* Duke University Press.

School for the Contemporary Arts. (2021, January 9). *Dance area talk: Devi Dee Mucina* [Video]. Vimeo. https://vimeo.com/508074413

Schott, N. (2021). *Pro-Ana/Mia performance ethnography: Remaking responses to psychiatric relations to "eating disorders".* [Doctoral dissertation, University of Toronto]. ProQuest Dissertation Publishing.

Slee, R. (2018). *Inclusive education isn't dead, it just smells funny.* Routledge.

Stiker, H.-J. (1999). *A history of disability* (W. Sayers, Trans.). University of Michigan Press. (Original work published 1997)

Titchkosky, T. (2011). *The question of access: Disability, space, meaning.* University of Toronto Press.

Walsh, S. (2022). *Re-thinking rights: Experiences of disability in an AODA Ontario.* (Publication #29063946). [Doctoral dissertation, University of Toronto]. ProQuest Dissertations Publishing.

Weiss, G. (2015). The normal, the natural, and the normative: A Merleau-Pontian legacy to feminist theory, critical race theory, and disability studies. *Continental Philosophy Review, 48*(1), 77–93. https://doi.org.10.1007/s11007-014-9316-y

Wilson, J. C., & Lewiecki-Wilson, C. (Eds.). (2001). *Embodied rhetorics: Disability in language and culture.* Southern Illinois University.

PART I

DISAPPEARING DISABILITY: DEMONSTRATIONS IN THEORY AND PRACTICE

EDITORS' INTRODUCTION

The chapters in this opening part demonstrate that while there are many ways to do disability studies, a focus on the way disability appears in the history of policy, in personal experience, and in political protests has much to do with what version of disability will be made to disappear. Working the tension between disappearance and appearance is difficult to do, and thus there is a need for both social theory and reflective practices. We aim at the same time to nurture an interest in doing disability studies. Whatever else disability studies *is,* it is a form of inquiry that grapples with how disability is made meaningful—this too needs theory and practice. In this sense, the work collected here is not about being an expert but is about attending to shifting relations, and the complexity that follows expanding ways of knowing and theorizing life together and the conflicts within. The chapters of this part turn to historical depictions of exclusion, to personal narrative, and to the Black Lives Matter political protest to better understand the appearance and disappearance of disability. These chapters also demonstrate that social theory and practice are ways to address power and help us continue to wonder about how disability dis/appears as it does.

In the first chapter, "DisAppearing Promises: The University's Unfortunate Framing of Disability," Tanya Titchkosky draws on work from Paul Gilroy and Sylvia Wynter as they articulate how race and racism function to maintain the status quo, revealing how conceptions of disability as unexpected and unfortunate are used to support the status quo within university bureaucracies. Making use of historical examples of how disability appears in the university environment, Titchkosky turns to Gilroy's concept of "race-thinking" in order to invite readers to critically encounter the practices of inclusion in a historical context, steeped in the normalcy of excluding students, faculty, and staff who are disabled. This chapter demonstrates how a disability studies approach can offer an enriched sense of humanity in the midst of otherwise limited representations of the normal or expected white able-bodied participant in university work and life.

In "Nativity," Hanna Herdegen shows the many meanings of autism through creative non-fiction, woven from her own experiences of being asked to explain autism—that is, to explain herself. Using the metaphor of travel, Herdegen narrates how autistic people can be conceptualized as skilled travellers, tasked with navigating neurotypical culture. In narrating the many ways she travels through daily life with this cultural demand for explanation, Herdegen also brings to the fore her own interest: to narrate, and in doing so, bring self, other, the world, and their interrelation to the forefront. For example:

> When you are very young at school, they make you sit in circles and answer questions like:
>> *What is the weather like outside?*
>> *What day of the week is it?*
>> *What did you do yesterday?*
>> The first two are the easiest. You just tell the truth, and people are usually happy with you.
>
> But saying the true thing is not the same as saying the right thing.

In "Navigating Borderlands: Deaf and Hearing Experiences in Post-Secondary Education," Sarah Beck and Sammy Jo Johnson—one author deaf and the other a child of deaf adults (Coda)—navigate the borderlands of deafness within the university, with a particular focus on the classroom. Having met each other in a university course on inclusive education, they write of generating a "space where we could push back against compulsory hearing. Here we created a small signing space within the larger auditory classroom." This led them to question what inclusion means. The experience of disability, differences, and deafness is intimately related to how inclusion is organized—that is, to how it appears and disappears in the classroom and elsewhere. Their chapter exemplifies the need to question the normative demands of classrooms, inclusion, and the compulsory nature of hearing in educational institutions.

"The social world differs from the natural world in (at least) one fundamental respect; that is, human beings give meanings to objects in the social world and subsequently orientate their behaviour towards these objects in terms of the meanings given to them…. As far as disability is concerned, if it is seen as a tragedy, then disabled people will be treated as if they are the victims of some tragic happening or circumstance…. Alternatively, it logically follows that if disability is defined as social oppression, then disabled people will be seen as the collective victims of circumstance."

Oliver, Michael. *The Politics of Disablement.* London, UK: The Macmillan Press, 1990, p. 2.

These first three chapters investigate the white middle class organization of education and family as well as show how the building of alternative understandings of our lives with disability may arise. Rounding out this part we switch registers—to the streets, to protests, and to the need to remake white middle class norms of social organization as they relate to disability experience. Concluding this part, chapter four is a textual rendering of one of Thomas Reid's podcast episodes (2020), which in its original form is a veritable smorgasbord of sound. Reid, a blind Black podcast creator, orchestrates a conversation about how disability appears and disappears in "Let Me Hear You Say Black Lives Matter." The textual transcription of this podcast situates readers explicitly within and between the intersections of disability and race, bringing home the sense that dis/appearances of identity and difference are both numerous and everywhere. The power of anti-black racism is encountered, and Reid invites us to engage this as a way to address our history and its impact on our present conceptions of disability and race. For readers who may like to work in sound, check out Reid's work at reidmymind.com or wherever you listen to podcasts.

Guiding Questions

1. Over time, has disability appeared in your life in different ways?
2. Does your recognition of disability change from one context to the next, such as from school to the streets, or from parks to a political protest?
3. In what ways has disability been made to dis/appear from current political unrest?
4. In what ways does your understanding of disability influence how you read texts/stories about disability?

REFERENCE

Reid, T. (Host). (2020, June 17). Let me hear you say Black Lives Matter [Audio podcast episode]. In *Reid My Mind*. http://reidmymind.com/let-me-hear-you-say-black-lives-matter/

CHAPTER 1

DisAppearing Promises: The University's Unfortunate Framing of Disability

Tanya Titchkosky

Key Terms: Academia; Disability Thinking; Imagination; Misfortune; Normal Man; Paul Gilroy; Race-Thinking; Sylvia Wynter; University of Toronto Accessibility—1981

INTRODUCTION

This chapter explores the appearance of disability in the academy by considering university responses to disability over time while questioning how such responses support and inhibit the overall project of critical inquiry. I understand *disability* itself to be a shifting set of responses to impairments within environments that have established ways of doing things and demarcated who or what belongs. Such an understanding provokes a need to attend to the situation of the appearance of disability together with non-disability by focusing on relations and responses as they make disability appear in particular ways. The following is one such conundrum of concern—the appearance of disability within North American university environments typically marks the spot where critical work stops and where regular Western knowledge regimes of science and bureaucratic management dominate.

Before turning to a few historical examples from the 1960s and 1980s, I briefly delineate how disability appears in university life today so as to illustrate the crucial conundrum of interest. I show how diminishing the life of disability is part of the ongoing racist structure of modernity. Following Paul Gilroy's (2002, 2005) lead, I demonstrate how the (de)valuation of human difference makes some people appear as failed biology of negative economic value, and this sense of human difference is used by established powers to sort, order, and control people. This belief in the lesser human supports the economic advantage of a few over the many. Yet, if we follow Gilroy's (2005) provocation to "commit acts of imagination" (p. 53), it is possible to begin to respond to disability and nurture a more promising relation to the differences that we are or can become. The hope is that, by denaturalizing the normalcy of disability as devalued and simply a problem or fodder for management, we can nurture a sense of disability as promise or possibility (Titchkosky, 2011).

"With this genre of the human being ... both the peoples of African hereditary descent and the peoples who comprise the damned archipelagoes of the Poor, the jobless, the homeless, the 'underdeveloped' must lawlike be sacrificed as a function of our continuing to project our collective authorship of our contemporary order onto the imagined agency of Evolution and Natural Selection."

Wynter, Sylvia. "Unsettling the Coloniality of Being/Power/Truth/Freedom: Towards the Human, After Man, Its Overrepresentation—An Argument." *CR: The New Centennial Review* 3, no. 3 (2003): 257–337; p. 317.

THE NATURALIZATION OF DISABILITY AS MISFORTUNE

There are various responses to disability within the university that confine it to a singular sense—it is a problem. And disability studies (DS) scholars have studied its constitution as such (Michalko, 2002, 2008; Mitchell & Snyder, 1997; Oliver, 1990, and many others). Disability's status as a problem is typically naturalized, making it seem unthinkable to imagine disability otherwise. Across Canada today, the existence of DS programs, courses, or content from one university to the next are not guaranteed; yet, on every campus, there are accessibility and health services tasked with ascertaining and managing impairments as their method of including disabled students, faculty, and staff. Those who already have a more secure place within the university typically address the issue of disability as a problem and receive pay cheques, research grants, and/or accreditations to do work *on* disability as such. A nearly universal response to disability across university campuses is to understand it as inviting medical research. The medicalizing of disability in policy is matched by disciplinary knowledge of all sorts that studies disability as an issue for cure, care, and containment (Finkelstein, 1998; Saltes, 2020; Zola, 1977). These responses mean that disability appears less like a life lived than it does as an unwanted problem, often indistinguishable from disease, illness, and injury (Slee, 2018). The chance of thinking *with* disability alongside disabled colleagues typically remains an unfulfilled promise. Thus, it is far more likely that disability enters our work lives wrapped in a sense of misfortune more so than injustice (Michalko, 2002; Shklar, 1990).

Misfortune is one of the dominant Western ways to frame different minds, bodies, senses, and sentiments, and it is ubiquitous throughout university environments. DS, however, offers an alternative by questioning what is *organizing this perception of disability* and *what are the consequences*—"Who or what does this conception of disability serve?" From the perspective of disability studies, *revealing* how disability is perceived and responded to—including among university knowledge producers—is key to denaturalizing the taken-for-granted sense of disability-as-problem and to opening up the possibility of other perceptions (Stiker, 1999).

Examining the ways in which disability is perceived and responded to in texts produced by the university reveals the frame of misfortune as it operates within the university environment. This frame is a key way disabled people are constituted as a health-management issue, typically addressed by non-disabled staff. This attention to frames means that DS aligns with Black studies, critical Indigenous studies, and feminist, queer, and trans studies insofar as they denaturalize ontological inferiority by revealing how knowledge about people is produced. To illustrate the construction of knowledge about disability taken as a management problem in university work-life, I turn to the 1960s, a time characterized as building a more just society.

UPHOLDING NORMAL "MAN"

"I want to talk about what it means to struggle to maintain that marginality even as one works, produces, lives if you will at the centre. I no longer live in that segregated world across the tracks. Central to life in that world was the ongoing awareness of the necessity of opposition. When Bob Marley sings 'we refuse to be what you want us to be, we are what we are, and that's the way it's going to be' that space of refusal, where one can say no to the coloniser, no to the downpressor, is located on the margins. And one can only say no, speak the voice of resistance, because there exists a counter language."

hooks, bell. "Choosing the Margin as a Space of Radical Openness." *Framework* 36, no. 36 (1989): 15–23; pp. 20–21.

During the 1960s, protests erupted on university campuses, raising questions of who belonged where, who could study, what could be studied, and how education and governance of universities might be handled differently. Questioning institutional power and knowledge served to highlight some of the conservative socio-political underpinnings of universities. Sylvia Wynter (2003) has suggested that the North American university of the 1960s generated and preserved a Western bourgeois conception of the human—Man—and, further, university work overrepresented this Man "as if it were the human itself" (p. 260). University knowledge can be read for the way it secures (conserves) the "well-being and the full cognitive and behavioral autonomy" of this singular version of being human to the detriment of the interests of the "empirical human" (Wynter, 2003, p. 262). Still, the 1960s was when knowledge that protected the unquestioned place of Man, be it in university administration, research, or teaching, was opened to critical inquiry.

Wynter (2003) suggests that, "before the sixties, the enforced segregation of the Black population in the South as the liminally deviant category of Otherness" (p. 259) encoded white Man as master. Critiqued by anti- and post-colonial theorists, this Man is also examined within DS as Normal Man or (since the 1990s) the Normate[1]—the position with power to define those who are its outsiders as the inferior. Normate Man stands in contrast to its Other, namely, the so-called lesser humans inclusive of "the Poor, the jobless, the homeless, the 'underdeveloped'" (Wynter, 2003, p. 317). Responding to its lesser Other, Normate Man relies on university knowledge production that naturalizes the sacrifice of many people— damned are those who lack a function that also props up a belief in the Natural Evolution of Man as a body-of-functions. It was during the sixties, according to Wynter (2003), that this over-representation of Man as if it were the human itself had a "vigorous discursive and institutional re-elaboration" (p. 262), tempting the "best and the brightest" to prop up a singular version of the human (i.e., Man) as true and wear his cloak of power (Wynter, 1994, pp. 47, 53, 59).

In *Claiming Disability*, Simi Linton (1998) suggests that the hope for a new world order represented in the 1960s would disrupt the sense that disabled people are lesser humans. And, from the perspective of the present, there did appear some radical forms of hope following the wars and polio epidemic where injured veterans and disabled students, even those in iron lungs, appeared on campus and in the classroom (Gabel & Danforth, 2008; Galer, 2018; Stone, 1984). One Canadian example of this burgeoning promise was that not only were all first-year students allowed into the stacks of the University of British Columbia (UBC) library in 1966, but on April 4, 1968, the Crane Memorial Library for blind and visually impaired students at UBC was established.[2]

Times seemed to be changing.

Despite this hope for change regarding who could study, what could be studied, and how knowledge might be shared, the bourgeois conception of Man as the human itself remained over-represented and relatively untouched.[3] Given the ongoing anti-Black racism, sexism, and the damning of the poor and the Indigenous, it is possible to say that the 1960s did not fulfill its promise (Million, 2013; Wynter, 1994, 2003), and the societal approach to disability-as-problem can be understood as propping up this conservatism. The issue of disability in the 1960s was more an issue to be managed than an impetus for inquiry, blocking further critique of "Man."

Turning now to how disability appears in the 1960s' university work-life, I am attentive to moments of including disability where critical inquiry ends and management of the unfortunate Other begins, a particular form of dis/appearance. The University of Toronto (U of T) is my example throughout.

INCLUSION OF DISABILITY—1965–1966

A sense of ordinariness was lent to excluding disabled people from participating in the university environment by assuming arbitrary capacities as "naturally" necessary for participation. For example, in 1965–1966, to enroll in dental hygiene, the U of T's Faculty of Dentistry required not only a medical examination but also that the applicant "must register for and satisfactorily complete a swimming test" (University of Toronto Archives, 1965, p. 14). Mandating the ability to swim as an entrance test, like eating with the proper fork at high table, is a way to weed out disabled people as well as anyone not firmly ensconced in white middle class culture.

The 1960s annual President's Reports included faculty updates—who was hired, who retired, and who became disabled and had to leave[4]—as well as lists of publications, new research, and other achievements over the year. These reports also included the number of medical tests conducted on campus and a numerical sketch of the results. These tests went far beyond assuring the absence of an infectious disease since they also recorded the percentage of the student population able to participate in "athletics and physical training"—participation rates hovered around the 95 per cent range.

Far more explicit uses of disability as a mechanism of exclusion were also employed within the university. Consider U of T's 1966–1967 (11) Course Calendar of the Institute of Child Study:

> In order to work with children it is necessary for the student to be in good physical and mental health and free from any form of infectious disease. Therefore every applicant who will have contact with children must have a complete medical examination at the University Health Service, preferably before the course opens.... Since physical stamina and freedom from

disabilities are essential for successful work in the preschool laboratory, the student is expected to discuss this matter before selection of his area of concentration. (University of Toronto Archives, 1966, p. 11)

Free from infectious disease is one thing, but freedom from disability is quite another. The Calendar carries the message that disability is an unfortunate condition that necessarily limits success and is as detrimental to working with children as is infectious disease. This message is pedagogical in that it suggests that it is normal to believe that Health Services can measure stamina and disability *in* individuals and can determine whether or not someone is suited for child studies. The Institute does not hide this version of a lesser human as its grounds for exclusion. Interestingly enough, the structure that housed the Institute of Child Study in the 1960s remained physically inaccessible until January 2018 when a new addition to the building increased access. The 1965–1966 instruction to students does not mention disabling environments as impinging on success, stamina, or participation decisions. Without addressing the built environment, the already-included participants are given tacit permission to respond to disability as if its absence is normal, even natural and unrelated to the material and ideological environment of the day (Slee, 2018).

These few examples are enough to suggest that the 1960s, while witness to many changes in university governance and areas of study, did little to awaken the need to reinvigorate its conception of disability and disabled people. Instead, it seems rather ordinary to exclude disabled people from university work and life. It was a common practice, and legal in Canada and other countries, in the 1960s to discriminate against people if they were disabled. This conserves the idea that there are lesser humans whose inclusion is questionable even as their management is necessary. From a DS perspective, such discrimination is ongoing in the design of programs, policies, physical structures, and everyday language.

To further understand the role of disability discrimination in sustaining contemporary social order, I turn to a historical moment when the legality of disability exclusion was interrupted.

LEGAL INCLUSION OF DISABILITY—1981–1982

Every university has its stories of individual disabled people who were included, but these stories are the exception that prove the rule of the normalcy of exclusion. The advent of the United Nations International Year of Disabled People (UN IYDP) in 1981, accompanied by other changes in law (Prince, 2009), disrupted this norm of the exclusion of disabled people. In Canada, signing on to the UN IYDP was soon accompanied by the passage of the Canadian Charter of Rights and Freedoms

(Canada, 1982). The Charter represents the highest law in Canada meant to guide all other laws. The Charter made it illegal to discriminate on the basis of disability, a practice that nearly every university had been engaging in as a matter of course.[5]

The Canadian Charter of Rights and Freedoms asserts that:

> Every individual is equal before and under the law and has the right to the equal protection and equal benefit of the law without discrimination and, in particular, without discrimination based on race, national or ethnic origin, colour, religion, sex, age or mental or physical disability. (Canada, 1982, s 15 (1))

The status of disability changes with the passing of the Charter, as exclusion on the basis of disability is no longer legal in Canada. This change aligns with the 1981 UN declaration that asked signatory countries to make plans for the "equalization of opportunities, rehabilitation and prevention of disabilities" in order to maximize "participation and equality" for "persons with disabilities" (United Nations, 1981). Universities across Canada also responded: U of T, for example, issued its first statement affirming the inclusion of disabled people in 1981. This document was circulated at meetings, distributed to faculties, and published in the student newspaper and other newsletters. Now buried in the administrative archive, this document marks an historical moment worth presenting in its entirety.[6]

Approved in principle by Governing Council on March 26, 1981

The University and Accessibility for Disabled Persons

The University of Toronto, with a very large number of old buildings and sprawling urban campus, can present a formidable challenge to disabled persons. Adaptations have been made to Erindale and Scarborough, but the situation on the St. George campus remains difficult. The task of reviewing the University's facilities in terms of physical accessibility, assigning priorities for improvements, and finding funds for the changes that will be necessary is equally formidable. The financial aspect is particularly troubling at a time when the University's needs in so many areas are acute, its resources eroded and its prospects for relief in the near future dim.

Given these constraints, it must be recognized that progress will be slow. However, the University has made a beginning, and intends, to the extent that is possible, to take the following steps toward improving accessibility in the months and years ahead.

1. The University endorses in principle the objectives of the United Nations General Assembly resolution proclaiming 1981 as the International Year of Disabled Persons.
2. The University will continue to develop administrative procedures to facilitate the integration of disabled persons into the University community including academic, administrative and support services.
3. The University will encourage faculty and staff to make accommodations for the requirements of disabled persons.

-2-

4. The University will seek funding with a view to ensuring that its buildings, services, and programmes are made accessible where feasible. The goal shall be a major improvement in accessibility within ten years according to a list of priorities established in consultation preferably with recognized groups of disabled persons at the University of Toronto, or failing such groups, with disabled members of the University community. When significant structural alterations are made or new facilities are built the needs of disabled persons will be considered.
5. The University will consult and work with other academic institutions in the province in the belief that the needs and issues require a co-operative effort on a system-wide basis.
6. The administration will place before the Budget Advisory Committee on an annual basis an appreciation of the University's progress in making the campus accessible to the physically handicapped and a set of recommendations for continuing improvements.

Office of the Vice-President—
Personnel and Student Affairs
February 12, 1981

After U of T issued this statement, it becomes difficult to find explicit articulations of the normalcy of excluding disabled people in university administrative texts. Still, what version of inclusion appears in the university life and work?

Aligned with the 1981 UN IYDP recommendation, the appearance of disability in this statement is wrapped up in a plan for management. Plans will be made for future inclusions because whatever else disability is, it is difficult to include and financially a burden; thus, "progress will be slow." This statement reminds the community that change will be difficult and, further, including disabled people is expensive. Regardless of little change, the statement suggests that it endorses the objectives of the UN declaration whereby the "equalization of opportunity" becomes a plan for future action of possible inclusion *if* it is not too difficult, *if* money is to be found, and *if* continued plans for administrative procedures of integration continue.

While much is said to dim the promise of the future inclusion of disabled faculty, students, and staff, the widely circulated document does cast light on U of T's first official version of including disability. It is a burdensome problem. As such, inclusion is difficult, seemingly optional, and highly precarious given the formidable needs of the university. Disability, as in the 1960s, is included, but not as essential to the workings of the university. Instead, it is positioned as essentially a problem of lesser humans whose inclusion may be administered if there is enough goodwill and resources. This inclusion is dependent on the more explicit promise that exclusion will remain an up-front possibility. "At a time when" other needs are pressing, disability may disappear.

The access statement represents inclusion as an act tied to the always present probability of exclusion—disability is included as always potentially excludable. As such, the figure of disability reveals how Man "over-represented as if the human itself" upholds Normate participants and their normal order of things. This widely circulated and archived statement on Access demonstrates that there is a plan for future acts of inclusion when time, space, inclination, and money permit, and it also teaches that this is reasonable for the managerial class for whom the university has already made buildings, services, and programmes fit.

I conclude by opening up explicit connections between this conception of disability and race-thinking as they both sustain the contemporary social order.

CONCLUSION—DISABILITY AND RACE-THINKING

"Something like the steep stairs outside of a university lecture hall can be critiqued as a spatial and architectural feature that excludes; the stairs can also be understood as making a rhetorical argument or sending a message at the same time; and also at the very same time the stairs should push us to understand that other features of the institution that may not be as immediately recognizable to us, also set up steep steps—and these can range from the subject matter being spoken about in that lecture hall, to the rote, stand-and-deliver model of pedagogy and its toll on many students and many teachers, to the actual cost of being in that lecture hall in the first place. When we bring together a study of rhetorical space, institutional critique, and disability studies, we *have* to understand all of these things as connected."

Dolmage, Jay. *Academic Ableism: Disability and Higher Education.* Ann Arbor, MI: University of Michigan Press, 2018, pp. 10–11.

Paul Gilroy (2005) tells us that the ongoing proliferation of "race-thinking" not only includes the "hatreds forged" by the tracing of the colour line but also includes boundary building accomplished through "genomics, biotechnologies and self-conscious biocolonialisms" (pp. 37–38). Gilroy reminds us that biological conceptions are invoked to make powerful distinctions among people that are used to empower some against others. This boundary building, which Gilroy (2005) calls *race-thinking*, not only makes lesser types of humans appear but also makes these boundaries appear *as if* ordained by nature. Race-thinking is Gilroy's way of referring to the process whereby racial hierarchies are established by the systems of power that make some people appear to fit and others to teeter on the edge of degradation and exclusion.

Through ever new ways of "doing" racial division we have the brutal proliferation of people classified as less-than-human. As Gilroy (2005) puts it, race is made to indicate those with an "unadorned inferiority"; the "lowest ontological rung"; the bare life of so-called *real* difference (p. 49). While race and disability are often spoken of as distinct categories of the human, Gilroy's critique of hierarchies that are based on biological concepts allows for disability to be understood as an expression of race-thinking. Today, *disability* is used to refer to an assumption of ontological inferiority making disability appear as an unnecessary biological condition. Occupying a low ontological rung are those people whose presence is made dependent on extra time, leftover money, special resources, exceptional programming, and a host of other things whose allocation is dependent on the luck of running into the goodwill of the superior. The notion of a lesser human, moreover, has been very profitable for those who manage not to appear as such.[7] As a naturalized unfortunate problem, *disability* serves as a term through which the race-thinking that Gilroy writes about continues today.

Race-thinking functions best if the *terms* of its production remain taken for granted. Societal responses to disability serve race-thinking since disability is naturalized as a problem that does not engender social critique but only management, and questions of injustice are left behind in favour of laments of misfortune. If race-thinking, propping up the power of Normate Man, was not still so much at play through the term *disability*, then special education classes would not be filled with racialized and Indigenous students with disabilities (Erevelles, 2000; Pickens, 2019); if it were not so, universities would have many more disabled faculty, students, and staff; if this were not so, 60 per cent of human rights complaints lodged by people in Canada would not be done on the basis of disability (Canadian Human Rights Commission, n.d.) and short- and long-term disability protocols would not serve as the easiest way to manage women, trans, Indigenous, and racialized people "with problems," essentially removing them from workplaces. These examples suggest that disability remains the "really wrong" (ontologically inferior) and thus *rightly* used category to make and mark the line between the unjustly treated and the necessarily excludable.

Critical studies, suggests Sylvia Wynter (1994), needs to "understand the rules governing our human modes of perception and the behaviours to which they lead" (p. 69). This means that we need to attend to who is perceiving disability, how, when, and to what end. I hope that the few examples that I have offered throughout this chapter are enough to trigger a memory of what we already know too well; namely, that in contemporary social order, *disability* is a key term used to manage and to naturalize the not-necessarily-present, the not-normal, the readily-excludable. Today, disability studies needs to work along with critical studies of all kinds to honour the promise found in rethinking what it means to be human (Goodley et al., 2019; Pickens, 2019). This chapter has sought to offer an invitation to *do disability studies* in the places we find ourselves as a way to pursue the promise of disability and disability studies.

NOTES

1. The Normate, according to Thomson (1997), "designates the social figure through which people can represent themselves as definitive human beings [and] ... can step into a position of authority" (p. 8). Linda Ware (2020) provides a history of the term's genesis (p. xiii). See also Goffman's (1963) concept of "the normals," whose stereotypical reaction to others with unexpected attributes makes for a category of the lesser human, namely, "the stigmatized."

2. Further illustrations of this promise include Ed Roberts and his iron lung (USA), Mike Oliver's sociology career after becoming a wheelchair user (UK), and Audre Lorde and her struggle in and for Black feminist-informed education as a legally blind woman (USA).

3. In the summer of 2020, the Black Lives Matter movement vigorously expanded across the globe, renewing a promise of change by undoing the anti-Black colonial power that produces the Americas in their current form. As in the 1960s, there are still signs that this necessary movement toward change is somehow caught manufacturing its lesser human, e.g., disability included as the "crippled" and "crippling" character of white Power. Including disability in this way may serve only to (re)confirm Man over-represented as if the human itself.

4. The year 1966 also marks the first year of disability insurance policies for faculty at the University of Toronto.

5. For a list of policy developments in Canada, consider the Eugenics Archive: https://eugenicsarchive.ca/discover/encyclopedia/535eeb377095aa000000021b.

6. Office of the Vice-President – Personnel and Student Affairs (1981).

7. This begs the question—does one's critical analysis require a lesser and damnable Other who has been forced into this job?

REFERENCES

Canada. (1982). *Canadian Charter of Rights and Freedoms*, Part 1 of the *Constitution Act, 1982*, being Schedule B to the *Canada Act 1982* (UK), 1982, c 11. https://laws-lois.justice.gc.ca/eng/Const/page-15.html

Canadian Human Rights Commission. (n.d.). *Rights of people with disabilities*. https://www.canada.ca/en/canadian-heritage/services/rights-people-disabilities.html

Erevelles, N. (2000). Educating unruly bodies: Critical pedagogy, disability studies, and the politics of schooling. *Educational Theory, 50*(1), 25–47. https://doi.org/10.1111/j.1741-5446.2000.00025.x

Finkelstein, V. (1998). Emancipating disability studies. In T. Shakespeare (Ed.), *The disability reader: Social science perspectives* (pp. 28–49). Cassell.

Gabel, S. L., & Danforth, S. (2008). *Disability and the politics of education: An international reader.* Peter Lang.

Galer, D. (2018). *Working towards equity: Disability rights activism and employment in late twentieth-century Canada.* University of Toronto Press.

Gilroy, P. (2002). *Against race: Imagining political culture beyond the color line.* Harvard University Press.

Gilroy, P. (2005). *Postcolonial melancholia.* Columbia University Press.

Goffman, E. (1963). *Stigma: Notes on the management of a spoiled identity.* Prentice Hall.

Goodley, D., Lawthom, R., Liddiard, K., & Runswick-Cole, K. (2019). Provocations for critical disability studies. *Disability & Society, 34*(6), 972–997. https://doi.org/10.1080/09687599.2019.1566889

Linton, S. (1998). *Claiming disability.* New York University Press.

Michalko, R. (2002). *The difference that disability makes.* Temple University Press.

Michalko, R. (2008). Double trouble: Disability and disability studies in education. In S. L. Gabel & S. Danforth (Eds.), *Disability & the politics of education: An international reader* (pp. 401–415). Peter Lang.

Million, D. (2013). *Therapeutic nations: Healing in an age of Indigenous human rights.* University of Arizona Press.

Mitchell, D., & Snyder, S. (1997). *The body and physical difference: Discourses of disability.* University of Michigan Press.

Office of the Vice-President – Personnel and Student Affairs. (1981). *The university and accessibility for disabled persons.* Thomas Fisher Rare Book Library Collection (A95-0014/Box 007 – File #12). University of Toronto Archives, Toronto, Canada.

Oliver, M. (1990). *The politics of disablement.* Macmillan.

Pickens, T. A. (2019). *Black madness :: Mad blackness.* Duke University Press.

Prince, M. J. (2009). *Absent citizens: Disability politics and policy in Canada.* University of Toronto Press.

Saltes, N. (2020). Disability barriers in academia: An analysis of disability accommodation policies for faculty at Canadian universities. *Canadian Journal of Disability Studies, 9*(1), 53–90. https://doi.org/10.15353/cjds.v9i1.596

Shklar, J. (1990). *The faces of injustice.* Yale University Press.

Slee, R. (2018). *Inclusion isn't dead, it just smells funny.* Routledge.

Stiker, H.-J. (1999). *The history of disability* (W. Sayers, Trans.). Foreword by D. T. Mitchell. University of Michigan Press.

Stone, D. A. (1984). *The disabled state.* Temple University Press.

Thomson, R. G. (1997). *Extraordinary bodies: Figuring physical disability in American culture and literature.* Columbia University Press.

Titchkosky, T. (2011). The promise of disability. In C. Rolheiser, M. Evans, & M. Gambhir (Eds.), *Inquiry into practice: Reaching every student through inclusive curriculum* (pp. 16–17). Ontario Institute for Studies in Education of the University of Toronto. https://www.oise.utoronto.ca/oise/UserFiles/File/ITE_PUB_2011_COMPLETE_LR1.pdf

United Nations. (1981). *Declaration of the international year of disabled persons.* https://www.un.org/development/desa/disabilities/the-international-year-of-disabled-persons-1981.html

University of Toronto Archives. (1965). *University of Toronto academic divisions calendar, 1965–1966,* p. 14, P78-0024. https://archive.org/details/uoftcalendaracad1965af/page/n671/mode/2up?q=Dentistry

University of Toronto Archives. (1966). *University of Toronto academic divisions calendar, 1966–1967,* pp. 11–12, P78-0024. https://archive.org/details/uoftcalendaracad1966af/page/n625/mode/2up?q=stamina

Ware, L. (Ed.). (2020). Introduction. In L. Ware (Ed.), *Critical readings in interdisciplinary disability studies: (Dis)Assemblages* (pp. ix–xiv). Springer.

Wynter, S. (1994). No humans involved: An open letter to my colleagues. *Forum: N.H.I. Knowledge for the 21st Century: Knowledge on Trial, 1*(1), 42–73.

Wynter, S. (2003). Unsettling the coloniality of being/power/truth/freedom: Towards the human, after man, its overrepresentation—an argument. *CR: The New Centennial Review, 3*(3), 257–337. https://doi.org/10.1353/ncr.2004.0015

Zola, I. K. (1977). Healthism and disabling medicalization. In I. Illich (Ed.), *Disabling professions* (pp. 41–68). Marion Boyars Publishers.

CHAPTER 2

Nativity

Hanna Herdegen

Key Terms: ABA Therapy; Autism; Language; Rhetoric

It's summer.

My sister and I are sitting on the tile floor of my apartment kitchen. My heart needed a break from putting the groceries away. My sister did most of the reaching and bending for me, but my ears are still ringing. My body gets tired more easily in the heat.

The tile is cool against my palms. There are raspberries in the refrigerator. Maybe I'll put some in my yogurt later.

"I have to go to the city tomorrow for training," my sister says.

The dishwasher has just finished a cycle. The air smells strongly of damp and soap and fake lime.

The refrigerator hums.

I've been trying to think of what to say. My body feels miles long, my feet stuck in the silt at the bottom of an ocean, my head somewhere above where the air is thin, everything fizzing at the edges. Words are so far away, even on better days. I grip on tight, pump them up from underground.

"We can ask: how does identity itself become instituted through encounters with others that surprise, that shift the boundaries of the familiar, of what we assume that we know?"

Ahmed, Sara. *Strange Encounters: Embodied Others in Post-Coloniality.* London, UK: Routledge, 2000, p. 7.

I remember three things about my first day of school.

One. There was a long hallway with bright lights.

Two. I was screaming.

Three. After I'd finished screaming, a lady called Beth or Becky or Barbara tried to feed me Red Delicious apples. Red Delicious apples are, objectively, the worst apple. Like licking corduroy.

The slices were dressed up like mouths, spread with peanut butter and stuck full of crooked marshmallow teeth.

Beth-Becky-Barbara's mouth was lipstick pink. *Eat it. Go ahead, eat up. Eat up, don't you want any? What's wrong, don't you want any?*

The lights were long white swords in the ceiling, humming like bees.

I didn't scream again. My voice had already decided to pack up and leave for the day.

My sister and I go to the coffee shop across from the architecture building. They serve gluten-free things on Saturdays, and I get a piece of coffee cake and a lemon-lime Italian soda. She gets a latte with almond milk and waits by the counter for our things so I don't have to stand.

We sit near the back, next to the pair of summer students studying with their earphones half-in. They sip iced coffees and chat to each other over the offset walls of their laptop screens. It's technical writing, probably. They're saying something about memos.

The bell jingles over the door, and I look toward the painted windows at the front of the shop. Someone's dog is tied up to the bench outside, its tail wagging as the people pass by on the sidewalk.

The radio plays the song from that Geico commercial with the googly-eyed stack of money.

Don't you want me, baby.

Don't you want me, ooooh.

A girl orders a peach smoothie at the counter. I brace for the grinding noise. I wish I'd brought my earplugs. I wish I felt like raising my hands to my ears.

The sound crawls inside my head. My sister brings me a fork for my cake.

The Italian soda sweats against my hands. "Did you know," I say, the fizz stinging my nose, my throat, "the guy who invented ABA [applied behavioural analysis] basically thought autistic people weren't people. He basically said, *Yeah, they've got eyes and hands and stuff, but there's nothing inside.* And he thought he was a big deal—like, using torture to make humans out of empty shells."

"Dick," my sister says.

"Yeah."

When you are very young at school, they make you sit in circles and answer questions like:

What is the weather like outside?

What day of the week is it?

What did you do yesterday?

The first two are the easiest. You just tell the truth, and people are usually happy with you.

But saying the true thing is not the same as saying the right thing.

What did you do yesterday? is not an easy question. This is because the true answer is not always the right answer. When people ask, *What did you do yesterday?*, they want to hear the right things, things like *I went to the park* or *I walked to the bakery with my mother.*

They do not want to hear things like *I spent a long time standing on a chair in front of the mirror, trying to understand how my face was attached to the rest of it.*

It's four hours from school to our parents' house in the northern part of the state.

I can't help my sister drive—I can't drive at all, because my heart sometimes drops me to the ground without warning—so she does it all herself while I navigate and charge the phones and work Spotify. We listen to the Eagles and then to a podcast episode about sexism and moral licensing.

The mountains remind me of Switzerland, the way the sun seems to set more suddenly here than in the open spaces closer to the water. We learned in fourth grade: piedmont, tidewater. Appalachian. My teacher was from the north and said it wrong. *Apple-ay-shin.*

"I don't know how to explain it," I say, watching the row of pines lining the road as they blur together behind the guardrail. "It's like those dreams you have where you know something terrible is coming toward you—like you can see a tornado coming across a field. But you can't run and you can't even feel your legs. And your bones feel staticky, and you're breathing, but your chest isn't moving. And it's like—I don't know, it feels like you're getting thinner, or, like, dissolving at the edges."

She's quiet for a while, and the road is mostly empty, and I wonder if it's because I've accidentally assumed something about me is universal when it isn't at all. I hate that. It feels like one of those slapstick tricks where you're minding your own business and then trip on the sidewalk and fall down a manhole.

"Okay, but what do we do?" she asks, finally. "I mean, it sucks, but he has to learn how to write sometime."

"No, he doesn't," I say. There is static buzzing in my elbows. "The whole point is that he doesn't."

I found Helen Keller when I was eight.

She was in a book in the classroom library. I had never met anyone before who screamed down the wall between them and the world.

It wasn't love, exactly. Or it might have been, if *love* can mean *the end of loneliness.*

On the back cover there were drawings of hands making the shapes of letters. I hid the book in my desk and memorized them during snack time.

I met Helen again when I was ten. It was a rainy Friday near the end of the year, when patience had run out for new things. We stayed inside from recess and watched *The Miracle Worker.*

Helen screamed and fought and threw things and ripped her pretty clothes, and I thought about how brave she was to do that out loud, where there were people who could hate her (who could hurt her) for it.

Then Teacher came, and I tried to imagine what it would feel like to be given words people could understand.

(*Like water underground,* Annie Sullivan said, and I thought maybe she could see Helen because she was seeing herself.

It's like the blind leading the blind, Helen's brother said, and I thought, *Yes. Yes, exactly.*)

Sometimes things stick inside my head like an echo.

Like water underground.

Like water underground.

Like water underground.

I made a place in my head, a place where Helen screamed and fought and threw things for me while I held myself still. I trapped words in my fingers so other people couldn't hear.

I was twenty-four when I found out that Helen thought some people like me were better off dead.

We're sitting out on the front porch in the dusky-blue early evening: me, my sister, and our friend Annie. It's just rained; the stone walkway is warm and wet under my bare feet. I can smell the heat of the day in the air still—like summer and bicycle tires. We've taken three lime popsicles from the freezer. Annie has some of the leftover yubu chobap on a plate she sets between us on the step.

The parents are inside, talking about things that are best left unlistened to.

"I don't know how you did it," Annie says, brushing stray rice from her hands. I met her when she was four years old, when she came home with my sister after preschool dance class and spent the afternoon running around the house in my old princess shoes. We've been as good as sisters for fifteen years.

"Did what?" I ask. I open my popsicle and try not to let it drip into my lap. It's half-melted already.

"How you sat at the adult table all those years," Annie explains, and my sister laughs.

"Yeah," she says, her feet resting in the mulch around the hydrangeas, "we used to be like, looking in from the kitchen, like, *Is Hanna okay in there?*"

"Thank you for sacrificing yourself for us," Annie says, giggling. "*We thank you for your service.*"

She makes me laugh. "No problem." I shrug. "You just learn what to talk about. And what to say. And when not to say anything." I've had a lot of practice with that. "Plus, I didn't really mind. Your dad tells good stories."

"They act like you're helpless, though," my sister says. "They feel sorry for you."

I know this. I've been sick for years now, and the worst thing is that people can't seem to get over being sad about it. About the way my life looks now. But it's rude to say *Get over it,* so I don't. Mostly.

"They're always telling me to hang out with you," my sister says. "Like I wouldn't just hang out with you because I want to. Like, we're *friends?* I *like* talking to you?"

I guessed this, but I didn't know. Not for sure. It's nice to know for sure.

"Thanks," I say. "Me too."

"How long has it been, now?" Annie asks. Some of her popsicle is escaping down her arm. We forgot napkins.

I'm not sure what she means, but I take a guess. "Since POTS?"

She nods.

"Three years since diagnosis. But five years since I first started feeling weird all the time."

"I remember you used to faint in church," my sister says. "Your eyes rolled back into your head. And Dad had to carry you out."

"Yeah. That was rough." The first time it happened I was seven. I woke up in my grandfather's arms with the entire congregation gathered outside on the steps, watching. The priest stood in front, making the sign of the cross in the air as we walked away, his vestments flapping in the wind. Green for Ordinary Time.

My heart is so much easier to explain than my head.

And even then, it took them years to believe me.

The first time I remember hearing the word *autism,* I was in the third grade. We were assigned interest projects: we had to choose a topic that interested us, do some research, interview an "expert," and present our findings to the class. I did mine on English springer spaniels, which I thought were the best kind of dogs.

A girl called Mary did her interest project on autistic children. Her sister, an ABA therapist, came to speak as her expert. I don't remember learning what "autism" meant, but there were puzzle pieces glued to Mary's poster board, and

Mary's sister talked about her patients like they were strange and sad and far away, like the children on the St. Jude's videos we watched every year during the Math-A-Thon. Except the St. Jude's children had faces.

I don't remember anything else. Joe Manny made a planetarium inside a refrigerator box. I spent most of recess wondering what it might feel like to be brave enough to sit inside. Would it really look like stars?

They're talking about cases at dinner again.

A little boy at the clinic screams every time he has to sit on a toilet.

A little girl at the clinic puts soap in her mouth instead of in her hands.

I'm eating broccoli in small bites. The chicken is too dry.

Ellen Samuels says, *Crip time is time travel.*

For disabled people, she says, time moves at altered speeds: assembled rifts instead of a stream. Disjointed moments arrest us, age us, leave us behind, meld together at odd angles.

A little boy at the school won't learn to tie his shoes.

A little girl at the school rubs her saliva between her fingers. *Disgusting.*

Eggplant and red peppers. Brown rice. Pass the salt.

I'm all the people I've ever been, screaming at once: *Listen, would you please just listen to me.*

Bettina Judd says we live in haunted houses.

She says medicine tries us—it *finds* us.

Innocent. Guilty.

She says verdicts are handed down in bloodlines. She says:

I don't feel innocent here lurking with the ghosts.

Our ghosts aren't exactly the same. I don't know how much the difference matters.

Zucchini. Corn. Sausage.

A little girl can't spell her name.

I'm the only expert on this subject sitting at this table, and they're not even looking at me.

The second time I remember hearing the word *autism* was on an episode of *House.* I was about fourteen or fifteen, and I had decided that I was going to become a veterinarian. I watched old *House* episodes on the little staticky TV in my basement room at night, the headphone cord wrapped around my fingers, a pencil in my hand. Every time they said a word I didn't know I would look it up in my mother's illustrated medical dictionary. The words would stick in my brain like song lyrics. I had *thrombocytopenia* on the back of my tongue for weeks.

In this particular episode, the case of the week centred on a young autistic boy who had unexplained fits. It turned out he had parasites in his eye from eating sand. He had been telling everyone about this all along. But nobody listened. In the end, of course, House figures it out, and in the final scenes of the episode the boy thanks House for saving his life by giving him his GameBoy and (!) looking him in the eye. The boy's mother watches tearfully.

The B plot involved House's colleagues debating amongst themselves about whether House—because he was irritable, impersonable, and single-minded— might also be autistic. They conclude that he probably isn't. I don't remember why.

They'd defined *autism* often enough in the episode that the word felt familiar to me by the end. But there was something about the boy's hands, I think, that made me take out the medical dictionary and flip through the As.

Or maybe it was the screaming and screaming and screaming and nobody hearing a thing.

One of the two.

We're driving home for Thanksgiving. I've been reading M. Remi Yergeau's *Authoring Autism* in my rhetoric class.

"They're writing in an autistic register," I say, because it's what it feels like: reading a native language. I didn't know I had a native language before last week.

"What's an autistic register?" my sister asks.

"There's just—a way of understanding that exists apart from meaning." I've been thinking about a metaphor, plotting it out in my head so I can use it in class after break. I don't know for sure, but I think I'm the only autistic person in the class. In discussions I've been swimming between two ports. Tell them nothing. Tell them everything.

Against meaning, Yergeau says.

They're a rhetorician—how can they be against meaning? we discuss. *Isn't that antithetical to the whole project of rhetoric?*

Tell them nothing. Tell them everything.

We're driving down route 460, between the orange pools of light from the streetlamps.

"It's like listening to a song in a language you don't speak," I say, slowly, carefully, gripping the soda in my lap so it doesn't spill. The twist-off cap doesn't twist back on. "There's something that sits under the words." The autumn stars are smoky above the town. They'll get clearer as we pass through the mountains. "That's what it's like. Being under the words."

There are whole worlds in that book I never knew existed anywhere but under my own skin.

Is this what it's like to live in a familiar place? To see someone and recognize them immediately?

Maybe that's why people like looking strangers in the eye.

I studied abroad in the spring of my junior year of college.

When you're preparing to go abroad, they make you go to meetings (and meetings, and meetings) where they tell you what to expect and how to behave.

Most of the students in my program were interested in the practical things:

How much shampoo should I pack?

How do you tip the waiters?

What happens if I miss my flight?

But most of what they'll tell you (in the meetings, and meetings, and meetings) is this:

It is a strange world out there. You are going to meet people who do things you don't understand, who expect you to behave in ways that don't make sense, whose way of being in the world is very different from yours.

And what you have to remember is that you are as much a stranger to them as they are to you. Be patient. Be kind. Be respectful.

Everyone warns you:

It's going to make you homesick. You're going to feel out of place. You might even feel angry that nobody does things the way you're used to. And that's fine. That's normal. We'll be here for you if you need to talk.

Remember:

Everyone feels like that. It's nothing to be ashamed of.

We're in the parking lot of the Mediterranean restaurant, and she says, "Yes, but how can we have a conversation?" She's locking the car, looking at me across the roof, her breath fogging the air as she frowns. "Like, how do you communicate things without meaning?"

People are very worried about functionality.

> "'Fixing' is a messy business, one for which the goal is not simply a stable and final resolution, but rather an illumination of process, a reckoning of forces, a continuing of the conversation about who we are and why we arrived here."
>
> Frazee, Catherine, Kathryn Church, and Melanie Panitch. "Enshrined: The Hidden History of a Circus Program." In *Mobilizing Metaphor: Art, Culture and Disability Activism in Canada*, edited by Christine Kelley and Michael Orsini, 25–53. Vancouver, BC: University of British Columbia Press, 2016, p. 52.

"Okay. Yeah," I say, putting my hands in my pockets. My keys are still cold from the walk after class. "There are times when understanding specific things can be important. Like *I'm in pain* or *I don't want that.* But the thing is that people say that 'autistic tantrums' or whatever, are because the kid needs to learn to communicate. But if you're actually—" I sigh. I want to say what I mean. "Okay. It's not that the kid needs to learn to communicate. They're already communicating. It's just that nobody's listening."

I don't say, *So of course they're screaming,* because I feel like that's obvious, but: *Of course we're screaming.*

The restaurant door opens, closes. Voices spill out. There's light and heat inside, and we're walking slowly.

I still haven't answered the question, so I try again. "They're already having conversations that mean things. But conversations don't have to be *about* meaning. Like—they can just be: I walk into the room, hand you my phone with a picture of a dog on it, and leave. That's a conversation. I jump up and down when you ask me a question. That's a conversation. You're talking to me, and I like the word *purple* so I shout PURPLE! That's a conversation." I stop on the sidewalk. I won't be able to hear once we go inside. "It's just ... decentring meaning, in the neurotypical sense." My hands are cold. "I don't need to be legible to be valuable."

> "With word and deed we insert ourselves into the human world, and this insertion is like a second birth, in which we confirm and take upon ourselves the naked fact of our original physical appearance. This insertion is not forced upon us by necessity, like labour, and not prompted by utility, like work ... its impulse springs from the beginning which came into the world when we were born and to which we respond by beginning something of our own initiative."
>
> Arendt, Hannah. *The Human Condition.* 2nd ed., Chicago, IL: The University of Chicago Press, 1998, p. 176.

We went to Germany and Ghana and Greece, and I kept waiting to feel it.

They kept saying: *You're going to encounter people who don't understand you. And that's frustrating. That's unsettling. It's okay. Just prepare yourself.*

We were in Switzerland and Italy and Turkey and Hungary. I kept waiting to feel what they said I should.

I never did.

(I never do.)

I felt the same in Mendrisio, in Accra, in Budapest as I have anywhere.

For the first time, people are telling me *It's okay to feel this*, and I don't feel it at all.

Maybe strangeness is a kind of home.

Maybe I'm native to myself.

At home, late at night, my sister knocks on my door.

"I'm so sorry," she says, before I can even really see it's her. She's brought her whole computer up two flights of stairs. The screen is glowing white against her wrists. "I read it, and, dude, I'm so sorry."

I make a face—I don't know which. My head swims from getting up too fast. "About what?" I ask, and the words are more breath than sound. My heart is beating so fast I can feel it in my teeth.

"I found that book you were talking about. And I was reading it, and they're talking about how they constantly have to answer all these questions about being autistic—like how being autistic is just, like, constantly answering questions." She tilts her head against the wall. The computer snaps shut, almost catching her fingers. "And I do that to you!"

The heat from the fire downstairs has filled the hallway outside my room. The air smells like Christmas already: smoke and cold, cinnamon and clove and orange from the cranberry sauce simmering on the stove. Our dad opens the back door to let the dog in.

I don't want her to be sorry.

"Well, yeah," I say, "they say that. And it's—" I put on a headliner voice "—*The Autistic Experience*, T. M. Like, *whoa*." I shrug. "But it's different when you do it." I lean against the edge of the open door. The wood is cool against my cheek. I close my eyes. My ears are ringing. "You're actually listening to the answer. You actually want to know."

"Relationality encompasses complex relations to the earth, cosmologies, living and non-living beings, and all other matter…. With this inextricable interdependence and interconnectedness comes a responsibility to live in ethical relationality with more-than-human others, where humans are not figured in hierarchical order."

Martin, Karen. "Here We Go 'Round the Broomie Tree': Aboriginal Early Childhood Realities and Experiences in Early Childhood Services." In *Early Childhood in Australia: Historical and Comparative Contexts*, edited by Jo Ailwood. Frenchs Forest, NSW, Australia: Pearson Education, 2007, p. 102.

It's summer.

We're sitting on the floor of my apartment kitchen. My heart needed a break from putting the groceries away.

I've been talking for fifteen minutes, and I'm not sure I've actually managed to get to what I'm trying to say. Not yet.

"They're saying things," I say. "They're all *already* saying things. And I *hate* that that's … not what people think. I hate that we're always the ones who have to explain ourselves, and no one's even listening. We're the ones doing the work, always, and nobody's even hearing us."

I have to take a break to breathe. It's almost time for the next dose of salt pills. My sister is quiet for a long time.

The refrigerator hums.

"Can I ask you a question?"

I look around for my water. It's hard to see in the dark. "Yeah."

"When did you know?"

SOURCES

Callis, J., Oakey, P., & Wright, P. A. (1981). Don't you want me baby [Song recorded by The Human League]. On *Dare*. Virgin Records.

Judd, B. (2014). *Patient: Poems*. Black Lawrence Press.

Merrick, M., Gibson, W. (Writers), & Tass, N. (Director). (2000, November 12). The miracle worker (Season 4, Episode 4) [TV series episode]. In P. M. Green & C. Hirschhorn (Executive Producers), *The wonderful world of Disney*. Fountain Productions; Walt Disney Television.

Samuels, E. (2017). Six ways of looking at crip time. *Disability Studies Quarterly, 37*(3). https://dsq-sds.org/article/view/5824/4684

Shore, D., Hoselton, D., Davis, P. (Writers), & Siegel, N. T. (Director). (2006, September 26). Lines in the sand (Season 3, Episode 4) [TV series episode]. In P. Attanasio, K. Jacobs, D. Sackheim, D. Shore, & B. Singer (Executive Producers), *House, M. D.* Heel & Toe Films; Shore Z Productions; Bad Hat Harry Productions; NBC Universal Television.

Yergeau, R. M. (2017). *Authoring autism: On rhetoric and neurological queerness*. Duke University Press.

CHAPTER 3

Navigating Borderlands: Deaf and Hearing Experiences in Post-Secondary Education

Sammy Jo Johnson and Sarah Beck

Key Terms: American Sign Language; Audism; Deaf Culture; Education; Inclusion

INTRODUCTION

This chapter reflects on both of our stories as university students, focusing on our experiences straddling deaf and hearing worlds. We tell our stories to raise questions about how the university campus becomes accessible to some bodies and ways of being while remaining highly inaccessible to others (Titchkosky, 2008). As one deaf[1] and one hearing author, our stories expose dramatic differences around accessibility. However, telling our stories side by side also reveals some parallels, specifically the demand to behave as *hearing* university students. By bringing attention to the demands placed on hearing, our stories also make visible some of the ways audism—defined on the Canadian Association of the Deaf (2015) website as the "direct, indirect, and/or systemic discrimination … or prejudice against Deaf people"—is manifest on campus. Audism, as Bauman (2004) has shown, is a complex system of oppression that also results in hearing privilege. Telling stories about different deaf and hearing experiences on campus can bring attention to the many ways audism operates in the university, identify hearing privilege that is too often unrecognized in this space, and demonstrate the importance of creating more inclusive spaces in post-secondary education (Ramirez-Stapleton & Duarte, 2021; Stapleton & Gillon, 2021).

"Deafness has been investigated for a long time (in some cases, as far back as the late nineteenth century) and ... conceptualizations of deafness and d/Deaf communities have changed over time. We use the word d/Deaf to capture the distinction often made between the word deaf, which describes an audiological status, and the cultural identity of Deaf, which is generally used by individuals who not only are deaf, but also claim Deaf as an identity reflecting their membership in a culture centered around the experience of deafness and the use of sign language to communicate.... As the investigation of deafness and d/Deaf communities grew in the latter part of the twentieth century ... the conceptualization of deafness has become more complex."

Mauldin, Laura, and Tara Fannon. "The Sociology of Deafness: A Literature Review of the Disciplinary History." In *Sociology Looking at Disability: What Did We Know and When Did We Know It*, edited by Sara E. Green and Sharon N. Barnartt, 193–225. Bingley, UK: Emerald Group Publishing, 2016, p. 194.

Sarah received a diagnosis of hearing loss during her undergraduate degree, after several years of university as a hearing student, and has since been introduced to the deaf community, deaf culture, and American Sign Language (ASL). In the first section Sarah examines her experience navigating the university as a student with relatively new hearing loss, which granted certain (speaking) privileges but also created additional barriers limiting her inclusion on campus. She shares the pressure she experienced to communicate and behave in ways acceptable to the dominant hearing culture, even when it was at the cost of her own access. Sammy Jo is a Child of deaf adults (Coda) and was raised in close proximity to the deaf community in Edmonton, although this distance has increased during her time in university. In the second section Sammy Jo explores her own language use on campus and how her hearing identity is intertwined with the hearing-centric structure of the university. This discussion brings attention to the ways hearingness is required and privileged on campus and in other educational institutions, and to the marginalization and exclusion of ASL in post-secondary education (see Robinson & Henner, 2018; Trowler & Turner, 2002).

In the final section of this chapter, we examine the class in which we met, where an alternative story emerges. In this classroom we created a smaller signing space where the demands to behave as hearing students were sidestepped, and where ASL and deaf culture could be seen on campus.[2] While we describe how this space was distinctively inclusive, we also identify some of the limitations of this reconfigured classroom.

"As my friend Thomas King has so aptly put it, inconvenience is what turns special needs into a nuisance. My leaving every day at lunch, my turning up in a makeshift wheelchair, my being depleted in a way that occasionally made it hard to engage in class—unbeknownst to me, all these things were grating on my teacher. Maybe she saw my presence as disruptive to the rest of the kids in class; maybe it was my sudden absence every afternoon. Whatever the cause, she started to view the accommodations I needed as an inconvenience. From there, her thinking followed the path Thomas outlined: as the supposed cause of the inconvenience, I was an annoyance, a nuisance.

"I know she felt that way because she told me, in front of the entire class."

Wente, Jesse. *Unreconciled: Family, Truth, and Indigenous Resistance.* Toronto, ON: Penguin Random House, 2021, p. 31.

SARAH'S STORY

In my undergrad I was diagnosed with a bilateral hearing loss and immediately fitted with my first pair of hearing aids. Shortly after, I realized that listening through a device was not the same and that I could no longer fully trust or rely on auditory information alone. I began using sign language interpreters in the classroom and, over time, developed a deep appreciation for, and identification with, ASL and deaf culture. This identification clashes with the dominant medical model of deafness, which views deafness primarily as an audiological issue (see Ladd, 2003). According to the medical model, the deaf body must be brought in line with hearing standards, and this is perhaps most evident when looking at the structural barriers to learning ASL faced by deaf children and their families (Snoddon & Underwood, 2014, 2017). The view that deaf people "must be encouraged (or even forced) to become as much like non-deaf people as possible" rests on a rejection of the languages, cultures, and communities of deaf people (Canadian Association of the Deaf, 2015). As a student with hearing loss, I was treated differently. My instructors and peers no longer saw me as "Sarah"; they saw me as disabled, and too often I was referred to as "the deaf girl" in class.[3] This label identified me only by my hearing loss, and it carried with it audist assumptions about my capabilities as a student.

On various occasions course instructors have not allowed me to participate in class activities. In one of my courses, students were divided into groups to discuss the week's readings. While other students were assigned groups, I was instructed to hop from group to group, observing my classmates as they discussed the topics and themes from the readings. As I sat there watching the other students, I could not help but feel that my opinions and contributions were not valued. When restrictions, such as this, are placed on deaf students, the opportunity to engage with other students and to demonstrate our knowledge is severely compromised. These decisions, which had a great impact on my learning, were typically made by my professor alone, and gave me no opportunity to negotiate my access. This example demonstrates different "levels of audism" as identified by Bauman, including "*individual audism*"—the negative assumptions about my ability to participate as a deaf student held by this professor—and "*institutional audism*"—the privileging of hearing ways of participating in the post-secondary classroom (2004, p. 242, italics in original).

Much of the exclusion that I faced at university was from my peers. Students rarely chose to sit next to me, often avoided my table, and I was seldom included in social chit-chat during breaks. When it was time to break into groups or sign up for presentations, I always had to be placed into a group by the course instructor. As I internalized these events, I started to see myself as a burden. I became cognizant of my behaviour and made changes to ensure that I did not become a burden to others.

I would refrain from asking questions in class, and I would instruct my interpreters not to interrupt even if they had missed information or needed clarification. I knew that by asking for clarification, it would only slow down the lecture or discussion. I was worried that if I interrupted too often, I would be perceived as slow or incompetent by my peers and the instructors. I sat there, at times, not fully grasping what was going on around me, and I often had to read the class notes to understand what had taken place in class even though I was present.

In a system that is built and functions around the ability to hear and excludes those who do not, deaf people are pressured to make themselves closer to the hearing by adapting to hearing norms. I often felt pressured to use speech over sign in class as all classroom activities were conducted in spoken language and functioned to exclude, isolate, and disadvantage me for using ASL. For instance, time-restrictions placed on presentations failed to take into consideration the added time needed when language is passed through an interpreter. Even so, using my voice in class made negotiating accessibility cumbersome. It was like my hearing peers and instructors would "forget" I had issues hearing. They would call my name to get my attention, often look away when speaking with me, and got annoyed with me when I did not respond. The frustration that comes with sitting on this border between not being hearing but not being deaf drove me to "turn off" my voice.

When navigating the campus outside of class, I was left to negotiate independently within these spaces, as interpreters are not immediately present and rarely provided. There are very few deaf people on campus and even fewer that sign. Without access to interpreters and having few deaf students or faculty, there were limited opportunities to use ASL on campus, further distancing deaf students from ASL and reinforcing a reliance on spoken language. Whether I was ordering a coffee on campus or asking for help finding a book in the library, there was a substantial amount of pressure to use speech over all other forms of communication as hearing staff and students were often reluctant to accommodate me, even after identifying myself as deaf. My speaking ability has often been used as "evidence" to deny my deaf identity and to reinforce the use of speech as the only acceptable form of communication. These negative interactions not only caused anxiety in the moment but occured with high regularity that I limited my interactions with hearing people on campus. Where I once attended events and participated in social clubs, social rejection and isolation became my new norm, to the point where I was rarely seen on campus at all.

SAMMY JO'S STORY

My story as a hearing university student involves a process of moving away from the deaf spaces and connections that filled much of my childhood. While Codas can and do stay connected to deaf communities beyond childhood, we are expected to transition—to "disappear"—into the hearing world as adults (Hoffmeister, 2008, p. 191). My own disappearance as a Coda is deeply intertwined with language, and in this account of my story I look specifically at my language use in the university. It may seem quite obvious that, as a hearing individual, I navigate university life using spoken language. The reliance on spoken language—at the exclusion of sign language—in my education has been made to seem natural and inevitable when in actuality my language usage serves to reinforce my membership in the hearing world. Moreover, it is not just my hearing identity that is reinforced but the hearing-centric structure of the university. That is, the disappearance of my Codaness as well as the dominance of spoken language within post-secondary education hinge on the marginalization of sign language from this space.

As a Coda I am both connected to and separate from the deaf community—the specific community I grew up in and other deaf spaces I have come into contact with. Hoffmeister (2008) describes Codas as "living on the 'border'" (p. 189). This borderland space involves a sense of being a part of something beyond the hearing world and that something being a part of me. In Preston's 1994 study involving 150 adult children of deaf parents in the United States, many partici-pants expressed a deep sense of inhabiting a space between the binary of deaf/hearing. As one participant put it: "I'm not deaf but I'm not hearing. [Signs: *I don't know I'm not deaf or hearing. Both, I guess.*]" (Preston, 1994, p. 236). Despite this sense of "both," my borderland Coda position is oddly temporary.

Hoffmeister (2008) explains that Codas are "groomed" for departure from the deaf world and communities of our childhoods (p. 201), and part of this transi-tion centres around our language usage. Preston (1994) found that for many adult Codas "speaking was used in public" and "signing was used conversationally at home and among friends" (p. 134). However, as a child, while certain spaces (like school) were reserved for spoken language, the divide between public/private was blurred as I used ASL inside and outside of my deaf home daily. This blurriness is different from Davis's (2000) account as a child of deaf parents, where he em-phasizes a distinct sense of belonging to the hearing world as a child; yet Davis describes a sense of loss in adulthood that resonates with my own story.

As a young adult, when I moved from Edmonton to Toronto to begin my mas-ter's degree at the age of 21, I experienced a sudden and painful disconnect from my deaf home, community, and ASL. Despite such feelings, my abrupt separation from ASL was one that I, at least at first, faced without question. It seemed natural that moving away to start graduate studies involved moving more fully into the hearing world. After all, I had always, with the exception of a preschool program specific to Codas, used English in my education.

I have benefitted from a linguistically accessible education in hearing schools, whereas this has not been the case for many deaf students. ASL has been sys-tematically excluded from educational institutions across North America for over a century, including post-secondary (Robinson & Henner, 2018). Many schol-ars have described the increased marginalization, policing, and restriction of sign language in education, beginning in the late nineteenth century (Baynton, 1996; Lane, 1989 [1984]). Many deaf children still face limited access to educa-tion in signing and culturally rich environments (Murray et al., 2018; Snoddon & Underwood, 2017). The exclusion of ASL from universities in Canada is part of this long and complex history. In the past several decades ASL has found space on many campuses across North America in the form of ASL classes; however, these classes are largely available to hearing, non-signing students (Brueggemann, 2009; Robinson & Henner, 2018).

The opportunities to use ASL in the university outside of the ASL class-room are severely constrained by a "system of compulsory able-bodiedness" (McRuer, 2006, p. 2). According to McRuer (2006), the system of compulsory able-bodiedness positions able-bodiedness as the only acceptable embodiment and way of being in the world. Harmon (2010) discuses "compulsory hearing" and the demands placed on deaf people to conform to the norms and expectations of the hearing side of the hearing/deaf binary (p. 33). The demands of compulsory able-bodiedness/hearing also limit the ways I move through the university as a hearing (Coda) student. As McRuer (2006) explains, this system gives the "appearance of choice" when there is none (p. 8): what appears to be a choice between two languages I am fluent in—English and ASL—is actually highly restricted. My reliance on spoken language in the university contributes to my disappearance as a Coda and my appearance as a hearing university student.

This is not to say I fully leave behind the deaf spaces of my childhood; rather, there is very limited space to be "both." As Kafer (2003) notes, the system of compulsory able-bodiedness "throws suspicion" on any identification with or as disabled when one passes as able-bodied (p. 80). This system works to make any personal connection to the deaf community, or longing for such connection that I may have, invisible: I continually find my Coda-ness masked by the ways I move through the classroom and larger campus. As I talk (in spoken English) about my connection to the deaf community in disability studies courses, conferences, and student events, I am never sure the significance is conveyed. What remains sure and certain is my membership in the hearing world.

Given the way I use language in the university, especially as a student who is fluent in English and ASL, I am implicated in perpetuating the dominance of English in educational settings. When I use English at the exclusion of ASL the status quo remains unchallenged; ASL remains relegated to the private sphere of my deaf home, and spoken English remains the language used in places of learning. This double removal of sign language, both from my everyday life as a hearing student and from post-secondary education, appears as natural.

A DIFFERENT STORY

In the fall of 2019 both authors met in a graduate course focused on inclusive education. This classroom became a space where we could push back against compulsory hearing. Here we created a small signing space within the larger auditory classroom. While this space became distinctively inclusive as we related to one another using ASL, we do not mean to suggest that this resolved the inequities discussed throughout this chapter. Indeed, deaf/hearing interactions on campus take place within larger institutional settings where spoken language and hearing norms are privileged (Trowler & Turner, 2002), and simply increasing spaces to use ASL without addressing barriers that exclude deaf people from all levels of higher education leaves its audist structure largely unchanged (Robinson & Henner, 2018).

The idea of inclusive education brings with it questions and issues when related to the education of deaf students, especially around mainstreaming in K–12 education. When deaf students are placed in mainstream schools, this raises concerns around the "linguistic rights and cultural identity" of deaf students as they are separated from deaf schools, which have provided spaces to develop and transmit language, identity, and culture (Murray et al., 2018, p. 693; Snoddon & Underwood, 2017). Murray et al. (2018) discuss different examples of inclusive education in primary and secondary schools around the world "that meet deaf children's linguistic and cultural needs" using various combinations of signing and non-signing environments, deaf and non-deaf teachers (p. 699). In post-secondary education, "support services such as interpreters, notetakers, and tutors" are often put in place, but this does not guarantee an inclusive setting (Foster et al., 1999, p. 225). In our university classroom there came to be a combination of methods that produced an environment that was both inclusive and exclusive.

A significant feature of this reconfigured class was how we understood one another. We are not just talking about the mode of communication used (sign language). Rather, it was through our use of ASL that we were able to create a space that did not demand conformity to hearing norms as described above (see Harmon, 2010). Our signing space, into which we brought a shared language and culture, directly challenged the medicalization of deafness in the university. For Sarah, rather than constantly police and monitor her behaviour to fit into the hearing classroom, she was able to be "just Sarah." For Sammy Jo, this space provided an opportunity to embody part of herself formerly absent from the university classroom, and she was, for the first time in her university experience, known by her sign name.

The importance of communicating in ASL in the university classroom, with fluent users, cannot be overstated. As Foster et al. (1999) point out, for deaf students in mainstream settings there can be great difficulty accessing "informal exchanges among hearing students regarding instructor expectations, study tips, and unspoken rules for class behaviour and organization" (p. 226). In our small signing space, we were able to navigate some of these barriers. For instance, we were able to participate in our own brainstorming, teamwork, and social interaction directly in ASL.

However, this space was not perfect, and one limitation we experienced related to using ASL beyond informal discussions between the two of us. For our group presentation we decided we would both present in ASL. However, due to the constraints around language discussed throughout this chapter, which manifested as additional work required to balance deadlines and coordinate communication with others in the class setting, this ended up not being possible. In the end, Sammy Jo spoke during the presentation, which meant her contributions (and those of the rest of the group, as well as all lectures and class discussions for that matter) were made accessible to Sarah only following interpretation.

Another limitation was that interaction with peers remained restricted for Sarah. To have the possibility of unrestricted interaction with only one student meant Sarah did not have a fully inclusive classroom experience. Our signed conversations were accessible only to the two of us; while not ideal in an inclusive setting where we can imagine everyone would sign, in these moments the dominant status of spoken language in the classroom was destabilized.

While this signing space was unprecedented in our experiences as university students, Sarah was still navigating a largely inaccessible space in ways Sammy Jo was not, and it is here that hearing privilege becomes especially apparent. In this classroom we negotiated a signing space that was natural and comfortable to us; nevertheless, outside factors continued to privilege hearingness and discourage signing, resulting in very different levels of inclusion.

CONCLUSION

"But if we are now to consider a collective pursuit of change which liberates us from these oppressions [racism, heterosexism, disablism, and audism] we cannot simply do this by adding one experience to another or differentiating between them. These experiences are all dimensions of our existence through our person or through our Other, and as long as they remain conceptually separate, there is a risk that we continue to argue that one is more important or more valuable and therefore more powerful than the other. Discourse is something which joins us and separates us, and locates us firmly in the world of social processes. Perhaps this is the unifying concept to take us forward."

Corker, Mairian. *Deaf and Disabled, or Deafness Disabled? Towards a Human Rights Perspective.* Buckingham, UK: Open University Press, 1998, p. 143.

By telling our stories we sketch some of the ways we navigate post-secondary education as one deaf and one hearing Coda student. When, by chance, we enrolled in the same course, we were able to create a space where we could push back against the constraints of compulsory hearing, yet audist practices and hearing privilege did not disappear from the classroom. We hope that the stories told here help to make visible some of the ways the university demands and privileges hearing ways of being, as well as the need for more meaningful inclusion of deaf persons and ASL across campus.

NOTES

1. Here "deaf" describes Sarah's identity as an individual with a hearing loss who uses ASL for communication access at a post-secondary institution and identifies with deaf culture.
2. For discussion of deaf culture see Padden and Humphries (1988) and Ladd (2003).
3. A similar experience is described by Duarte, who writes about being referred to as the "Deaf-Blind student" and the removal of individual "identity" when seeking accommodations in the university (Ramirez-Stapleton & Duarte, 2021, p. 15).

REFERENCES

Bauman, H.-D. L. (2004). Audism: Exploring the metaphysics of oppression. *The Journal of Deaf Studies and Deaf Education, 9*(2), 239–246. https://doi.org/10.1093/deafed/enh025

Baynton, D. C. (1996). *Forbidden signs: American culture and the campaign against sign language*. University of Chicago Press.

Brueggemann, B. J. (2009). *Deaf subjects: Between identities and places*. New York University Press.

Canadian Association of the Deaf / Association des Sourds du Canada. (2015, July 3). *Audism*. http://cad.ca/issues-positions/audism/

Davis, L. J. (2000). *My sense of silence: Memoirs of a childhood with deafness*. University of Illinois Press.

Foster, S., Long, G., & Snell, K. (1999). Inclusive instruction and learning for deaf students in postsecondary education. *The Journal of Deaf Studies and Deaf Education, 4*(3), 225–235. https://doi.org/10.1093/deafed/4.3.225

Harmon, K. (2010). Deaf matters: Compulsory hearing and ability trouble. In S. Burch & A. Kafer (Eds.), *Deaf and disability studies: Interdisciplinary perspectives* (pp. 31–47). Gallaudet University Press.

Hoffmeister, R. (2008). Border crossings by hearing children of Deaf parents: The lost history of Codas. In H.-D. Bauman (Ed.), *Open your eyes: Deaf studies talking* (pp. 189–215). University of Minnesota Press.

Kafer, A. (2003). Compulsory bodies: Reflections on heterosexuality and able-bodiedness. *Journal of Women's History*, *15*(3), 77–89. https://doi.org/10.1353/jowh.2003.0071

Ladd, P. (2003). *Understanding Deaf culture: In search of Deafhood*. Multilingual Matters. https://doi.org/10.21832/9781853595479

Lane, H. L. (1989). *When the mind hears: A history of the deaf*. Vintage Books. (Original work published 1984)

McRuer, R. (2006). *Crip theory: Cultural signs of queerness and disability*. New York University Press.

Murray, J., Snoddon, K., De Meulder, M., & Underwood, K. (2018). Intersectional inclusion for deaf learners: Moving beyond General Comment no. 4 on Article 24 of the United Nations Convention on the Rights of Persons with Disabilities. *International Journal of Inclusive Education*, *24*(7), 691–705. https://doi.org/10.1080/13603116.2018.1482013

Padden, C., & Humphries, T. (1988). *Deaf in America: Voices from a culture*. Harvard University Press.

Preston, P. (1994). *Mother father deaf: Living between sound and silence*. Harvard University Press.

Ramirez-Stapleton, L. D., & Duarte, D. L. (2021). When you think you know: Restorative justice between a hearing faculty member and a Deaf+ student. *New Directions for Student Services*, *2021*(173), 11–26. https://doi.org/10.1002/ss.20374

Robinson, O., & Henner, J. (2018). Authentic voices, authentic encounters: Cripping the university through American Sign Language. *Disability Studies Quarterly*, *38*(4). https://doi.org/10.18061/dsq.v38i4.6111

Snoddon, K., & Underwood, K. (2014). Toward a social relational model of Deaf childhood. *Disability & Society*, *29*(4), 530–542. https://doi.org/10.1080/09687599.2013.823081

Snoddon, K., & Underwood, K. (2017). Deaf time in the twenty-first century: Considering rights frameworks and the social relational model of Deaf childhood. *Disability & Society*, *32*(9), 1400–1415. https://doi.org/10.1080/09687599.2017.1320269

Stapleton, L., & Gillon, K. (2021). Audism and hearing privilege within higher education: A snapshot into the lives of diverse deaf communities. In K. Hinton, V. Grim, M. F. Howard-Hamilton, & O. Gilbert Brown (Eds.), *Unleashing suppressed voices on college campuses: Diversity issues in higher education* (2nd ed., pp. 27–44). Peter Lang.

Titchkosky, T. (2008). "To pee or not to pee?" Ordinary talk about extraordinary exclusions in a university environment. *The Canadian Journal of Sociology / Cahiers Canadiens de Sociologie, 33*(1), 37–60. https://www.jstor.org/stable/canajsocicahican.33.1.37

Trowler, P. R., & Turner, G. H. (2002). Exploring the hermeneutic foundations of university life: Deaf Academics in a hybrid "community of practice." *Higher Education, 43*(2), 227–256. https://www.jstor.org/stable/3447544

CHAPTER 4

Let Me Hear You Say Black Lives Matter

Thomas Reid

Key Terms: ACB; Advocacy; African American; Anti-Racism; Black Lives Matter; Blind; Colour Blind; George Floyd; NFB; Police Brutality; Protest; Racist; Solidarity

"Let Me Hear You Say Black Lives Matter" is a podcast episode from Black, blind artist and podcaster Thomas Reid. As you read or listen to Reid's part of our collection, you will notice that at times there are descriptions of noises and sounds in the background. We have decided to keep Reid's podcast as you might hear it in order to blur the lines of how we encounter the written word, as well as re-imagine the act of reading itself.

Thomas Reid (TR):
The title says it all! It's the place we have to start if we are really going to make change in this country and world. I'm talking about individuals as well as society. And included among that group are the blindness consumer advocacy organizations: ACB (American Council of the Blind) and NFB (National Federation of the Blind). While there are differences in the founding philosophies of each, at the core both of these groups strive for Blind people to have the same rights as our sighted peers. Do they really mean all Blind people? I want to believe they do, but I guess I'm going to need to hear them say it: Black Lives Matter!

I'm trying to remain optimistic, but right now, it really takes a lot of effort to be hopeful. I was reminded of a story from the *Reid My Mind Radio* archive that in a way illustrates some of what needs to happen in order to really move forward.

Audio: *Music ... "Mission Start"*

TR: Welcome to or back to the podcast! My name is Thomas Reid, and I'm the host and producer of *Reid My Mind Radio*—the podcast bringing you compelling people impacted by all degrees of blindness and disability. Sometimes I share experiences of my own as a man adjusting to becoming Blind as an adult. Today, well, it's right there in the title. That is, the place we have to start if we are really going to make change. I'm talking about individuals, society and, yes, blindness and disability advocacy organizations.

Let's go!

Audio: *The final voice says: "Yo, Black Lives Matter!"*

TR: Like a lot of families, meals are a time to come together. Not only to prepare and enjoy the food but also to check in with one another. In the Reid household, we established some rules years ago around what was acceptable during meals. Like we don't answer phone calls, we don't look at our devices, but rather we stay in the moment while we are eating together.

Audio: *News commentator on the killing of George Floyd and protests*

TR: Unfortunately, no matter how much I would like the rule to be in effect, just while we're eating, there are times we can't really afford to keep them. The most recent murders of Ahmaud Arbery and George Floyd, the protests, and, of course, the self-described nationalist in the White House have caused us to rescind the rules. Both of my kids need to discuss all of this.

Riana, who will be 23 soon, is extremely passionate when it comes to issues around social justice. She needs to be active, and she's figuring out the best ways for her to do that. For example, donating to protester bail funds, continuing to educate herself through reading and research, and sharing resources with her network. Raven is younger, more internal, and is really figuring out how to articulate her thoughts. Her friend groups are very diverse, and she recognizes the differences and really appreciates them. Recently, she had to deal with the outing of a classmate, one in particular which has garnered a lot of national attention. This young 17-year-old made very public awful racist comments. Listen to the statement from a young girl from Generation Z. Some thought this would be the post-racial generation, free from racism. Notice how deliberately she shares her revelation.

If you are triggered by little racists using the N-word, skip ahead about 34 seconds.

17-Year-Old Racist: "So, I've been seeing this video going around about why Brown people should be able to say the N-word. So I'm here to tell you why white people should be able to say the N-word. Because we made it up, and none of you guys would be able to say that word if my ancestors didn't decide to call you Black people Niggers all the way back in those old days. And so what do you guys do to try and show your appreciation, for coming up with your best word to call your best friend Nigga as you pass each other in the hall? You do what all good Black people do, you stole it. So all I'm doing here is trying to take back what's already ours."

TR: If it was shocking to you because you never heard this sort of language, it's time to acknowledge your privilege. It's not a time to pat yourself on the back because you raised your children to be colour blind. It's not a time to feel the need to share how you cried when Dr. King was assassinated or even you know someone who is Black. That doesn't work toward a solution, which makes you part of the problem.

Not even the four walls of our comfortable home can keep my family protected from the reality of violence against Black men, women, and children. Like trying to explain to my kids how Trayvon Martin's murderer was not going to face prison. Michael Brown's killer would just walk free.

Riana has goals of moving out on her own. Meanwhile Breonna Taylor, a 26-year-old Emergency Medical Technician, gets shot eight times in her own home by police who wrongfully busted in her house in search of a suspect already in custody. Raven right now is learning to drive, and I have to think of Sandra Bland and the others who ultimately have fatal encounters with police because they're driving while Black.

A word of caution: What you're about to hear is an example of the trauma and fear associated with police brutality.

Audio: *Woman passionately trying to help a young Black man while he is being surrounded by police. We find out her boyfriend was also killed by police. The audio ends with her sobbing for them to simply put their guns away while begging the young man not to move.*

TR: Y'all know this isn't about my privileged dinnertime, right?

For Black people, it's not only the threat of violence and interactions with police, but not dealing with the feelings around these murders is like allowing a virus to infect our bodies. We can wash our hands regularly, sanitize every package that comes into our homes, eat organic food ... but how do we protect ourselves from feeling as though we don't matter?

Audio: A woman saying "Black Lives Matter"

TR: Being totally Blind doesn't stop the images of these horrible killings from being ingrained in my mind. I don't need to see a video of Michael Brown's body left on the street after being murdered; I don't need to see Ahmaud Arbery being shot down or this deranged so-called officer kneeling on George Floyd's neck to understand what that looks like. In fact, these images involuntarily flash in my mind without ever having seen them.

Recently I tweeted that I was waiting to hear a show of solidarity from the blindness organizations. I soon read one from NFB and then specifically questioned if ACB was going to show their support. They did. They also directed a tweet to me that they were waiting on a review before posting. My response was that I was happy to see them done but the real statement will be seen in their actions, like representation on their boards and in leadership positions and outreach. Both statements were weak. In general, any solidarity statement at this point in time that does not include the simple phrase acknowledging that Black Lives Matter doesn't have much weight in my opinion.

Audio: Fire engine racing toward a burning building

TR: If a house was burning on a block of 10, should the fire department show equal attention to each house? Wouldn't it be fair to first put the one fire out? Save the family in the house. Apparently, some would prefer the fire department drive right past the burning house in order to make it clear that all the houses on the block are important. Meanwhile, do you all smell that smoke? The other homes on the block are beginning to burn.

Audio: Young man says "Black Lives Matter!"

TR: If a solidarity statement had to be generated by the Black or multicultural segment of the organization, it's starting from the wrong place. Is that because some Blind people like to think their blindness makes them immune to racism? Funny thing is most Blind people have had sight at some point. In fact, most Blind people aren't even totally Blind. You're not being honest with yourselves if you think racism doesn't affect you. As if you don't benefit from white supremacy.

Audio: *Do Blind People See Race …*

From Tommy Edison's YouTube Channel: *"Martin Luther King always talked about 'don't judge a man by the colour of his skin but by the content of his character.' And I have to be honest with you I think people like myself and other Blind people are the best at that because we don't see the colour of their skin."*

From YouTube, "Can Blind People See Race?", Freedom is Mine Official: *"Can Blind people see race? Given that we identify a person's race primarily by their appearance, what elements do the visually impaired use to perceive race? Several studies have been done into this area, and the conclusion is definitely yes, visually impaired people can perceive race."*

TR: History has shown when it comes to so-called racial issues, America is all about weak statements. America doesn't want to examine their role. You know what, let me say that again to not sugar coat it.

Audio: *Music …*

TR: White America doesn't want to do the work to fix racial injustice. I see the same right now from blindness organizations. Asking Black people to lead this effort isn't the fix. Rather, once again for Black people, our dinnertime with our families is being interrupted.

Why not start with a real self-evaluation. Have a conversation among the organization's leadership and board about race. Whether personal but more specifically as it relates to the organization. Look back; how many members are even in the organization? How often does the leadership interact with them and what have those interactions been about? How often do we hear from Black people at our meetings and conferences? Have we ever truly done any outreach or did we wait for those Black people in the organization to recruit others?

This is a problem that existed in this country for 400 years and won't be fixed with one statement. It won't be fixed in our lifetimes. It requires a lot of work that starts with honest self-examination.

To be clear, I think it's time for these organizations to truly look at the intersections between disability and other identities. The majority of police brutality cases impact Black people with disabilities. Women with disabilities experience an overwhelming number of sexual attacks; LGBTQ and trans communities have a significant population of people with disabilities. And Black transgender men and women need our support. Honestly, if you have a problem with that then you need to ask yourself if you're really about justice.

All the organizations that are either of or for the blind want the same thing: independence, security, opportunity for all Blind people. Who does this really include? For some, blindness skills training isn't going to be enough to have an opportunity to reach that goal.

For me personally to believe these organizations and others are really about independence for all, I'm going to have to see them lead the way. That leadership needs to come from those in power right now.

I'm going to need to hear them simply say it: "Black Lives Matter."

Audio: Audio montage of individuals saying "Black Lives Matter!" Concludes with all simultaneously saying it.

TR: In producing this podcast, I'm always searching for the right mix of education, resource sharing, and entertainment. As I usually believe our stories have more to offer outside of those adjusting to blindness, I recalled this travel story from the *Reid My Mind Radio* archive episode titled "Traveling Zen."

Audio: The Notorious B.I.G.: "I Got a Story to Tell"

TR: Just this past Thursday I was travelling to Mobile, Alabama—yes, Mobile, Alabama.... Why? Well, that's not really for this discussion. In fact, let's go revisit the day.

Audio: Car pulling to curb

TR: Exiting the chauffeur-driven Suburban I'm met by one of the Allentown Airport staff responsible for assisting travellers through the airport. I refer to them as the "Meet and Greet" staff.

Normally, I have to get to the check-in counter in order to request this, but luck just had it, a very nice gentleman by the name of Tom was waiting on the curb for someone who needed assistance.

Audio: Sound of airport—check-in/security

TR: Smoothly clearing the check-in process and security, Tom informs me that my flight is delayed just as we reach the gate. It was close to 12 p.m. And my flight was

originally scheduled to leave at 1 o'clock and arrive in Atlanta at 3 p.m. for a connecting flight to Mobile at 5:15 p.m.

OK, no worries. A departure at 2 is fine; I'll get to Atlanta by 4. No problem,
even though Atlanta's airport is huge, I'd still have time to make my flight. And I'd
rather wait in Allentown Airport, which is way smaller and more comfortable.

At 2 o'clock I'm told we're now departing at 2:30. Now this is a potential problem! With a connecting flight at 5:15 ... there's a good chance I'll miss my flight. I go
over to the ticket agent to see what I can do about this potential dilemma. Rosita,
the ticket agent, schedules me for the later flight, which leaves Atlanta at 9:15, in
the event I missed the 5:15 flight.

Requiring the assistance of a Meet and Greet means I'm one of the last people
off the flight. This adds to the probability that I may miss my connection. On the flip
side, I'm one of the first on the plane!

I'm pretty relaxed already, but now I decide it's time for me to go into a Zen
state of mind. One thing about adjusting to blindness, it means becoming accustomed to waiting.

The ticket agent announces over the PA that it's time to board.

I grab my coat, bag, and cane and proceed to the counter. I board with one of
the ticket agents. I ask her if she could somehow call ahead and make sure a Meet
and Greet is there when we arrive so I can exit the plane quickly and make my connection. She takes my boarding pass and says she would do that.

Sitting in the window seat, I strike up a conversation with my seatmate when
he arrives on board Delta Flight 5387. I tell him about my connection issue. He
seems to think I have a strong chance of making the flight. We chat a little more.
I put my headphones on and open my Audible app to read my book. I'm good, I'm
pretty relaxed and calm.... I accept what I can't control!

At around a little after 4, the pilot announces that we're about to descend and
we're scheduled to arrive on time, 4:40. My seatmate nudges me.

"I think you're gonna make it," he says.

Knowing what I know about the wait for a Meet and Greet I tell him, "Meh, we'll
see! I'll still have to wait for assistance."

At 4:45 we're on the ground taxiing to the gateway. I take out my phone and
check the Delta app to determine the status of my next flight. There's significant
bad weather so I'm hoping my next flight would be slightly delayed. Nothing. The

pilot announces we're going to Terminal C, Gate 33. By 5 p.m. we're still on the tar waiting to be directed into our new gate, D33.

My seatmate is excitedly telling me I can make that flight. "Just run out of here, you can make it," he says.

I'm thinking, Did he not hear me when I said I need to wait for assistance?

I check the app again; it now says my next flight is boarding and scheduled to leave on time. At gate D29. I tell my seatmate.

"Aww, you can do it!" he says as he stands up to retrieve his bags from the overhead. I ask him to pass me my backpack and folded up cane.

"Is this yours too?" he asks.

"A folded up white cane?" I ask.

"Yes!" Now he sounds confused.... I think it sinks in.

"My man," I say, "Do you think you can help me get to D29? It has to be right near this gate."

I didn't think it would be a bother; he wasn't connecting to another flight.

"Yeah!" he exclaims.

I say to him, "Get in front of me and let me hold onto your right elbow."

He complies. I grab my bag, and we take off.

Audio: Victory music

TR: My seatmate is now ripping through the narrow aisle. And my shoulders knocking into chairs and walls. He apologizes.

"Bro, I can take a hit; let's do this. Turn it up."

"Yeah," he exclaims again, now even more determined to accomplish his goal.

We zoom past the flight attendants who say something about an assistant. I don't bother responding; no time for that. My seatmate and I are now a team and we're on a mission.

"He's my blocker," I think to myself, "and we're gonna score this touch down."

"We can do this," I hear him say as we rip past the ticket agent at Gate 33. As we're quickly and purposefully walking, in search of gate D29—

I hear my name—"Paging Mr. Reid, Thomas Reid."

"That's me," I tell him.

"He's here, he's here," yells my Blocker.

"He's here, he's here," says the ticket agent at D29 into a telephone.

We get to the podium at Gate 29 ... touchdown!!!

As if rehearsed, we do a two-hand high five, chest bump, all while the ticket agent and bystanders applaud.

OK, that would have been the movie version celebration.

Instead, the ticket agent asked for my boarding pass. I retrieve my boarding pass, thank my teammate, and I'm hurried onto my next flight.

I didn't get his name or even have the chance to shake his hand, but man, I appreciated him.

Sitting on my final flight to Alabama considering how through that entire process I felt quite comfortable and calm with just going with the flow, I thought about the first part of that very well-known serenity prayer: "God, grant me the serenity to accept the things I cannot change; courage to change the things I can; and wisdom to know the difference."

This experience reinforces what I believe is the power of teamwork. I thought about how this pertains to lessons for those adjusting to blindness or, for that matter, adjusting to any sort of change.

I've always been one to think of that very broad definition of independent as "doing something by myself."

Could I have done this by myself?... Some may quickly say no, others may argue yes, with the right circumstance, as in accessible information. Like a good indoor navigation app. But honestly, it was way more fun with a team!

Audio: Music starts ...

TR: My seatmate, and ultimately my teammate, for a few minutes at least, was as far as I can tell a white guy. We worked together. I was in a position where I needed him to be out in front if I wanted to make my flight. It wasn't my only option, but missing that flight would have meant a really long and possibly very uncomfortable delay. Not for him, but rather, just me.

Reid My Mind Radio will be back on August 4th. I have some really good episodes planned for the second half of the year, but right now, I need to do a little recharging. If you're new to the podcast, feel free to check out the archive. We have over 100 episodes, and they don't expire.

You can get that just by subscribing to *Reid My Mind Radio* wherever you get your podcasts. None of my stuff is behind a paywall, because I really do want it to be an accessible resource for those adjusting to blindness.

Transcripts, resources, and more are over at ReidMyMind.com. And yes, that's *R* to the *E-I-D* (**Audio:** *"D, and that's me in the place to be!" by Slick Rick*), like my last name.

Audio: Reid My Mind Radio *Outro*

TR: Peace! And I really mean that!

Audio: *Headphones dropping on table*

PART II

DISAPPEARING DISEMBODIMENT

EDITORS' INTRODUCTION

This section, "DisAppearing DisEmbodiment," focuses on the ways in which the reality of our bodily existence is mediated by culture; there is no appearance of our bodies that is not situated in culture and reflective of it. Of embodiment, Margrit Shildrick (2020) suggests that the Western assumption of a stable and autonomous singular subject with a "body whose integrity is so unquestioned that it may be forgotten" (p. 303) is a myth when we consider that embodiment "is never gender-neutral, ageless nor universal" (p. 306). Centring the experience of how embodiment appears and disappears, especially in educational settings, the chapters collected in this part exemplify that "theorizing non-normative morphology, not as a failure of form (inviting therapeutic modification), but as an-other way of being" is not only possible but also desirable (Shildrick, 2020, p. 306). It is remarkable that non-normative morphology, or bodily difference, is universal. And yet, things we learn about the body and our movement through social space makes it seem like every-body is the same. Disability studies helps to open the cultural paradox supported by the myth of having the same body and helps us re-encounter our unique bodily integrity.

"Disciplinary society consists of settings and institutions of confinement. The family, schools, prisons, barracks, hospitals and factories all represent disciplinary spaces that confine. The disciplinary subject changes from one milieu of confinement to the next. In doing so, it moves within a *closed system*. The inhabitants of milieus of confinement can be ordered in space and time."

Han, Byung-Chul. *Psychopolitics: Neoliberalism and New Technologies of Power.* London, UK: Verso, 2017, p. 17.

Madeleine DeWelles, in "Between Peace and Disturbance: Anorexia, Control, and Embodiment," illustrates how young adult novels teach us about the normative body. She suggests that in being taught the norms of the body, young adults are introduced into a form of education where "a desire to keep the peace of the normative body" arises. Exploring the appearance of anorexia in a young adult novel as disturbing and yet also peaceful enables an analysis that is not stuck on reiterating a medicalized way of making anorexia appear as only a sense-less disease. Instead, DeWelles holds peace and disturbance in tension in such a way that the complexity of the meaning of anorexia, and even the tensions between illness and disability, the body and its conditions, come to the fore.

Following this, Maria Karmiris's chapter, "Disabling Curricular Encounters: The Barriers in Barrier-Free Access," discusses the many contradictions that arise within an annual barrier-free sporting-day event. Karmiris narrates her experience of this day with a young student, Nadine, and Nadine's mother and draws on various social theories that help us encounter embodied experiences to make sense of designed in(ex)clusions. Karmiris notices dozens of developmental disability classes from 20 different schools at this sporting event, which appears at first glance to be designed for students like Nadine, who acquired a diagnosis of autism and intellectual disability. Provocative and ironic, Karmiris details the inaccessibility of this school event while also uncovering the imagined version of impairment the sporting day makes apparent and supports—much better than it supports Nadine.

The topic of disembodiment, and its multiple manifestations, arises again in Helen Rottier, Ben Pfingston, and Josh Guberman's "Ghosts, Mice, and Robots: Disappearing the Autistic Person." Through expressions of autism found in literature, science, and technology, the authors (who identify as autistic) interact with cultural mediations of autism that they metaphorically characterize as ghosts, mice, and robots. Each one of these metaphors makes autism appear in research and rhetoric in particular ways, and yet, ironically, these appearances *disappear* a variety of experiences of the embodied reality of the authors' ways of being. The authors explore the impact of this disappearance on disability studies and academia more broadly while rematerializing their own autistic subjectivities through their incisive analysis. This analysis ultimately raises the provocative question of the nature of "the humanity of an institutionalized definition of personhood that casts autistic people as less human than non-autistics and machines alike." As Karmiris does in her chapter, this chapter too demonstrates how, by describing one's own experience and regarding this description "as good to think with," the complex cultural assumptions organizing embodied experience can be revealed (Michalko, 2002, p. 165).

In the next chapter, Satsuki Kawano demonstrates how dyslexia is represented and performed in Japan. While the extensive use (and critique) of disability labels is a prevalent trope in Western education, Kawano's work begins by highlighting an occasion where such labelling does not readily appear. In the Japanese context of a "radical under-recognition of dyslexia," Kawano explores an inaugural international advocacy event held in 2016 at the Asia-Pacific Dyslexia Festival in Yokohama, Japan. As a way to address what happens to disability-experience that does not appear as such to others, Kawano draws on concrete ritual processes that involve disabled people "coming out" at this festival. Making use of her experiences at the festival, Kawano demonstrates that, by attending to both the appearances and disappearances of dyslexia, we are offered the possibility of encountering the ways in which embodiment, including our mindedness, is culturally organized and experienced.

Concluding this section is a poem titled "Tuning Goes Frig," written by Sid Ghosh, a young autistic man with Down syndrome. A video from the 2020 United Nations World Down Syndrome Day Conference shows Ghosh's creative process. Sitting in a beige dining room chair, Ghosh wears a long-sleeved grey shirt. His left hand clutches the tawny muslin tablecloth draping the table, and his right hand holds a pencil as if ready to write on paper. We are unprepared, perhaps, for how Ghosh begins to tell a story with his pencil, away from paper, guiding the eraser end of his pencil to various points on the board. A conductor with his baton, Ghosh assembles words and brings together sentences and plays us a poem.

Sami Schalk: "When we began to discuss texts such as Audre Lorde's *The Cancer Journals* … Meri Nana-Ama Danquah's *Willow Weep for Me* and Bebe Moore Campbell's *72 Hour Hold*, students easily comprehended how the intersection of race and disability made life more difficult for the disabled Black women in these texts; however, they struggled to understand the relationship of ableism and racism…. Disability quickly lost its social, material and political significance as a category of oppression and became merely a synonym for 'disadvantage.' I pushed students to use disability to refer to impairment, identity, discourse or a social system/social construct, but again and again the same conflating phrases appeared.

"The challenge I see in teaching Black DS [disability studies] is to help students understand how racism and ableism collude in a variety of ways in contemporary society, not only in the lives of Black disabled people, but also Black people collectively as discourses of disability continue to be used as means to control and do harm to racialized populations."

Dunhamn, Jane, Jerome Harris, Shancia Jarrett, Leroy Moore, Akemi Nishida, Margaret Price, Britney Robinson, and Sami Schalk. "Developing and Reflecting on a Black Disability Studies Pedagogy: Work from the National Black Disability Coalition." *Disability Studies Quarterly* 35, no. 2 (2015).

Guiding Questions

1. How does shame, hunger, being perceived as different, or as too much or too little, have an impact on how you feel about your body?
2. Does being in the classroom, or online, or on the phone lead you to experience your body in different ways?
3. Given structures in the physical environment, in what ways do you encounter your body such that it seems as if every-body is supposed to be the same?
4. How does the cultural assumption of sameness make disability appear and disappear? And how do assumptions about "normalcy," or what is perceived as normal and not normal, organize how you perceive bodily difference?
5. What needs to disappear, or be forgotten or ignored, when people think that disability is located inside bodies, minds, senses, emotions, comportment, or some other aspect of an individual? Can disability be imagined as not a problem to be fixed in the doctor's office, in the classroom, in rehabilitation settings, in the news, and in the media?

REFERENCES

Michalko, R. (2002). *The difference that disability makes.* Temple University Press.
Shildrick, M. (2020). The self's clean and proper body. In J. A. Weinstock (Ed.), *The monster theory reader* (pp. 303–329). University of Minnesota Press.

CHAPTER 5

Between Peace and Disturbance: Anorexia, Control, and Embodiment

Madeleine DeWelles

Key Terms: Anorexia; Control; Disturbance; Embodiment; Peace

> *I allow myself a small smile. Death won't desert me. It's waiting for me, beckoning. And I'm ready, taking sure steps toward my final act. An intricately choreographed scene that will amaze. I will face the audience and with a glimmering cloud of smoke—poof! I will disappear.*
> —Stevie; in Meg Haston, *Paperweight*

This quotation, from Meg Haston's (2014) young adult novel *Paperweight*, illustrates a young woman's desire for anorexia, as well as her desire to *disappear*. *Paperweight* draws connections to the relationship between the body, its appearance, and the desire for its disappearance. But in Haston's words, something different happens—something that shifts orientations to anorexia. A comfort is taken in the act of disappearing—a certain *peace* is found in anorexia and the disappearance that it promises. That is, the relationship between peace and disturbance is released (Baldwin, 1962, as cited in Standley & Pratt, 1989, p. 21).[1]

Anorexia, in many ways, disturbs the peace that comes with culturally constructed ideals of the body. This may be where anorexia begins—with a desire to keep the peace of the normative body. Despite so much regulation and cultural control over the body, it is often surprising when anorexia appears. Is it not confusing, then, for anorexia to be positioned as a disturber of the peace, when it is also represented as *keeping the peace* of the controlled body? Anorexia can be engaged as a phenomenon situated, caught even, between the dis/appearance of peace and disturbance.

In this chapter, using a disability studies framework and guided by examples from the young adult novel *Paperweight* (Haston, 2014), I begin by showing how anorexia makes the controlled body appear while also making it disappear. The question then becomes: As what does anorexia appear? As what does control appear? How is control controlled? As I ask these questions, I consider the complexities and tensions of food, eating, the body, and embodiment. I am also influenced by Zygmunt Bauman's (2000) *Liquid Modernity*. Bauman (2000) comments on how the orders of modern life put us in a state of constant, fluid change. Bauman (2000) challenges the notion of a "postmodern" period, claiming that society is always in a fluid process of sociocultural change and subsequent control. This includes the control of the self and control of the physical body. Additionally, control takes on the form of many characters; control comprises much of our lives and our embodied relations. Often, we find peace in control—maybe this is why we constantly seek new ways of finding it, of making it appear. This chapter considers the tensions between the dis/appearance of anorexia-as-peaceful and anorexia-as-disturbing, articulating *how* anorexia might offer the notion of "the controlled body" a sense of peace, while also disrupting and disturbing it. Anorexia and its representations are perhaps ways for us to come closer to how our bodies are tied to our embodied relationships and experiences, as well as appearances and disappearances in modern life.

ANOREXIA AND ITS TREATMENT

"[If] disabled people and their knowledge were fully integrated into society, everyone's relation to ... [their] real body would be liberated."

Wendell, Susan. "Toward a Feminist Theory of Disability." *Hypatia*, no. 4 (1989): 104–126; p. 104.

Anorexia is spoken of in terms of treatment. "How is anorexia treated?" is often made to mean "How is anorexia gotten rid of?" or "How is anorexia made to disappear?" What if the question "How is anorexia treated?" changed into *How is it understood? How is it shaped? How is it represented?* These questions form the basis of this section, where I briefly provide some context of anorexia and its appearances.

According to James C. Harris (2014), Sir William Gull introduced "anorexia nervosa" in 1868, describing it as "a peculiar form of disease occurring mostly in young women, and characterized by extreme emaciation" (Gull, 1874, as cited in Harris, 2014, p. 1212). Since then, anorexia and related disorders (eating disorders) have become a large area of historical, medical, feminist, and sociocultural interest.[2] Consider, for example, the appearances of anorexia in the medical community where it is conceptualized as "a disease with an underlying organic cause to be treated and cured" (Urwin et al., 2002, p. 652). A quick Internet search of the term "anorexia nervosa" brings up several results. Consider, for instance, Mayo Clinic's (2018) definition:

> Anorexia nervosa … is an eating disorder characterized by an abnormally low body weight, an intense fear of gaining weight and a distorted perception of weight. People with anorexia place a high value on controlling their weight and shape, using extreme efforts that tend to significantly interfere with their lives. (para. 1)

Fox, Ward, and O'Rourke (2005) note that anorexia has also been theorized in sociological and feminist scholarship. These models tend to look toward familial, social, and cultural contexts as the *cause* of anorexia, such as cultural ideals of thinness, as well as systemic oppressions, such as sexism and patriarchy (Bordo, 1989, 2003; Brumberg, 2000; Fox et al., 2005; Gremillion, 2003; Orbach, 2009). Still, anorexia is written as a means to an end—a problem of the body in need of a solution (Mitchell, 2002; Titchkosky & Michalko, 2009). What appears to be held in common amongst these orientations is that control and anorexia are inextricably tied. The medical model emphasizes an individual's control of weight; the sociocultural model emphasizes the social and systemic controls of body weight and appearance.

Sometimes, control (or lack of it) is represented as the *cause* of anorexia. For instance, Tiggemann and Raven (1998) note that "although anorexics may achieve rigid control over food and weight, they paradoxically experience themselves as out of control and may seek weight loss to achieve a sense of effectiveness in at least one area of their lives" (Lawrence, 1979, as cited in Tiggemann & Raven, 1998, p. 66). Here, there is an assumption that anorexia is a peaceful control appearing within an otherwise disorderly life. Anorexia, then, can be represented as a way to control disorder, while simultaneously be represented as a controlling disorder. This is a fascinating conundrum, which I engage now through a discussion of *controlling* representations of the controlled body.

REPRESENTATIONS OF THE CONTROLLED BODY: MEG HASTON'S *PAPERWEIGHT*

"We are vulnerable, variable, stubbornly and inevitably different from each other, in bodies and under conditions that continually change.... What do we want to produce?"

Schweik, Susan. "Disability and the Normal Body of the (Native) Citizen: The Body and the State: How the State Controls and Protects the Body, Part I." *Social Research* 78, no. 2 (2011): 417–442; p. 442.

The meanings we have of each other, ourselves ... of everything ... are controlled. This is inescapable. Maurice Merleau-Ponty (1962) writes, "Because we are in the world, we are condemned to meaning" (p. xix). Following Merleau-Ponty, perhaps we are also condemned to control. Control is not something to fear; I am not suggesting that we need more or less control. Love, trust, safety, care—these are ways of nurturing relationships, and all come with a degree of control. Given that control surrounds us, what controls control? Meg Haston's *Paperweight* tells us much about the body, control, and its relationship to embodiment.

Paperweight is about a young woman's desire for anorexia. Interestingly, there is a double meaning in the title *Paperweight*. Paperweights can be both heavy and light. For instance, *paperweight* might be understood as the weight of a piece of paper—something that is very light. On the other hand, *a paperweight* is heavy—something that holds down the lightness of a piece of paper, keeping it from floating away. In a subtle yet beautifully complex way, the relationship between lightness and heaviness is blurred—it is not that lightness and heaviness are opposite.[3] Rather, this title shows that there is a heaviness (or disturbance) that comes with the lightness (or peace) that anorexia and control appear to promise.

A character named Stevie is the protagonist of *Paperweight*. She is described as trapped in her life, which is made worse at the treatment centre where she is made to go. As the novel progresses, we learn that Stevie's brother has died, and that Stevie wants to die, too. Throughout the novel, Stevie recalls experiences with her family, such as her mother leaving and her father forcing her to go to an eating disorder treatment program. We also encounter Stevie's relationship with her therapist, who represents control but, at the same time, complicates control.

There are many representations of control in Haston's novel, and these representations also release the complexities of control.

At the beginning of the novel, Stevie is introduced to a team of clinicians. There are two doctors, a therapist, and a dietician. At their first meeting together, the dietician says: "This is *your* treatment, Stevie. We want you to be an active participant in your own healing" (Haston, 2014, p. 60). The phrase "active participant" appears as a way of *giving* control to Stevie. It is almost as if the more control Stevie gets through her treatment, the less control she will have over her eating disorder. It is fascinating that control becomes *both* a problem and a solution (Michalko, 2002; Mitchell, 2002; Stiker, 1999; Titchkosky & Michalko, 2012) of eating disorders. In response to her dietician, Stevie thinks, "*My* treatment. She is telling me that if this doesn't stick, it will be my fault and mine alone." She then says out loud, "You know I'm being forced to stay here, right?" (Haston, 2014, p. 60).

Stevie's eating has been individualized and conceptualized as "[her] fault and [hers] alone." The scene between Stevie and her clinicians, however, is a collective one. It is a social scene that ends in individualization. The social makes individualization possible. Such individualization is manifest in the relationship between fault and blame—or perhaps, control and blame. Stevie makes a connection between control and blame, demonstrating the insidious nature of her dietician's comment. Control, then, becomes a tool that represents Stevie's premonitory failure and blame. Furthermore, if Stevie has control, it is then *her fault* if she lets it slip away from her. She (mis)controls control.

THE (MIS)CONTROL OF CONTROL

"Sanism may include individual experiences of discrimination, violence and stereotyping.... In addition, sanism ... certainly denies psychiatrised children as 'knowers'. As such, sanism helps us to understand the oppression that may be faced by children diagnosed with 'mental illness', and the very naming of sanism helps us to deconstruct assumptions regarding rationality, normalcy, madness, and the ways in which a range of human emotions, behaviours and thoughts are classified either narrowly or as part of a wide spectrum of what it means to be human."

LeFrançois, Brenda A., and Vicki Coppock. "Psychiatrised Children and Their Rights: Starting the Conversation." *Children & Society* 28, no. 3 (2014): 165–171; p. 166.

What does "the (mis)control of control" mean? To address this, consider Rod Michalko's (2009) "The Excessive Appearance of Disability." Michalko (2009) theorizes how disability is represented "as excess, as too much and not enough" (p. 65). As Michalko (2009) discusses the excessive appearance of disability under modernity, he notes:

> From not enough sight, not enough use of our legs ... to too much embodied difference, too grotesque, too many letters scrambled in our brains; disabled people are excessive; we are too much and not enough. (p. 71)

Following Michalko (2009), anorexia appears as too much and not enough. *Anorexia* is often represented as *too much* control and *not enough* food, *not enough* body. Still, control over the body appears as a solution, yet there are normative ways to *control* control. Furthermore, there are instances of the (mis)control of control.

Consider another of Stevie's experiences. Stevie's dietician advises her how to control food intake, saying, "For now, let's focus on getting you through refeeding. After that, it's my recommendation that we put you on a weight-gain meal plan, instead of maintenance" (Haston, 2014, p. 62). Stevie, relieved, thinks to herself, "Good. Maintenance is for the bulimics and the girls who have half-assed attempts at anorexia" (Haston, 2014, p. 62). Stevie feels proud, and perhaps with this pride comes a sense of peace and comfort. Stevie's interpretation of the maintenance diet also reveals that she has not (mis)controlled control. She believes she has controlled her body into having anorexia, unlike other girls who have achieved only "half-assed attempts at anorexia" (Haston, 2014, p. 62). However, Stevie then receives news that completely disturbs the peace that anorexia has promised: "Dr. Singh begins to speak. When I hear the word *diagnosis*, the room sharpens. I watch his thin, purple-tinged lips for the words I expect to hear.... He does not say what I need him to say" (Haston, 2014, p. 64). Instead, Dr. Singh says, "I am ... changing your Axis One diagnosis in part. It seems that *bulimia nervosa* would be a better diagnostic fit, given that you are not currently below eighty-five percent of your ideal body weight" (Haston, 2014, p. 65).

Diagnosis is a tool of control, and Stevie is enraged when she learns of her new diagnosis. "'Bulimia!', Stevie thinks, 'A slur, when I've worked so hard to become what I am'" (Haston, 2014, p. 65). This is a powerful illustration of how medicine attempts to control, define, and treat eating disorders. At the same time, Stevie is represented as controlling her diagnosis as well. Stevie also identifies with diagnoses, taking pride in and clearly desiring the diagnosis of anorexia. A diagnosis of bulimia makes the hoped-for diagnosis of anorexia completely disappear. For Stevie, this is very disturbing. Stevie wants to *be* anorexia; there is an identity of anorexia that takes shape in Stevie's desire. But the construction of identity does not happen to Stevie and Stevie alone. That is, the diagnosis of anorexia or any eating disorder becomes a social situation *of the body*. As Simone de Beauvoir writes, "it will be said that the body is not a *thing*, it is a situation ... it is the instrument of our grasp on the world, a limiting factor for our projects" (de Beauvoir, 2011, p. 46). The responses from Stevie's clinicians, her family, other patients in the treatment centre, and even her own memories of her brother all indicate the situation of Stevie's body and the complexity of eating, of death, of life, and of embodiment.

Later, we encounter Stevie again, staring at her reflection on a blank television screen. "The girl on the screen is impotent," Stevie muses. "She has no control; she has allowed impulse and hunger to rule her" (Haston, 2014, p. 66). Hunger controls us all, yet when anorexia appears, the relationship between hunger and control is pronounced much further. This example shows not that Stevie has *no* control. Rather, it is that she has (mis)controlled control. Impulse and hunger had *too much* control; Stevie did not have *enough* control. Her body did not *disappear enough*. The appearance of bulimia and the loss of anorexia represents not only a loss of control for Stevie but also a loss of peace. Furthermore, control was never gone. Stevie might feel as though she (mis)controlled control, but Stevie's diagnosis was controlled by her doctors, by medicine, by normative expectations of control that also control normative expectations of the body (Titchkosky, 2009; Titchkosky & Michalko, 2009). Stevie's diagnosis was just the beginning.

After Stevie gets her bulimia diagnosis, her treatment begins. This includes being weighed, having her meals supervised, and attending what is called "group," which is like group therapy. During her first group session, Stevie is with her therapist, her dietician, and other girls who have binged on various foods.[4] In this session, Stevie's therapist and dietician have spread out foods that the young women in the group have binged on—fried chicken, fruit punch, and salt and vinegar chips (Haston, 2014). At first, Stevie is enraged—she hates being in the group with the girls who have lost control over these foods—these scary foods, these forbidden foods. At one point, Stevie sees a girl pour fruit punch into a cup (Haston, 2014). The red syrup reminds Stevie of her mother's lips; similarly, the salt and vinegar chips sitting on the table remind Stevie of her brother, who loved but no longer loves those chips.

In this example, Stevie is angry at being in a group session that seems to control binging (or control what is defined as out-of-control). But then, there is Stevie's connection of food to family. Food is intimately tied to family, control, desire, childhood, memories, and even the forbidden. Then again, with the forbidden, there is also a sense of peace. Whether this peace comes from eating these foods or avoiding them altogether, peace is present. For instance, at one point during this group session, Stevie wishes that all the other girls could leave so that she could be all alone with the food, just one more time. There is desire here, but also a sliver of peace. Yet, this peace is controlled. Stevie wants to be alone with the food *just one more time;* so too is Stevie encouraged to eat this food, but only *in moderation.*

As we engage with the complexity of embodiment, I turn to Bauman's (2000) *Liquid Modernity* and its relation to the body, control, and embodiment.

LIQUID MODERNITY AND THE COMPLEXITY OF EMBODIMENT

Zygmunt Bauman begins *Liquid Modernity* (2000) by discussing what change means in the context of a modern, ever-in-flux society. Bauman (2000) writes, "The modern mind was after perfection.... Early on, change was viewed as a preliminary and interim measure, which it was hoped would lead to an age of stability and tranquility—and so also to comfort and leisure" (p. x). Bauman suggests that we must go through change in order to achieve peace. Furthermore, Bauman (2000) does not agree with the term "post-modernity" and instead writes, "What was some time ago dubbed (erroneously) 'post-modernity', and what I've chosen to call, more to the point, 'liquid modernity' is the growing conviction that change is *the only* permanence and change is *the only* certainty" (p. viii, emphasis in original). Furthermore, he notes, "A hundred years ago, to be modern meant to chase 'the final state of perfection'—now it means an infinity of improvement, with no 'final state' in sight and none desired" (Bauman, 2000, pp. viii–ix). Following Bauman, if there is constant change and if change is the only certainty, what does this mean for the body, which is also changing? How might Bauman's provocations take us deeper into Stevie's experiences?

For Stevie, anorexia comes with pride, peace, and disturbance. Anorexia is represented as a way to *stop* change, or to control the change that occurs within our bodies. For Stevie, anorexia and death represented a certain "final state" that *is* desired. But as *Paperweight* shows, the desire to control the changing body is also controlled. Change is certain, as Bauman (2000) suggests, but so too is change controlled and constricted. In *Paperweight,* Stevie wants to change her body in order to achieve the peace of anorexia, or the peace that she believes will come with anorexia. At the same time, Stevie's doctors, therapist, and dietician see change as a way to achieve peace—but rather, change *away from* anorexia, bulimia, or any "disordered" eating. And with this change, there is much disturbance. Therefore, there is complexity and tension between change, peace, and disturbance. Sometimes, change is peaceful, just like control. Other times, it is deeply disturbing.

CONCLUSION

"Deep within myself, I had begun to worry that all this loving care we gave to the pink and white flesh-coloured dolls meant that somewhere left high on the shelves were boxes of unwanted, unloved brown dolls covered in dust.... At first they [hooks' parents] pointed out that white dolls were easier to find, cheaper. They never said where they found Baby but I know. She was always there high on the shelf, covered in dust—waiting."

hooks, bell. *Bone Black: Memories of Girlhood.* New York, NY: Henry Holt and Co., 1996, p. 24.

Anorexia does not simply disappear with the appearance of "recovery"; anorexia is not controlled simply with a diagnosis. Embodiment and our embodied relations comprise a myriad of appearances and disappearances, and so too does it comprise peace and disturbance. Appearances, disappearances, peace, and disturbance— these are tethered to our bodies, our relationships, and the worlds around us, and thus contribute to the beautiful complexity of embodiment.

NOTES

1. Please note that the relationship between peace and disturbance was also introduced to me in a roundtable presentation with Dr. Rod Michalko, Dr. Tanya Titchkosky, Dr. Devon Healey, and Miggy Esteban (OISE, University of Toronto, November 2019).
2. See, for instance, Bell, 2006; Bordo, 2003; Brumberg, 2000; Gremillion, 2003; Holmes, 2018; Orbach, 1986, 2009; Pugh and Waller, 2017; Urwin et al., 2002.
3. Many thanks to the *DisAppearing* team for drawing attention to the meanings of this title.
4. According to the National Eating Disorders Association (2018a, 2018b), a binge is defined as (1) consuming a large amount of food in a discrete period of time, and (2) feeling a loss of control during the consumption of this food. It is quite fascinating that in this definition (or diagnosis) *time* is in control yet the person "binging" is not.

REFERENCES

Bauman, Z. (2000). *Liquid modernity*. Polity Press.

Bell, M. (2006). Re/Forming the anorexic "prisoner": Inpatient medical treatment as the return to panoptic femininity. *Cultural Studies ↔ Critical Methodologies, 6*(2), 282–307. https://doi.org/10.1177/1532708605285622

Bordo, S. (1989). The body and the reproduction of femininity: A feminist appropriation of Foucault. In A. Jagger & S. Bordo (Eds.), *Gender/body/knowledge* (pp. 13–33). Rutgers University Press.

Bordo, S. (2003). *Unbearable weight: Feminism, Western culture, and the body* (10th ed.). University of California Press.

Brumberg, J. (2000). *Fasting girls: The history of anorexia nervosa*. Vintage Books.

de Beauvoir, S. (2011). *The second sex* (C. Borde & S. Malovany-Chevallier, Trans.). Vintage Books. (Original work published 1949)

Fox, N., Ward, K., & O'Rourke, A. (2005). Pro-anorexia, weight-loss drugs and the Internet: An 'anti-recovery' explanatory model of anorexia. *Sociology of Health & Illness, 27*(7), 944–971. https://doi.org/10.1111/j.1467-9566.2005.00465.x

Gremillion, H. (2003). *Feeding anorexia: Gender and power at a treatment centre*. Duke University Press.

Harris, J. C. (2014). Anorexia nervosa and anorexia mirabilis: Miss K.R. and St. Catherine of Siena. *JAMA Psychiatry, 71*(11), 1212–1213. https://doi.org/10.1001/jamapsychiatry.2013.2765

Haston, M. (2014). *Paperweight*. HarperTeen.

Holmes, S. (2018). *The role of sociocultural perspectives in eating disorder treatment: A study of health professionals, 22*(6), 541–557. https://doi.org/10.177/1363459317715778

Mayo Clinic. (2018, February 20). *Anorexia nervosa*. https://www.mayoclinic.org/diseases-conditions/anorexia-nervosa/symptoms-causes/syc-20353591

Merleau-Ponty, M. (1962). *Phenomenology of perception*. Routledge & Kegan Paul.

Michalko, R. (2002). *The difference that disability makes*. Temple University Press.

Michalko, R. (2009). The excessive appearance of disability. *International Journal of Qualitative Studies in Education, 22*(1), 65–74. https://doi.org/10.1080/09518390802581885

Mitchell, D. T. (2002). Narrative prosthesis and the materiality of metaphor. In S. L. Snyder, B. J. Brueggemann, & R. Garland-Thomson (Eds.), *Disability studies: Enabling the humanities* (pp. 47–64). The Modern Languages Association of America.

National Eating Disorders Association. (2018a). *Anorexia nervosa*. https://www.nationaleatingdisorders.org/learn/by-eating-disorder/anorexia

National Eating Disorders Association. (2018b). *Binge eating disorder.* https://www. nationaleatingdisorders.org/learn/by-eating-disorder/bed

Orbach, S. (1986). *Hunger strike: The anorexic's struggle as a metaphor for our age.* Faber and Faber.

Orbach, S. (2009). *Bodies.* Picador.

Pugh, M., & Waller, G. (2017). Understanding the 'anorexic voice' in anorexia nervosa. *Clinical Psychology & Psychotherapy, 24*(3), 670–676. https://doi.org/10.1002/cpp.2034

Stiker, H.-J. (1999). *A history of disability.* University of Michigan Press.

Standley, F. L., & Pratt, L. H. (Eds.). (1989). *Conversations with James Baldwin.* University Press of Mississippi.

Tiggemann, M., & Raven, M. (1998). Dimensions of control in bulimia and anorexia nervosa: Internal control, desire for control, or fear of losing self-control? *Eating Disorders, 6*(1), 65–71. https://doi.org/10.1080/10640269808249248

Titchkosky, T. (2009). Disability images and the art of theorizing normality. *International Journal of Qualitative Studies in Education, 22*(1), 75–84. https://doi.org/10.1080/09518390802581893

Titchkosky, T., & Michalko, R. (Eds.). (2009). *Rethinking normalcy: A disability studies reader.* Canadian Scholars' Press.

Titchkosky, T., & Michalko, R. (2012). The body as the problem of individuality: A phenomenological disability studies approach. In D. Goodley, B. Hughes, & L. Davis (Eds.), *Disability and social theory* (pp. 127–142). Palgrave Macmillan.

Urwin, R., Bennetts, B., Wilcken, B., Lampropoulos, B., Beumont, P., Clarke, S., Russell, J., Tanner, S., & Nunn, K. (2002). Anorexia nervosa (restrictive subtype) is associated with a polymorphism in the novel norepinephrine transporter gene promoter polymorphic region. *Molecular Psychiatry, 7*(6), 652–657. https://doi.org/10.1038/sj.mp.4001080

CHAPTER 6

Disabling Curricular Encounters: The Barriers in Barrier-Free Access

Maria Karmiris

Key Terms: Barrier-Free; Curriculum; Inclusion; Normalcy

INTRODUCTION

In this chapter I wonder how "Nadine," her mother, and I are impressed by Nadine's crying and running away from the circuit of activities during an annual barrier-free event for developmentally delayed elementary students in Toronto. I wonder how this annual Barrier-Free Event is encountered as overwhelmingly full of barriers for eight-year-old Nadine? In this sense, this chapter intends to explore the disabling impacts of curricular orientations in the everyday life of disabled[1] students like Nadine. The term *disabling curricular encounters* is deployed for the purposes of questioning, troubling, and resisting contemporary orientations within our schooling practices. In other words, I wonder how could an event whose stated goal is to include disabled children ultimately sustain mechanisms of exclusion? What mechanisms of exclusion are being sustained within this annual "Barrier-Free" Event? Similarly, how has this disabling curricular encounter for Nadine succumbed to the risks "of empowering dangerous readings that create pathological versions of childhood" (Goodley & Runswick-Cole, 2012, p. 53)? Throughout our day at this Barrier-Free Event, she is repeatedly read as out of line and unhappy in a manner that intersects with her racialized, gendered, and disabled embodiment. This chapter seeks to explore the types of repetitions that occur within our disabling curricular encounters that generate and sustain the conditions for Nadine's exclusion from a space that calls itself barrier-free.

DISABLING CURRICULAR ENCOUNTERS: RUNNING AND CRYING, CRYING AND RUNNING

> "I would argue that crip theory (in productive conversations with a range of disabled/queer movements) can continuously invoke, in order to further the crisis, the inadequate resolutions that compulsory heterosexuality and compulsory able-bodiedness offer us. And in contrast to an able-bodied culture that holds out the promise of a substantive (but paradoxically always elusive) ideal, crip theory would resist delimiting the kinds of bodies and abilities that are acceptable or that will bring about change."
>
> McRuer, Robert. *Crip Theory: Cultural Signs of Queerness and Disability.* New York, NY: New York University Press, 2006, p. 31.

My story of participation in this annual Barrier-Free Event is inextricably linked to Nadine and her mother who immigrated to Canada from Saudi Arabia about two years prior to my meeting them. Nadine is diagnosed with autism and an intellectual disability. During my time as her teacher, Nadine communicated predominantly through non-verbal mediums such as gestures and/or pictorial representations with the occasional use of a few words in both Arabic and English. While waiting for the school bus to take us to the venue for the Barrier-Free Event, I am actually hopeful that all of the students, staff, and parent volunteers in all three classes are about to embark on an enjoyable day trip. One of the reasons I am so hopeful is that while we are listening, watching, and interacting with our morning routine of songs, Nadine exclaims, "Ya Salam/ يا سلام." Nadine's mom explains that the translation for "Ya Salam/ يا سلام" is "That's wonderful." Before we leave for the trip that morning my sense of hope that the Barrier-Free Event will be a source of happiness and joy returns to Nadine's exclamation of "Ya Salam/ يا سلا" because I am captivated by Nadine's sense of wonder and her mother's joy.

Upon arrival at the venue, a representative from our group signs us in, and I am handed a package of information, which includes a map and schedule of events. Our group finds one of the few remaining fold-out tables to place our lunches and belongings. As the venue continues to fill, I notice that most of the school groups who arrive after us stake out spots on the floor as there are no more tables available. I look at the growing crowd of non-disabled and disabled adults and children, and I look at my itinerary. I count 45 developmental disability classes from 20 schools. I also notice that this Barrier-Free Event includes a rotation through 10 events, with an interval of 10 minutes at each event and a 40-minute break for lunch. There are two accessible washrooms labelled by gender for the hundreds of participants present today. I am relieved that at least our group has staked out a spot at one of the few fold-out tables. I look up from my papers, and I notice that the expression of joy on Nadine's face while we were at school has completely evaporated. As I have been looking at my papers outlining the itinerary, the venue has become increasingly crowded and noisy. As the organizers offer their preamble and as "O Canada" begins to play, Nadine's face is full of panic and then tears.

Nadine looks around at the crowd. She looks at her mother. She looks at me. She covers her ears as an endless stream of tears follows all of us while the foghorn blows at 10-minute intervals to move participants in this Barrier-Free Event along to the next activity station. Our group of three classes is moving in the circuit with four other classes from two different schools. I only know this because that is what I read on the list I have been given. I interact with neither the other disabled children nor the support staff and teachers from the other classes. We move in the same counter-clockwise direction to the different activity stations all day without knowing each others' names or interacting with each other in any way. At the wheelchair basketball station, I notice that some of the students in the other classes are wheelchair users, so they do not have to rush and find wheelchairs in order to play wheelchair basketball. Every 10 minutes we have to move along in the circuit, listen to a different set of rules for playing the game or using the particular equipment at that station. There is barely time to use any of the materials at each activity station before it is time to move on in the circuit. Nadine is simultaneously crying, trying to plug her ears, and running away from each activity station. Each of the staff members in our group takes turns along with her mother to try and engage her in the activities at each of the stations. Her mom gives her several hugs and reports that her heart is beating too fast. The foghorn blows again and again, and it is lunchtime.

"To be marked nonnormative or nonconforming—which is, to say, outside the limited protections of whiteness—is to be vulnerable to punishment, violence, surveillance."

Kelley, Robin D. G. "On Violence and Carcerality." *Signs: Journal of Women in Culture and Society* 42, no. 3 (2017): 590–600; p. 591.

It is at least a 20-minute wait to use the washrooms, so we take turns waiting in the line. The foghorn blows again to signal that lunch has ended and that it is time to return to our spot in the activity circuit. Nadine lets go of her mother's hand and runs away. Her mother and two of the support staff run after her trying to catch up. I stay with the rest of my students hoping that Nadine has not run too far. About 20 minutes later, Nadine, her mother, and the two support staff return to the group. Almost instantly, Nadine lets go of her mother's hand. She is running away again. This time I go after her. She is running toward the rock-climbing wall, which is out of bounds and not part of the activity circuit in this Barrier-Free Event. I am told by one of the nearby adults: "He is not allowed to climb that." The adult has read Nadine as presenting as a boy even though she is a girl. Even if it means climbing her way as far away as she can, Nadine is intent on leaving this circuit of events. I take her off the climbing wall before she gets too far up. She is crying. I sing "Five Little Ducks," which is one of her favourite songs. We find her mother sitting at the fold-out table where our group ate lunch. This area is relatively quiet as the majority of participants are still moving around the circuit of activities at 10-minute intervals. For the remainder of the trip we abandon following the circuit. Her mother and I sit with Nadine listening to her favourite songs on her mom's phone.

Her screaming, crying, and running away from the circuit of activities are read as disruptive and troublesome. After all, Nadine and the hundreds of children with intellectual disabilities present today should be happy at this attempt at inclusion during this annual barrier-free event. According to Ahmed (2008): "We become alienated—out of line with an affective community—when we do not experience pleasure from proximity to objects that are attributed as being good" (p. 11). This barrier-free event is valued as good for the ways it foregrounds inclusive practices through access to adaptive equipment and materials for engagement in physical activities. There is sledge hockey, sitting volleyball, wheelchair basketball, and parachute games, to name a few of the events organized *for* the students in the developmental disability classes. This event occurs once a year in the spring and is often one of the few field trips that developmental disabilities classes attend. Nadine and the other disabled children should be happily participating as this event is *for* them. Yet, Nadine is one of several students who is unhappy and out of line. She is not oriented to this barrier-free event in the ways that are expected (Ahmed, 2006). She encounters this barrier-free event as disabling, disorienting, and a source of unhappiness.

According to Ahmed (2010): "To be not happy is to be not in the eyes of others in the world of whiteness which is the world as it coheres around right bodies, or the white bodies" (p. 589). Extending Ahmed's work of troubling the taken-for-granted relationship between whiteness and happiness within disability studies, Goodley, Liddiard, and Runswick-Cole (2018) state: "Disabled people are similarly strangers at the neo-liberal able table that only recognizes self-sufficiency. To Ahmed's 'un' and 'not' we add 'dis'. To become disabled is to work against a normative ableist culture" (p. 211). The insights from both Ahmed (2010) and Goodley, Liddiard, and Runswick-Cole (2018) not only reveal the persistent barriers present in barrier-free events but also call into question pathological readings of Nadine. Spending the afternoon off the track with Nadine and her mom provoked me (and I hope you, too) to think about how barriers remain ever-present within this self-named barrier-free event. They remain present within this barrier-free event within the temporal nature of fold-out tables, not enough tables, and circuits timed by the relentless blow of the foghorn at 10-minute intervals. Nadine, however, is unhappily out of line and breaks away. Fortunately, she invites me to break away with her.

It is through Nadine's invitation to break away from the circuit that I can begin to question and disrupt what it means to participate in a barrier-free event. According to Baker (2010), current curricula foci are inextricably linked to the century's old hegemony of western colonial logics in a manner that should prompt both students and teachers to wonder "do 'we' organize curriculum and classes or does this history organize 'us'?" (p. 228). Her work serves as a reminder that the word "curriculum derives from the Latin *currere* meaning racecourse or track. Significantly, we are to understand this track not as linear but as circular where the ending meets back-up with the beginning" (Baker, 2010, p. 226). When Baker's insight about the ways in which current curricula are sustained through endless loops around the same track, participation in a barrier-free event for students with developmental disabilities can be read as a tangible enactment of that loop as necessarily excluding and marginalizing of Nadine and countless of her fellow participants. Today's barrier-free event tangibly revolves around a racetrack. Each of the 45 classes begins at a different point on the racetrack, yet the circular motion at 10-minute intervals returns each group to the same spot where they started. The 10-minute intervals at each station foregrounds both an efficiency in scheduling activities as well as little to no interaction between participants. At each station, the lead organizer of the activity explains the rules and points to the spot to either find equipment and/or wait in line for a turn to try the game. There is barely time to become engaged with an activity, let alone interact with other participants. While on the racetrack, there is an imperviousness within the direction of the circular motion. We are all supposed to be moving in the same direction, while simultaneously remaining unmoved by each other's presence as we follow the circular loop. Untouched by the countless embodied differences of race, gender, class, and disability, the circular motion of the barrier-free circuit sustains its hegemonic force. While on the racetrack, we are permeated with the touch of normalcy while remaining untouched by each other. Breaking away and getting off the track is Nadine's provocative invitation to me (and hopefully to you, too) to be touched differently through disabling curricular encounters.

DISABLING CURRICULAR ENCOUNTERS AND POSSIBILITIES WITHIN "YA SALAM/ يا سلام"

"The practices [of inclusion] reflect the long-term continuity of benevolence as a form of social and cultural control directed to the problems that arise from the economically poor and the marginal and the physically and mentally vulnerable."

Slee, Roger. *Inclusive Education Isn't Dead, It Just Smells Funny*. London, UK: Routledge, 2018, p. xi.

In experiencing the barriers within this barrier-free event with Nadine and her mom, I am troubled by how normalcy re-stories itself under the guise of barrier-free access as well as the tangible impacts of Nadine's disabling encounter with the curriculum. I am also provoked by Nadine's refusal to participate. While the running and crying and plugging her ears connote Nadine's unhappiness and distress, her refusal to participate disrupts the circuit of events in a manner that necessitates the need to stop and wonder (Titchkosky, 2011). Here I wonder about how Nadine is potently and powerfully communicating the ways in which the normative demands of schooling sustain exclusions.

Nadine's breaking away from the circuit offers fruitful opportunities to both confront the untenable constraints of the normative demands within western colonial logics and also consider the possibilities of imagining and inhabiting distinctly different human relations amidst, with, and through disability. Her disabling encounter with the curriculum is a moment to refuse capture through stopping and wondering about how our individual and collective human scripts have been shaped by colonial western logics (Titchkosky, 2007, 2011). Along with disability scholar Titchkosky (2007, 2011), Wynter's work is indicative of the

necessity of evoking the human imaginary in order to make and tell distinctly different stories. Through Wynter's work, the precarity of western science to be the
only voice that claims to represent "true" knowledge becomes increasingly evident.
Wynter (1984, 2003, 2015) contends that there is an urgent need to rewrite science to include a study of how our systems and structures are implicated in the
tales we tell ourselves and each other. Wynter states: "one cannot 'unsettle' the
'coloniality of power' without a redescription of the human outside the terms of
our present descriptive statement of the human, Man, and its over representation" (2003, p. 268). I would contend that within the need for redescription of the
human (Wynter, 1984, 1987, 1994, 2003; Wynter & McKittrick, 2015) lies the
integral role of disability and disabled children like Nadine.

When we finally return to school and our classroom, Nadine indicates her
relief by saying "Ya Salam/ يا سلام." I smile, understanding the context of her
declarative statement: "That is wonderful." Away from the crowded venue of
several hundred disabled and non-disabled people. Away from the relentless
circuit of activity stations, the noise of the foghorn, the noise of participants,
the unfamiliar faces, the new task demands coming at 10-minute intervals,
there is no wonder at Nadine's sense of relief that our day at the so-called
barrier-free event is over. Most of the time, Nadine communicates through non-
verbal gestures and the use of pictures. When she uses words to communicate,
she uses both Arabic and English. When she says "Ya Salam/ يا سلام," there are
times, like at the beginning or end of this field trip, that the wonder she is experiencing can be read as the joy of having her mother with her or the relief of
returning to a familiar and safe space.

Sometimes when Nadine says "Ya Salam/ يا سلام," I share in her exclamation
of wonder. For example, on rainy indoor recess days, we often walk through the
school hallways. There is a poster on the wall near the school nutrition room that
depicts dairy products. Nadine stops on one of our walks and points at the picture
of milk and says, "Halib/ حليب." I respond back: "Yes, halib/ حليب in Arabic, milk
in English." This exchange happens repeatedly during our walks. One day, Nadine
says: "Halib/ حليب/ Milk, Ya Salam/ يا سلام." That is, "it is wonderful, that this
white liquid is not just milk, but it is also halib/ حليب." This matters to Nadine as
her encounters with the world intertwine Arabic and English, as well as her embodied and visual modes of expression. When we walk in the hallways, she always
reaches her hand out and we hold hands. Sometimes, while we are walking, she
fills the silence with "Ya Salam/ يا سلام."

Stopping and wondering with Nadine involves attending to what she is communicating through her crying and running as she breaks away from the circuit; it

involves keeping the way she is tethered to both Arabic and English in the foreground; it also involves attending to her embodied expressions of joy and excitement. In the morning while we are waiting for the bus and in between the hugs she shares with her mom and the declarations of "Ya Salam/ يا سلام," Nadine stands up and jumps up and down while flapping her arms. Her mom asks me if there is any way to stop Nadine from engaging in the movements of jumping and flapping. Nadine's mom is familiar with the stares and glares directed toward her and her daughter. She has encountered the sting of being read as both strange and stranger. Her mom is surprised when I encourage her to accept her daughter's movements and motions as a component part of how Nadine communicates and expresses herself during this moment and time. Maybe in a few years her movements and motions will continue and/or manifest themselves with entirely different rhythms and motions. Maybe in a few years the movements and motions once read as strange and estranging will be read very declaratively as wonderful; "Ya Salam/ يا سلام." This exchange with Nadine's mom is representative of the ways in which the barriers Nadine encounters at the barrier-free event that we attend are representative of countless barriers Nadine and her mother confront on a daily basis—in the grocery store, at the park, in the elevator to their apartment, etc. In this sense my advice to Nadine's mom can be read as wonderfully unrealistic. In the short-term, it will not stop the stares and glares and/or the discriminatory or offensive comments. It will not stop the tears or the panic the next time Nadine's presence, her movements, her disability, and her black body are read as an unexpected surprise.

Yet, unexpected encounters perhaps hold the most fruitful possibilities to refuse, disrupt, and reimagine our relations with each other amidst disability. In keeping with Wynter's provocations to reimagine what it means to be human through our relations with each other and the stories we tell ourselves (Wynter, 1984, 1987, 1994, 2003; Wynter & McKittrick, 2015) and Titchkosky's provocation to inhabit our relations with disability as opportunities to wonder (2011), I am suggesting here that teaching and learning with Nadine is an opportunity to engage in a sincere questioning of the ways normalcy continues to limit the possibility for Nadine to encounter the world or a field trip as barrier-free. I have heard Nadine say "Ya Salam/ يا سلام" countless times, and even after a year of teaching and learning with her, there are moments when her declaration of "Ya Salam/ يا سلام" continues to leave me in the midst of wonder. The wonder occurs for me within the invitation of her outstretched hand on our walks or the gesture to sit with her and her mom to sing songs. I am in wonder that someone who has encountered so much exclusion within schooling can remain so willing to teach and learn. Nadine's invitation to engage with disability differently leaves me hopeful that there remain possibilities to reimagine our relationships amidst embodied differences differently.

Ahmed reminds her readers of the root word within happiness. According to Ahmed (2010, p. 574), "the etymology of the word happiness relates precisely to the question of contingency: it is from the Middle English word *hap*, suggesting chance." She also conveys the import of refusing to follow the paths of happiness as integral to questioning whiteness, heteronormativity, and classism. She states: "To deviate from the paths of happiness is to refuse to inherit the elimination of the word *hap*" (2010, p. 593). Amidst her declarations of wonder, amidst her rhythmic jumping and flapping arms, amidst her use of words in both Arabic and English, even amidst her crying and running, Nadine inhabits the contingency within *hap*: "Ya Salam/ يا سلام." Through my own encounters with Nadine, I hope for more invitations to engage in the *hap* of disabling curricular encounters.

CONCLUSION

"If ... there is an interrelationship between matter and discursive meaning, we need to more tangibly recognize the materiality of disability's active participation in the processes of meaning-making itself. This is not simply because disability must be resignified in more positive, affirming ways; but rather that disability provides the evidence of embodiment's shifting, kaleidoscopic dynamically unfolding agency."

Mitchell, David T., Susan Antebi, and Sharon L. Snyder. *The Matter of Disability: Materiality, Biopolitics, Crip Affect*. Ann Arbor, MI: University of Michigan Press, 2019, p. 2.

This chapter has explored the possibilities within disabling curricular encounters. Through the provocations of my experiences with one of my students at a barrier-free event, I have sought to trouble the ways current orientations toward normalcy within schooling practices continue to be encountered as disabling, exclusionary, and marginalizing for students like Nadine. I have also foregrounded the possibilities in breaking away from the seemingly endless circuit of repetition. Teaching and learning encounters with Nadine provoke the possibilities to wonder through forging distinctly different relationships. Her crying and running away from the limits of barrier-free conceptions of what it means to participate and engage with curriculum not only questions current schooling practices but offers fruitful possibilities to engage in other kinds of stories. Stories that inhabit the space in between Arabic and English, in between jumping up and down with arms flapping and listening to her favourite songs. Stories that are no longer about stares and glares at the stranger but rather stories that inhabit the unexpected wonder that comes with the refusal to follow normalcy. Thus, disabling curricular encounters evoke the kind of wonder that not only refuses normalcy but suggests that becoming human differently amidst disability is always and already a possibility. "Ya Salam/."سلام يا."

NOTE

1. While person-first language is the widely accepted and taken-for-granted practice within education, throughout this paper identity-first language (Liebowitz, 2015) is used. Identity-first language is offered as an invitation to provoke a consideration of how disability is integral rather than separate from our humanities.

REFERENCES

Ahmed, S. (2006). *Queer phenomenology: Orientations, objects, others*. Duke University Press.

Ahmed, S. (2008). Sociable happiness. *Emotion, Space and Society, 1*(1), 10–13.

Ahmed, S. (2010). Killing joy: Feminism and the history of happiness. *Signs: Journal of Women in Culture and Society, 35*(3), 571–594.

Baker, B. (2010). Provincializing curriculum? On the preparation of subjectivity for globality. *Curriculum Inquiry, 40*(2), 221–240.

Goodley, D., & Runswick-Cole, K. (2012). Reading Rosie: The postmodern disabled child. *Narrative: Approaches in Research and Professional Practice, 29*(2), 51–64.

Goodley, D., Liddiard, K., & Runswick-Cole, K. (2018). Feeling disability: Theories of affect and critical disability studies. *Disability & Society, 33*(2), 197–217. https://doi .org/10.1080/09687599.2017.1402752

Liebowitz, C. (2015, March 20). *I am Disabled: On identity-first versus person-first language*. The Body Is Not an Apology. https://thebodyisnotanapology.com/ magazine/i-am-disabled-on-identity-first-versus-people-first-language/

Titchkosky, T. (2007). *Reading and writing disability differently*. University of Toronto Press.

Titchkosky, T. (2011). *The question of access: Disability, space, meaning*. University of Toronto Press.

Wynter, S. (1984). The ceremony must be found: After humanism. *Boundary, 2*, 19–70. https://doi.org/10.2307/302808

Wynter, S. (1987). On disenchanting discourse: "Minority" literary criticism and beyond. *Cultural Critique*, (7), 207–244. https://doi.org/10.2307/1354156

Wynter, S. (1994). No humans involved: An open letter to my colleagues. *Forum NHI Knowledge for the 21st Century, 1*(1), 42–73.

Wynter, S. (2003). Unsettling the coloniality of being/power/truth/freedom: Towards the human, after man, its overrepresentation—an argument. *CR: The New Centennial Review, 3*(3), 257–337. https://doi.org/10.1353/ncr.2004.0015

Wynter, S., & McKittrick, K. (2015). Unparalleled catastrophe for our species? Or, to give humanness a different future: Conversations. In K. McKittrick (Ed.), *Sylvia Wynter: On being human as praxis* (pp. 9–89). Duke University Press.

CHAPTER 7

Ghosts, Mice, and Robots: DisAppearing the Autistic Person

Helen Rottier, Ben Pfingston, and Josh Guberman[1]

Key Terms: Autism; Academic Ableism; Neurodiversity; Research Ethics; Rhetoric

INTRODUCTION[2]

Whether due to or despite "awareness" campaigns, nearly everyone is "aware" of autism. Yet, due to or despite these campaigns and the hyper-visibility of autism as an epidemic (Gernsbacher et al., 2005) and an opponent against which society is morally obligated to war (McGuire, 2016), autistic people are regularly disappeared from conversations about our lives. In the academic sphere, autism is often discussed without input from autistic people, inserting distance between the condition and those affected. This disappearance can be understood as a form of ableist[3] violence that dehumanizes autistic people.

> "Attending to the normative and normalizing nature of such [pathologizing, 'crisis'] stories of autism and advocacy enables us to ask difficult and important questions about the premises and practices of acts of advocacy and, more broadly, about the culture in which we live. Critically attending to such stories allows us to ask, for example, the following: How do dominant versions of autism that characterize it as a condition of human life instead of a lived human condition—a some 'thing' and not a someone—allow for and even catalyze a collective failure to recognize violence against autistic people as a significant and pressing sociocultural problem?"
>
> McGuire, Anne. *War on Autism: On the Cultural Logic of Normative Violence.* Ann Arbor, MI: University of Michigan Press, 2016, p. 10.

This chapter's authors are autistic, early-career academics who met at the Autistic Self Advocacy Network's Autism Campus Inclusion program. We use the pronouns we and our when discussing the autistic community. Additionally, we use identity-first language when referring to autistic individuals and communities; this is the community's overwhelming preference (Gernsbacher, 2017; Kenny et al., 2016). We each practice self-advocacy on campus through our academic work and our community organizing. This chapter arose from the realization that metaphors used to erase autistic people and knowledge are central to each of our respective areas of scholarship. Helen, coming from disability studies, examines the rhetorics of ghostliness. Ben comes from psychology and explores how mice serve as a replacement for autistic people in the human sciences. Josh draws on work in human-computer interaction, wherein autistics are at once like robots but also less human than them. These three metaphors are meant to serve as a cross-sectional view of how autistic people are articulated and understood in research.

This chapter examines the ways autistic people are disappeared from academia and society—their bodies and knowledge—through rhetoric and research. Drawing upon examples of ghosts, mice, and robots as objects that disappear the autistic human subject, we explore this disappearance and its implications. We address disappearance by rematerializing or reappearing the autistic person as subject and academic and sharing methods for advancing autistic thought in and around academia. We conclude by calling upon academia to support autistic researchers' scholar-activism, value autistic knowledge, and address ableist disappearance in society.

GHOSTS

"I seek to explore the ways in which normal, everyday and typical understandings of the human being are, in reality, incredibly exclusionary: including some and omitting others. And this potential for the human category to divide and rule—to let in some and force out others—is a category currently, worryingly and deplorably being rewritten in popular discourse.... The consequences are potentially wide-reaching and terrifying. And so our responses have to be immediate but not bereft of thought."

Goodley, Dan. *Disability and Other Human Questions*. Bingley, UK: Emerald Publishing, 2020, p. 23.

Avery Gordon (1997) introduces ghosts as a tool through which we can understand disappearance. Gordon uses the ghostly to signify both present absence (one who is present but rendered ineffectual) and absent presence (one who is absent but has an impact on the social and historical contours of the present). Autistic individuals inhabit both present absences, through tokenism of autistic representatives in organizations, and absent presences, through the ableist presumption that autistics are not already embedded in academia, policy, and other change-making positions. Autistic individuals are often disappeared from society into literal, figurative, and rhetorical ghostliness. This section will explore autistic disappearance through deadly violence, mourning narratives, and arhetoricity and gesture toward the autistic subject's reappearance through autistic knowledge production. The following includes a discussion of violence, filicide, and suicide.

Autistic individuals are concretely disappeared through life-ending violence. Each year, autistic communities and allies gather for Disability Day of Mourning to remember the lives of over 600 disabled people killed by parents and caregivers. This tradition was started by the Autistic Self Advocacy Network (ASAN) in 2012 following the murder of George Hodgins, an autistic man. Subsequent media coverage further ghosted Hodgins by portraying his murder as inevitable and an act of mercy (ASAN, n.d.a).

Another instance of ghostly violence against autistic people is suicide. Autistic people are 10 times as likely to die by suicide than non-autistic people. Although this violence is self-enacted, it is rooted in ableism and bullying; researchers continue to explore the impact of social isolation and bullying on suicidality in autistic people.

Autistic individuals, particularly autistic children, also disappear through mourning narratives that position autism as worse than death. Mourning narratives are upheld by parents and professionals who grieve the loss of a typical child, centring the non-autistic child and disappearing the autistic child. Autistic self-advocate Jim Sinclair (in Bascom, 2012) proclaimed, "Don't mourn for us," and addressed how mourning narratives perpetuate myths about the humanity and potential of autistic individuals. Sinclair explains that the "vision of [the autistic child] is obscured by the ghost of a child who never lived" (in Bascom, 2012, p. 15) and that the act of mourning disappears the autistic individual's capacity for life.

The autistic subject is rendered ghostly through disappeared intentionality or ability to make arguments. Rhetorical ghostliness prevents the autistic person from making claims about their lives. M. Remi Yergeau (2018) introduces the concept of demirhetoricity, in which one is simultaneously too autistic and not autistic enough to speak to autistic experience. Sinclair (in Bascom, 2012) describes a similar strategy used to discredit self-advocates: first, deny the person's membership in the group ("not really autistic"); second, claim that the person is an extraordinary case ("high-functioning") and thus does not speak for all members of the group; and third, claim that the person is incapable of understanding and is arhetorical. Each of these tactics is a way of disappearing autistic advocacy from society, and functioning language is an especially violent method of erasure for people labelled either high-functioning or low-functioning. As Ellen Murray (2016) explains, "'High functioning' is used to deny support. 'Low functioning' is used to deny agency." Arhetoricity also renders the autistic academic ghostly and incapable of knowledge production. The academy is built upon the rhetorical potential of the scholar; thus, autistics are disappeared from academia and ghosted from knowledge production.

The implications of the autistic subject's disappearance into ghostliness are felt in the present absence and absent presence Gordon describes as haunting. When autistic people are in the room, we are still disappeared, ignored, and silenced. When we are absent, the ableism responsible for our disappearance continues to haunt. How do we reappear the ghostly autistic subject? Gordon (1997) developed a formula: By "providing a hospitable memory for ghosts out of a concern for justice" (p. 60), we can reckon with hauntings and prevent further disappearances. Memorializing the dead, (re)inviting the absent, and listening to the silenced is only the first step; we must also strive to disrupt the ableism that disappears the autistic subject from society.

By valuing autistic modes of knowing and being, we can create a more inclusive and less haunted academia. Disability studies pioneers this work by emphasizing knowledge translation, neurodivergent literacies, and emancipatory research methods to rematerialize the autistic subject as a source of knowledge. Autistic scholars, allies, and collectives are central to this reappearance. Following their lead, we can disrupt ableist rhetoric that silences autistic and disabled perspectives and (re)value autistic knowledge production in the academy.

MICE

"Through the corporeal metaphor, the disabled or otherwise different body may easily become a stand-in for more abstract notions of the human condition, as universal or nationally specific; thus the textual (disembodied) project depends upon—and takes advantage of—the materiality of the body ... while such contested oppositions emerge with similar urgency in debates pertaining to other familiar categories of identity (race, class, gender) disability may be especially effective in crossing the boundaries of identity categories, potentially restructuring critical approaches."

Antebi, Susan. "Caliban and Coney Island: Spanish American Narratives of Corporeal Difference and Performance." *Disability Studies Quarterly* 25, no. 4 (2005).

Autistic people are disappeared within the academy through model organism research. Described as having an "autism phenotype," BTBR mice[4] are commonly used as a model for autism in research settings (Ruskin et al., 2013). For example, Ruskin et al. (2013) reported that a ketogenic diet decreased repetitive behaviours and increased social interaction in mice bred to mimic autism. Model organisms are used in medical or behavioural research because of their short generation times, manipulability, small size, and other factors (Ankeny & Leonelli, 2011; National Institute of General Medical Sciences, n.d.). Overall, the use of mice models in autism research contributes to autistic disappearance through literally disappearing autistic bodies, as well as the limited capability of mice to represent autism and the failure of research to reflect the autistic community's values.

First, using mice disappears autistic bodies from the academy in a literal sense. Model organisms, including mice, can only ever mimic certain aspects of a disability, not the entire experience (van der Staay et al., 2009). As such, using mice as a model organism could be seen as an attempt to simulate autism. Simulations, defined by Titchkosky et al. (2019), serve as only a partial representation of the imitation's focus, and often, such representations fall short in what they teach about the actual experience. This is because a simulation aims to propose what it is like to experience something, not what it actually is. Additionally, the knowledge that simulations of disability produce often fails to create understanding alongside it, further alienating people's thoughts about disabled people from disabled peoples' actual, lived experience (Titchkosky et al., 2019). Model mice represent the main behaviours associated with autism, and due to this, their epistemic potential is limited; they only (re) produce a form of knowing without facilitating experientially valid understanding.

The fact that model organism research uses simulations contributes to autistic disappearance in research and calls into question the applicability of the findings. If model mice only serve as a partial representation of autism, then it is improbable that the research will transfer effectively to autistic people. Additionally, researchers are alienated from the actual autistic experience, replacing potential understanding with incomplete and myopic knowledge. However, the conclusion drawn from this critique should not be that autistic people should be used in the place of model mice for the same research. Models are often used for good reason, such as protecting participants from unforeseen risks associated with the research conditions. Model organism research falls short in more significant ways, further contributing to autistic disappearance in academic science.

Additionally, model organism research vanishes autistic people from scholarship metaphorically: research using model organisms does not reflect the community's values. Most research done with mice reflects the medical model of disability, which defines disability as an individual medical problem that should be "helped" with medical intervention. Medical model research fundamentally assumes that autism and disability are abnormal, wrong, and a burden on oneself and others. It considers the primary cause of suffering for autistic people to be autism itself, not environmental and cultural factors that hinder autistics. The medical model also empowers practitioners to improve disabled people's lives, all while expecting disabled people to seek out self-betterment (Retief & Letsosa, 2018). Such research aims to use medicine or treatment to "fix" autism in some such way, including fully curing autism or simply targeting specific "deficits." Ruskin et al. (2013) illustrate how mice studies medicalize autism and frame it as an illness to be cured or treated.

The medical model is inconsistent with the lived experiences of many autistic people, who reject the notion of a cure and the medical perspective of autism (Bagatell, 2010). Many see autism as a fundamental part of their personhood; being non-autistic would mean being a different person. Members of the community identify the source of suffering—if they suffer to begin with—to be societal attitudes that push for them to conform (Bagatell, 2010). This push to conformity is the purpose of medical model research. As such, mice research fails to meet its own goals, further contributing to autistic disappearance rather than alleviating it.

Kevin Elliot (2017) described several values of consideration for scientists, including transparency, representativeness, and engagement. Representativeness indicates that research reflects ethical principles and values, especially for those who are most affected by such research, and is mostly absent from model organism research (Elliot, 2017). Regardless of who researchers are, scientists should make the perspectives of those most affected by their research a priority. By following the traditional medicalized model, which is something that disappears autistic people and their values, the use of model mice in autism research does not meet Elliot's criteria for representative research.

Instead, researchers using models actively prioritize the principles of doctors, family members, and other non-autistic stakeholders. As such, model organism autism research systemically contributes to building barriers. Due to the various ways model organism research disappears autistics from academia—particularly in science and medicine—from a literal, physical disappearance to the devaluation of our voices and values, this kind of research should not be taking place at all, on animal or human subjects.

Autistic people and researchers affiliated with the community are pushing back against the current system, with allied researchers advocating for community-based models for years. More recently, ASAN has positioned itself against cure-based research, instead supporting research centred around autistic communication, education, and health care (ASAN, n.d.b). Alongside ASAN, the

Academic Autism Spectrum Partnership in Research and Education (AASPIRE) champions research that actively involves autistic individuals and focuses on the community's priorities, such as improving employment opportunities and health care experiences (AASPIRE, n.d.a, n.d.b). However, model organism research remains and continues to contribute to the perpetuation of ableist, medicalized autism research, ultimately contradicting these community-based efforts and continuing to disappear autistic presences from academia.

ROBOTS

"Science is a social institution about which there is a great deal of misunderstanding, even among those who are part of it. We think that science is an institution, a set of methods, a set of people, a great body of knowledge that we call scientific, is somehow apart from the forces that rule our everyday lives and that govern the structure of our society. We think science is objective. Science has brought us all kinds of good things.... At the same time, science, like other productive activities, like the state, the family, sport, is a social institution completely integrated into and influenced by the structure of all our other social institutions. The problems that science deals with, the ideas that it uses in investigating those problems, even the so-called scientific results that come out of scientific investigation, are all deeply influenced by predispositions that derive from the society in which we live. Scientists do not begin life as scientists, after all, but as social beings immersed in a family, a state, a productive structure, and they view nature through a lens that has been molded by their social experience."

Lewontin, Richard C. *Biology as Ideology: The doctrine of DNA*. Toronto, ON: Anansi Press, 1991, p. 3.

Robots represent another physical and rhetorical engine for the disappearance of autistic subjects. As technological research and development for autism interventions surges, many researchers turn toward robots (Spiel et al., 2019). In this popular research area, robots are often used to support existing interventions such as applied behaviour analysis (ABA; see Spiel et al., 2019). ABA is an intensive intervention program that attempts to reward behaviours deemed socially appropriate while punishing behaviours considered troublesome. ABA shares an unfortunate history with "conversion therapy" (see Yergeau, 2018) and is considered incompatible with the neurodiversity paradigm adopted by autistic self-advocates and communities (see DeVita-Raeburn & Spectrum, 2016). Generally, the interventions noted by Spiel and colleagues (2019) use robots as tools in researchers' and clinicians' efforts to lessen the visibility of autism by training autistic children to act in less autistic and in normatively "human" ways.

While the use of robots in autism therapies is a recent development, discussions about robots and their relationship to autism have a long history. Following the development of autism–robot comparisons, Yergeau (2018) traces mechanical descriptions of autism to Bruno Bettelheim's 1959 article, "Joey: A 'Mechanical Boy.'" Bettelheim (1959) described his autistic subject, Joey, as an unskilled infant but a successful machine. As early as 1974, scientists like Joseph Weizenbaum (1983) brought autism into conversations about computers. Weizenbaum described simple computer programs, typewriters, and "infantile" autistics as having similar conversational capacities (i.e., none whatsoever). Today, when autistic children communicate verbally, they are still described as doing so in a machine-like (Paul et al., 2005) or robot-like (Centers for Disease Control and Prevention, 2015; National Institute on Deafness and Other Communication Disorders, 2015) manner.

Describing autistics as more similar to machines than to humans, even just rhetorically, has serious implications. Autistics do communicate, even if not verbally (see, e.g., Baggs, 2007). If a computer makes bothersome noises or flashes indecipherable text on its screen, one may simply ignore the machine, rather than attempt to understand it. Configuring autistic behaviour as machine-like disappears the agency and personhood behind autistic communication and justifies negligence toward autistics.[5] For if autistics are more like machines than humans, if there is no person behind their sounds and motions, then recognition and understanding of our motions and sounds are of little concern. Computer-like understandings of autistics distance us from not just humanity but from the realm of the living altogether. Autistics are not computers, of course. We are living, breathing people. And yet, our communications are routinely treated as unimportant unless or until we meet ablenormative standards for communication.[6]

Contemporary autism–robot research inherited the notion that autistics resemble machines more closely than people. The autism–robot studies explored by Spiel and colleagues (2019) often justify themselves on two premises. The first premise states that autistics prefer technology to other people. The second premise claims that autistics will be more interested in and able to imitate robots emulating human behaviours than living conversation partners. Lucy Suchman (2011) explores how, in research intending to contribute to a greater understanding of humans, researchers sometimes use robots as stand-ins for people. Through this work, humans and humanoid robots co-create meaning of and with each other. Roboticists design robots to behave humanlike. To elicit human behaviour, roboticists program robots based on models thought to explain the same behaviour in humans. When robots behave as expected, roboticists take this success as evidence of their models' correctness for how/why humans behave as they do. So, as robots behave more humanlike, models for human behaviour become more robot-like.

In autism–robot therapies, autistic children are meant to become less autistic with the help of robots, but neither the robots nor their creators are to be affected by the autistic subjects. The robot's meaning is predetermined via the aforementioned discursive, co-constituting practice of building robots that act like humans. These humans are, in turn, defined by the same robots for which they served as templates. This process renders the robots intelligible to their human counterparts, who can assume a behaviour means a specific thing, whether performed by a human or humanoid robot (Suchman, 2011). Autism–robot research appears unconcerned with achieving shared understanding between autistic children, robots, and/or non-autistic clinicians and caretakers (Spiel et al., 2019). Instead, a primary purpose of robot studies can be understood as an effort to render the autistic child intelligible to the non-autistic other. The socialized robot now plays a role in the ablenormative socialization of the autistic child. In this research, there exists a hierarchy in which humans and robots have the capacities to act upon one another, but wherein autistics can only be acted upon. Autistics are configured as so "epistemically absented" (Yergeau, 2018, p. 54), so distant from intelligibility, that we have less agency and capacity for sense-making than the robots to which we are compared.

These therapies serve to coerce, through the deployment of normative violence, autistic children into a less autistic (and ostensibly more human) state. The end-goal is to mould a new child, one regarded as normatively human enough to act upon and shape other entities. Through this work, the academy contributes to the continued disappearance of autistic existences and perpetuates the notion that there exists some recoverable, non-autistic child underneath the child's autism (see Yergeau, 2018, for an exploration of this notion of recovery). When researchers try to materialize a normal child from within an autistic person, they are actively working to disappear the child that already exists (see Sinclair, 2012).

Autistic self-advocates challenge the underlying premises (a) that autistic differences render the expressions of their humanity less valid and (b) that these differences warrant normalizing interventions (see, e.g., Bascom, 2012). Within a neurodiversity framework (Kapp et al., 2013), it is not the humanity of autistic children that is suspect. Rather, it is the humanity of an institutionalized definition of personhood that casts autistic people as less human than non-autistics and machines alike. Contemporary explorations of robots as therapeutic aids for autistics and historical autism–robot discourses cleave a wedge between autistics and humanity. Nevertheless, autistic personhood reemerges despite these erasures.

While there is little room for autistic agency and knowledges within autism–robot interventions, autistic agency and knowledges do exist. Recognition of autistic knowledges, however, troubles the status quo wherein autistic communication is ignorable and autistic subjects exist to be acted upon. As machines, we cannot possess threatening knowledge nor construct alternative meanings of research about us. As people, our knowledge challenges the ethicality and validity of entire areas of study. Until such a time that the academy recognizes autistic self-determination and autistically produced knowledges, we must continue to assert our worthiness through our resistance to our disappearance.

CONCLUSION

In this chapter, we described the ways that ghosts, mice, and robots disappear the autistic human subject from academia, through rhetoric, research, and applied technology. The implications of this disappearance include dehumanizing research and policy outcomes and the haunting of dominant narratives around autistic (non)personhood. Using ghostliness as an analytic, we show that violence, mourning narratives, and alleged arhetoricity disappear autistic subjects. Use of model organisms disappears autistic people from research, which fails to reflect autistic experiences and uphold autistic community values. Technological interventions for autism involving robots disappear autistics and their agency by configuring them as non-human. However, (re)appearance is possible through (re)valuing of autistic knowledge, perspectives, and modes of being. Autistic scholars and allies are the leaders of the resistance and reappearance of autistic knowledge. Critically, these knowledges and perspectives must be recognized as wholly valid without assimilation to academic norms and rigour and will continue to push back against ableism in academia, medicine, and society.

NOTES

1. The authors are listed in the order their respective sections appear. Each author led the writing of one section, and all authors contributed equally to the overall chapter.
2. This work is supported by the National Science Foundation (grant #DGE-1256260).
3. Ableism is the systemic oppression of people with disabilities (see Campbell, 2015). Ableist violence stems from the expectation of ablenormative bodyminds.
4. BTBR mice are a form of genetically modified mice often used to model autism in preclinical research (see Meyza & Blanchard, 2017).
5. In ABA, such negligence is a primary form of punishment.

6. For example, communication is recognized as such when primarily conveyed across verbal/aural channels, when paired with non-autistic body language and facial affect, and when unaccompanied by stereotypy. Julia Bascom (2012) illustrates the lasting consequences of ABA and its practitioners forcibly quashing her autistic modes of communication.

REFERENCES

Academic Autism Spectrum Partnership in Research and Education (AASPIRE). (n.d.a). *Home.* https://aaspire.org/

Academic Autism Spectrum Partnership in Research and Education (AASPIRE). (n.d.b). *Partnership.* https://aaspire.org/about/partnership/

Ankeny, R. A., & Leonelli, S. (2011). What's so special about model organisms? *Studies in History and Philosophy of Science Part A, 42*(2), 313–323. https://doi.org/10.1016/j.shpsa.2010.11.039

Autistic Self Advocacy Network (ASAN). (n.d.a). *2022 Anti-filicide toolkit.* https://autisticadvocacy.org/projects/community/mourning/anti-filicide/

Autistic Self Advocacy Network (ASAN). (n.d.b). *Position statements.* https://autisticadvocacy.org/about-asan/position-statements/

Bagatell, N. (2010). From cure to community: Transforming notions of autism. *Ethos, 38*(1), 33–55. https://doi.org/10.1111/j.1548-1352.2009.01080.x

Baggs, M. (2007, January 14). *In my language* [Video]. YouTube. https://www.youtube.com/watch?v=JnylM1hI2jc

Bascom, J. (Ed.). (2012). *Loud hands: Autistic people, speaking.* The Autistic Press.

Bettelheim, B. (1959). Joey: A "mechanical boy." *Scientific American, 200*(3), 116–130.

Campbell, K. (2015). Ability. In B. Reiss, D. Serline, & R. Adams (Eds.), *Keywords for disability studies* (pp. 46–51). New York University Press.

Centers for Disease Control and Prevention. (2015, February 26). *Signs & symptoms of autism spectrum disorders.* http://web.archive.org/web/20200813000957/https://www.cdc.gov/ncbddd/autism/signs.html

DeVita-Raeburn, E., & Spectrum. (2016, August 11). *Is the most common therapy for autism cruel?* The Atlantic. https://www.theatlantic.com/health/archive/2016/08/aba-autism-controversy/495272/

Elliot, K. C. (2017). *A tapestry of values: An introduction to values in science.* Oxford University Press.

Gernsbacher, M. A. (2017). Editorial perspective: The use of person-first language in scholarly writing may accentuate stigma. *The Journal of Child Psychology and Psychiatry, 58*(7), 859–861. https://doi.org/10.1111/jcpp.12706

Gernsbacher, M. A., Dawson, M., & Hill Goldsmith, H. (2005). Three reasons not to believe in an autism epidemic. *Current Directions in Psychological Science: a Journal of the American Psychological Society, 14*(2), 55–58. https://doi.org/10.1111/j.0963-7214.2005.00334.x

Gordon, A. (1997). *Ghostly matters: Haunting and the sociological imagination.* University of Minnesota Press.

Kapp, S. K., Gillespie-Lynch, K., Sherman, L. E., & Hutman, T. (2013). Deficit, difference, or both? Autism and neurodiversity. *Developmental Psychology, 49*(1), 59–71. https://doi.org/10/f4k9fq

Kenny, L., Hattersley, C., Molins, B., Buckley, C., Povey, C., & Pellicano, E. (2016). Which terms should be used to describe autism? Perspectives from the UK autism community. *Autism, 20*(4), 442–462. https://doi.org/10.1177/1362361315588200

McGuire, A. (2016). *War on autism: On the cultural logic of normative violence.* University of Michigan Press.

Meyza, K. Z., & Blanchard, D. C. (2017). The BTBR mouse model of idiopathic autism—current view on mechanisms. *Neuroscience & Biobehavioral Reviews, 76,* 99–110. https://doi.org/10.1016/j.neubiorev.2016.12.037

Murray, E. [@ellenfromnowon]. (2016, March 9). *"High functioning" is used to deny support. "Low functioning" is used to deny agency.* Twitter. https://twitter.com/ellenfromnowon/status/707710248296046592

National Institute on Deafness and Other Communication Disorders. (2015, August 18). *Autism spectrum disorder: Communication problems in children.* https://www.nidcd.nih.gov/health/autism-spectrum-disorder-communication-problems-children

National Institute of General Medical Sciences. (n.d.). *Research Organisms.* https://www.nigms.nih.gov/education/fact-sheets/Pages/using-research-organisms.aspx

Paul, R., Augustyn, A., Klin, A., & Volkmar, F. R. (2005). Perception and production of prosody by speakers with autism spectrum disorders. *Journal of Autism and Developmental Disorders, 35*(2), 205–220. https://doi.org/10.1007/s10803-004-1999-1

Retief, M., & Letsosa, R. (2018). Models of disability: A brief overview. *HTS Teologiese Studies/Theological Studies, 74*(1). https://doi.org/10.4102/hts.v74i1.4738

Ruskin, D. N., Svedova, J., Cote, J. L., Sandau, U., Rho, J. M., Kawamura, M., Jr., Boison, D., & Masino, S. A. (2013). Ketogenic diet improves core symptoms of autism in BTBR mice. *PLoS One, 8*(6). https://doi.org/10.1371/journal. pone.0065021

Sinclair, J. (2012). Don't mourn for us. *Autonomy, the Critical Journal of Interdisciplinary Autism Studies, 1*(1).

Spiel, K., Frauenberger, C., Keyes, O., & Fitzpatrick, G. (2019). Agency of autistic children in technology research—a critical literature review. *ACM Transactions on Computer-Human Interaction, 26*(6), 1–40. https://doi.org/10.1145/3344919

Suchman, L. (2011). Subject objects. *Feminist Theory, 12*(2), 119–145. https://doi.org/10/ dzcdsr

Titchkosky, T., Healey, D., & Michalko, R. (2019). Blindness simulation and the culture of sight. *Journal of Literary & Cultural Disability Studies, 13*(2), 123–139. https://doi.org/10.3828/jlcds.2018.47

van der Staay, F. J., Arndt, S. S., & Nordquist, R. E. (2009). Evaluation of animal models of neurobehavioral disorders. *Behavioral and Brain Functions, 5*(11). https:// doi.org/10.1186/1744-9081-5-11

Weizenbaum, J. (1983). Eliza—A computer program for the study of natural language communication between man and machine. *Communications of the ACM, 26*(1), 23–28.

Yergeau, M. R. (2018). *Authoring autism: On rhetoric and neurological queerness.* Duke University Press.

CHAPTER 8

Performing Dyslexia in Contemporary Japan

Satsuki Kawano

Key Terms: Anthropology; Dyslexia; Japan; Learning Disability; Ritual

INTRODUCTION

The Asia-Pacific Dyslexia Festival took place in Japan in 2016, the first international awareness-raising event on dyslexia. It aimed to increase social recognition of people with dyslexia, as their challenges and experiences of normative reading and writing practices have remained largely under-recognized in Japan. In this chapter, while prioritizing the views of Japanese people who identify with dyslexia, I illuminate how disability appeared in multifaceted ways in this public forum. Dyslexia was visible in many sessions through the construct of discrepancy, which emphasizes the notable gap between a person's strengths and weaknesses. While specialists in research and education tended to highlight the urgent need for implementing inclusive support provision in regular classrooms, people with dyslexia legitimated their preference for using alternative modes of producing creative outputs rather than through reading and writing. By taking part in discussion sessions and exhibiting their projects, they juxtaposed their ways of engagement with normative outlets of production that take reading and writing for granted. My study thus explores how participants in the advocacy event both verbally and non-verbally performed dyslexia, thereby strategically making disability appear in certain ways. In doing this, I use Victor Turner's (1967, 1969) notion of liminality, which characterizes the transitional ritual process and has been employed to analyze the societal imposition of isolation and an ambiguous status on disabled people in the study of disability and ritual (Murphy, 1990 [1987]; Murphy et al., 1988; Willett & Deegan, 2001). By focusing on disabled people as co-designers of an advocacy event, however, I provide an alternative perspective on liminality, which they collectively used to authorize their own views of valued engagement in Japan's post-industrial society.

> "The disablist and disabling sociospatial environment produces a vivid, but unwanted consciousness of one's impaired body. Here, the body undergoes a mode of 'dysappearance' which is not biological, but social."
>
> Paterson, Kevin, and Bill Hughes, "Disability Studies and Phenomenology: The Carnal Politics of Everyday Life." *Disability & Society* 14, no. 5 (1999): 597–610; p. 603.

PERSPECTIVES ON RITUAL AND DISABILITY

While an abundance of anthropological studies has explored rituals as shaping normative life-course transitions from a cross-cultural perspective, there has been limited study of rituals created and performed by disabled people. By using Turner's notion of liminality, which refers to the transitional phase of a ritual (Ingstad, 1995; Murphy, 1990 [1987]; Murphy et al., 1988; Nicolaisen, 1995; Willett & Deegan, 2001), anthropological studies tended to highlight the societal imposition of isolation and an ambiguous status on disabled people. The original notion of liminality was developed to theorize the transitional stage of a rite of passage— betwixt and between—when participants have left a socially recognized status but have not yet occupied a new one. In a classic analysis of initiation rites (Turner, 1967, 1969), Ndembu boys were separated from other community members, lived together, submitted to their elders, and faced a range of ordeals to eventually rejoin society as young men. However, disability is an "in-between" state, "for the person is neither sick nor well" (Murphy et al., 1988, p. 238). Willett and Deegan (2001) note that, unlike the newly initiated, the reincorporation of disabled people may never occur (cf. Titchkosky, 2003, p. 231; she observed that "[c]laiming disability as one's place betwixt and between raises the possibility of inserting into the world alternative ways of being and alternative ways of knowing"). Despite the contributions of such works, it is striking that analyses of *concrete* ritual processes involving disabled people are extremely sparse.

Meanwhile, disability studies scholars have critically analyzed the representations of disability in public spectacles. In "freak shows," for example, spectators consumed the staged appearances of people with bodily differences in the United States during the 19th and the early 20th centuries (Thomson, 1996). Though some scholars have examined the creative and critical commentaries on disability produced in performances designed or enacted by disabled playwrights and artists (see, e.g., Mitchell & Snyder, 2005; Porco, 2014), few studies on ritual and disability have positioned disabled people as creators and performers of secular rites. As a culturally defined occasion for producing elevated contexts that authorize embodied and emplaced meanings (Kawano, 2005), rituals have been adopted as a tool by power-holders to impose their views on a minority group or by the oppressed to strategically construct their view to challenge dominant perspectives. A new life-course rite may be created by stakeholders when the society's ritual system excludes them (Kawano, 2010). Secular rituals (Moore & Myerhoff, 1977), such as public ceremonies and festivals, do not involve interaction with supernatural beings, yet they still provide culturally valued venues for constructing participants' identities. Using these perspectives on ritual, I analyze the Dyslexia Festival as an occasion that allowed diverse stakeholders to promote certain representations of dyslexia for their own ends. Unlike previous studies of ritual that noted the import of altering participants' bodily appearances to construct their transitional identities (Addo, 2009; Mauldin, 2004; Turner, 1967, 1969), however, I stress that the Dyslexia Festival involved the "de-masking" of participants' indiscernible identities, as people with dyslexia wear no widely recognized sign that denotes their impairment.

DYSLEXIA IN JAPAN: BACKGROUND

Dyslexia is under-recognized in contemporary Japan. Though scientific studies of dyslexia emerged as early as the 1950s, dyslexia was frequently discussed as a "rare disorder" in Japanese children in postwar Japan (e.g., Makita, 1968). By the 1990s, a category of neurodevelopmental disabilities known as "*hattatsu shōgai*" gained recognition by the state, which includes so-called high-functioning autism and Asperger's, attention deficit hyperactivity disorder, and learning disabilities such as dyslexia. The 2004 Act on Support for Persons with Developmental Disabilities was legislated to incorporate these disability categories into the nation's welfare and education systems, though dyslexia still remains relatively unknown in today's Japan.

While the revised special needs education system was implemented in 2007 to provide in-class support for children with developmental disabilities, only 0.16 percent of the total student population received support in part-time special needs classes (*tsūkyū*) for their challenges in speaking, listening, reading, writing, calculating, and/or reasoning in 2017 (Ministry of Education, Culture, Sports, Science & Technology of Japan, 2018). No established pedagogies exist to teach Japanese children with dyslexia. Academic accommodations are not routinely provided for them. Guidelines for diagnosing specific reading disorders in Japanese-speaking children exist, yet no clinical guidelines for diagnosing adults exist. It was in this context of extreme under-recognition of dyslexia that the first international advocacy event took place in 2016.

ASIA-PACIFIC DYSLEXIA FESTIVAL: CONTEXT

Held in Yokohama in June 2016, the Asia-Pacific Dyslexia Festival was a preliminary event for the 2020 World Dyslexia Forum in Okayama (postponed due to COVID-19) and part of a series of forums that have been organized by the United Nations Educational, Scientific, and Cultural Organization (UNESCO) and Dyslexia International since 2010. The Japanese advocacy group EDGE played a major role in organizing this festival. Established in 2001, this nonprofit organization has been providing support for people with dyslexia and their families. The Dyslexia Festival aimed to increase social recognition of dyslexia and to build a society where people with dyslexia are able to lead fruitful lives by using their strengths (from the guidebook by the Asia-Pacific Dyslexia Festival and Symposium Committee, 2016, p. 3; hereinafter referenced as Guide). "Diversity and Identity: An Ideal School" was the main theme of the event.

The Dyslexia Festival involved Japanese specialists, advocacy groups, parents, and people with dyslexia. As part of the prelude to the larger UNESCO event, participants included representatives of international organizations as well as advocates with dyslexia from other Asian societies. The event consisted of festival sessions organized mainly for non-specialist audiences and conference presentations by researchers as well as advocacy groups. What follows is my analysis of the Dyslexia Festival as a site for these diverse participants to construct dyslexia. During the event, dyslexia was often made discernable by invoking the construct of discrepancy. The strengths and accomplishments in certain areas of those with dyslexia were contrasted with the notable challenges they experienced in reading and writing.

PERFORMING DYSLEXIA: MAKING DISABILITY APPEAR ON STAGE

The opening session of the Dyslexia Festival set the tone for the event, crystallizing the gap between exceptional accomplishments and serious difficulties through an exchange between the mayor of Yokohama city and a young architect with dyslexia. He had been featured on a TV show hosted by the mayor when the latter had worked in media production. During this opening session, the young architect was first asked to read out a few paragraphs of text that were appropriate for Japanese second graders. Dyslexia was thus displayed as unexpectedly slow and awkward reading. To emphasize the man's challenges, the mayor commented that his reading skills had not improved since he last saw him during the TV show. The architect's reading aloud, which did not represent the normative fluency expected of a Japanese professional, was then followed by his skilled presentation on his award-winning designs. He spoke confidently and smoothly, contrasting his reading skills with his public speaking as well as his artistic talent. By showcasing the performance of his extraordinary professional accomplishments and growth alongside his lack of progress in reading skills, the young adult performed dyslexia for the session.

In the professional literature on dyslexia, it is often characterized by the discrepancy between strengths and weaknesses within an individual. Socially, however, the performance of dyslexia challenged the audience's expectations that a Japanese professional cannot possibly struggle with reading aloud texts for elementary school students. Reading and writing are taken for granted in Japanese social life, and schooling is widely believed to uniformly equip Japanese persons with reading and writing skills. Therefore, the architect's performance of dyslexia contested the audience's culturally specific expectation that ordinary people in Japan read and write in ordinary ways. An inquiry into disability, therefore, reveals not only "the social process of norming" (Michalko, 2009, p. 65) and "the hegemonic character of ordinary life" (Titchkosky, 2003, p. 23) but also the culturally specific forms that such dynamics take.

LEGENDARY FIGURES WITH DYSLEXIA AND INDIVIDUAL PURSUITS OF MEANINGFUL PROJECTS

During the festival, speakers sometimes mentioned the names of famous Westerners who presumably lived or currently live with dyslexia to make it appear as a source of genius as well as trials. For example, Albert Einstein, Winston Churchill, and actor Tom Cruise were mentioned during the event (no Japanese celebrities had publicly acknowledged that they had lived with dyslexia in 2016). Given that the notion of talent is often invoked when describing people with dyslexia at Japanese advocacy events, it makes sense that the festival committee wished to showcase the skill of people with dyslexia and their creative outputs at an event entitled "Dyslexia Talent Exhibition: Shine in Your Own Way."

When describing themselves during the festival, participants with dyslexia likewise contrasted their strengths and weaknesses, though they did not focus on the "extraordinary" talent associated with legendary Westerners with dyslexia. For example, one participant noted that he has difficulties with writing but enjoys raising animals and is keen to study insects in university (Guide, 2016). Another man stated that he is not good at "processing letters" but loves to create things, from software to homes. In these ways, participants engaged with the notion of discrepancy by stressing the importance of finding something they enjoy doing and developing their strengths, rather than using a medical deficit model or the notion of people with dyslexia as extraordinarily talented.

FOCUSING ON WEAKNESSES

The struggles of people with dyslexia were stressed in a workshop on how to teach children with dyslexia at home, a discussion on the effective use of assistive technology, and a panel on the development of remedial and specialized educational materials that allow learners to grasp characters and interact with them using multiple senses. During these sessions, presenters discussed how reading and writing difficulties manifest among learners with dyslexia and how alternative learning methods can be used to facilitate their learning.

A "mock LD [learning disabilities]" workshop, meanwhile, was held for non-dyslexic attendees to experience notable reading and writing challenges in a classroom-like setting. By deliberately creating exceptionally difficult reading and writing tasks, the workshop let them experience the consequences of learning struggles despite their serious attempts to complete the exercises within the allotted time. These sessions highlighted not only the technical struggles that learners with dyslexia face but also the affective experiences of disablement that result from the burden of reading and writing tasks. The instructor specifically asked attendees how they felt when peers completed the tasks and a new activity was given before they had completed their own work. In this workshop, therefore, dyslexia appeared as the gulf between, on the one hand, normative learning demands and an attendee's performance and, on the other, as the gap between the learner's performance in relation to their peers' in a classroom-like setting.

During the conference, scholars and advocacy groups discussed the need to urgently develop appropriate support processes, specialized programs, and curricula. It was in this context that dyslexia was discussed as a deficit from a medical perspective. Dyslexia was likewise regarded as an issue that must be urgently managed in classrooms. Discussions were held on the possibility of building a school for Japanese children with dyslexia, and this included the sharing of reports on some American schools that provide intensive support. Dyslexia thus sometimes appeared as a school issue to problematize the Japanese education system and classroom environments that fail to adequately educate children with dyslexia.

DYSLEXIA AND ALTERNATIVE MODES OF ENGAGEMENT

While researchers and therapists constructed dyslexia as a learning difference that requires appropriate accommodations, special curricula, and assistive technologies, participants with dyslexia went further and associated dyslexia with a preference for an alternative mode of *creation*, one that brings to the fore their agency, ingenuity, and productivity. In the advocacy event's pamphlet, one participant with dyslexia noted that people with dyslexia "are not unintelligent"; they simply use different methods of expression rather than those used by the majority (Guide, 2016, p. 28). Similarly, a woman with dyslexia commented that she dropped out of high school because she "couldn't stand her marginal progress in academics and felt she couldn't accept herself" (Guide, 2016, p. 28). However, she eventually discovered the art of doll making. An adult peer group also sent messages to visitors that linked discovering one's passion with a positive attitude (Guide, 2016). During one festival session, attendees with dyslexia shared modes of expression that they love, including illustration, photography, writing software, architecture, pottery, doll making, and collecting insects. At an exhibition held during the festival, some participants displayed their work. Finding alternative venues and modes of expression was seen as crucial in establishing a positive identity. Many attendees felt that finding alternative modes of self-expression was essential in life, for either personal pleasure or a career. "Show your strengths," "don't give up," "believe in your potential," and "keep searching for solutions" were the messages conveyed by participants with dyslexia to their peers.

"We must now collectively undertake a rewriting of knowledge as we know it. This is a rewriting in which ... I want the West to recognize the dimensions of what it has brought into the world—this with respect to ... our now purely naturalized modes or genres of humanness. You see? Because the West *did* change the world, *totally*. And I want to suggest that it is *that* change that has now made our own proposed far-reaching changes *now* as imperative as they are inevitable."

Wynter, Sylvia. *On Being Human as Praxis*. Durham, NC: Duke University Press, 2015, p. 18.

In their daily lives, disabled people navigate the gaps between themselves and normative expectations while cultivating "disability expertise" (Hartblay, 2020) as the "designers and experts" of the everyday world (Hamraie & Fritsch, 2019) in negotiating such disparities. The idea of focusing on one's strengths, at first glance, appears to lack a political stance to problematize the disabling influences of normative modes of engagement. The value of alternative modes of creation, however, cannot be understood fully without considering the normative demands of manual printing and the limited availability of alternative formats and methods in Japanese social life. Until recently, resumes had to be written by hand, and people are regularly expected to manually fill out a wide range of forms and applications in their daily lives. Primary and secondary schools typically do not allow students to access the Internet, and electronic devices are rarely used during lessons (though the Japanese government has recently emphasized the adoption of "cutting-edge technology for education" (Ministry of Education, Culture, Sports, Science & Technology of Japan, 2020). Students are repeatedly taught to swiftly and accurately copy their teacher's handwritten notes on the blackboard. Handwritten letters are highly valued, and some people even believe that handwriting expresses one's character. Although Japanese society prizes the production of print or handwritten materials and the evaluation of written work at school and work, people with dyslexia favour alternative forms of output and assessment. Though dyslexia did not appear with terms such as *disability rights* and *social justice* during the Dyslexia Festival, what may seem to be a politically neutral account of personal challenges and dreams reveals a critical commentary on reading and writing as dominant methods of valued creation in contemporary Japan.

STRATEGIC DE-MASKING TO MAKE DISABILITY APPEAR

By having people with dyslexia appear on stage, speak to attendees, and share their creative outputs, the Dyslexia Festival offered them occasions to celebrate who they are and how they shine. Significantly, the event provided a space for youth and adults with dyslexia to "come out" (the expression used to refer to the public recognition of a non-visible minority status in Japan). This disclosure is even more notable given that theirs is an identity that is doubly masked in today's Japan: first, as mentioned, there are no physical signs of dyslexia; second, dyslexia is still socially under-recognized in Japan despite the long-time work of specialists and advocacy groups. This brings me to explore how the participants of this secular ritual attempted to unveil their identities in their own ways by employing verbal and non-verbal performances.

Several studies of festivals have highlighted the impact of masking and the performance of minority identities involved in carnivals as civic rites (Mauldin, 2004), where the "political effects of masking and remaking personalities and identities through visually altering their signification are important" (Addo, 2009, p. 227). Male participants perform as women, or young ones transform themselves into old persons. Indigenous participants may likewise take part in events to highlight their difference and inclusion in post-colonial contexts. However, rather than masking, it is through the process of *de*-masking that festival participants made dyslexia appear during the advocacy event. They are not "masked" in daily life in the sense that they intentionally hide their identities by "passing" (Goffman, 1963). However, their impairments are visually unrecognizable in face-to-face interactions, and even when they struggle with reading and writing in their social life, such difficulties are often dismissed and are not readily linked to dyslexia in Japan. Participants engaged in the act of de-masking by taking part in the advocacy event—mainly through speaking in sessions and displaying their creations, produced through modes of engagement other than reading and writing.

The literature on civic rites has scrutinized the divide that exists between spectators and performers (Addo, 2009, p. 228). During the Dyslexia Festival, however, the division between the audience and the performers of difference was not always evident. People with dyslexia gathered to address dyslexia's limited social recognition in Japan, a country in which their presence and needs are rarely discussed. They collectively addressed the lack of alignment between themselves and the privileging of reading and writing in Japan's post-industrial society. By choosing to place themselves on stage, they performed their identity of difference on their own terms while also serving as witnesses of their peers' acts. This co-shaping of a moment of collective disclosure of their minority identity during the festival led to the experience of *communitas*, or undifferentiated togetherness in the classic Turnerian sense of liminality (Turner, 1967, 1969).

DISABILITY'S NON-APPEARANCE

What remained unaddressed, however, was the widely circulated notion that no schooled Japanese person could face literacy issues. A representative from UNESCO made note of literacy (*shikiji*) in her program greeting, but I did not hear this word again for the duration of the event. Though dyslexia appeared as a "school problem" due to the limited provision of accommodations, it did not appear as the nation's literacy problem that Japanese society should urgently address.

Furthermore, my fieldwork revealed that discussions on differences according to class, gender, and age were largely missing at the Dyslexia Festival. One panel featured representatives from an American private school with a specialized program for students with dyslexia. Though it was clear that the school catered to middle- and upper-middle-class families, the questions on the cost of such a specialized program were not discussed. In addition, the Japanese participants with dyslexia who performed their identities during the festival were predominately young males, though there were a few school-age girls and women. Due to the lack of awareness of dyslexia in Japan, many middle-aged and older people with notable reading and writing challenges remained under-recognized.

CONCLUSION

"Narrative is not just the simple transportation of language but of ideas of the self, and ideas of the self that contain negations of other people. What is it, then, to adopt or be indoctrinated into these narrative structures, those ideas, to come to know those ideas as your own, when you are the negated other people? The intravenous being, the being administered into being, through the idea of the universal that is, at the same time, self-negating?"

Brand, Dionne. *An Autobiography of an Autobiography of Reading.* Edmonton, AB: University of Alberta Press, 2020, pp. 27–28.

Diverse stakeholders took part in the Dyslexia Festival to make disability appear in certain ways through verbal and non-verbal performances. Though dyslexia often appeared as a discrepancy characterizing the distribution of "abilities" within an individual, a closer look at the constructions of dyslexia reveals notable variations. While youth and adults with dyslexia recognized the importance of appropriate support programs and assistive tools, their performances tended to construct dyslexia as a legitimate way of taking part in society through alternative means rather than through reading and writing. By taking advantage of the opportunities to self-stage their minority identity in public, participants thus used the event to foster a sense of solidarity as agents and to shape the transitional ritual process characterized by *communitas*, rather than embodying a permanently "betwixt and between" state of social isolation and ambiguity. Nonetheless, dyslexia failed to appear in certain ways: Literacy was not raised as a Japanese issue in framing dyslexia. Though individuals from economically disadvantaged families as well as older people were not purposefully excluded from the event, dyslexia's potential intersectionality in Japan remained largely unexplored.

My inquiry into the interface between ritual and disability reveals the multi-vocal and multifaceted ways that stakeholders made dyslexia appear. Rites are often examined as a formal way of sending messages by focusing on what they say (Moore & Myerhoff, 1977, p. 24). However, rituals arguably must also be analyzed in relation to what they do not say. To capture dyslexia's appearance, then, we not only need to read between lines but likewise need to read between acts.

REFERENCES

Addo, P. A. (2009). Anthropology, festival, and spectacle. *Reviews in Anthropology, 38*(3), 217–236. https://doi.org/10.1080/00938150903110625.

Asia-Pacific Dyslexia Festival and Symposium Committee. (2016). *Asia-Pacific dyslexia festival and symposium guidebook.*

Goffman, E. (1963). *Stigma: Notes on the management of spoiled identity.* Prentice Hall.

Hamraie, A., & Fritsch, K. (2019). Crip technoscience manifesto. *Catalyst: Feminism, Theory, Technoscience, 5*(1), 1–33. https://doi.org/10.28968/cftt.v5i1.29607

Hartblay, C. (2020). Disability expertise: Claiming disability anthropology. *Current Anthropology, 61*(21), S26–S36. https://doi.org/10.1086/705781

Ingstad, B. (1995). Mpho ya modimo—A gift from God: Perspectives on 'attitudes' toward disabled persons. In B. Ingstad & S. R. Whyte (Eds.), *Disability and culture* (pp. 246–263). University of California Press.

Kawano, S. (2005). *Ritual practice in modern Japan.* University of Hawai'i Press.

Kawano, S. (2010). *Nature's embrace: Japan's aging urbanites and new death rites.* University of Hawai'i Press.

Makita, K. (1968). The rarity of reading disability in Japanese children. *American Journal of Orthopsychiatry, 38*(4), 599–614.

Mauldin, B. (Ed.). (2004). *Carnaval!* University of Washington Press and Museum of International Folk Art.

Michalko, R. (2009). The excessive appearance of disability. *International Journal of Qualitative Studies in Education, 22*(1), 65–74. https://doi.org/10.1080/09518390802581885

Ministry of Education, Culture, Sports, Science & Technology of Japan. (2018). *Tokubetsu shien kyōiku shiryō, Heisei 29-nendo, Dai ichibu shūkei hen (Special needs education references for 2017, Summary statistics part 1).* https://www.mext.go.jp/component/a_menu/education/micro_detail/__icsFiles/afieldfile/2019/10/28/1406445_000.pdf

Ministry of Education, Culture, Sports, Science & Technology of Japan. (2020). *Ministry of Education, Culture, Sports, Science & Technology FY2020 budget highlights.* https://www.mext.go.jp/en/unesco/mext_00002.html

Mitchell, D., & Snyder, S. (2005). Exploitations of embodiment. *Disability Studies Quarterly, 24*(3). https://dsq-sds.org/article/view/575/752

Moore, S. F., & Myerhoff, B. G. (1977). Introduction. In S. F. Moore & B. G. Myerhoff (Eds.), *Secular ritual* (pp. 3–24). Van Gorcum.

Murphy, R. F. (1990). *The body silent.* W. W. Norton. (Original work published 1987)

Murphy, R. F., Scheer, J., Murphy, Y., & Mack, R. (1988). Physical disability and social liminality. *Social Science & Medicine, 26*(2), 235–242.

Nicolaisen, I. (1995). Persons and nonpersons. In B. Ingstad & S. R. Whyte (Eds.), *Disability and culture* (pp. 38–55). University of California Press.

Porco, A. S. (2014). Throw yo' voice out: Disability as a desirable practice in hip-hop vocal performance. *Disability Studies Quarterly, 34*(4). https://dsq-sds.org/article/view/3822/3790

Thomson, R. G. (Ed.). (1996). *Freakery: Cultural spectacles of the extraordinary body.* New York University Press.

Titchkosky, T. (2003). *Disability, self, and society.* University of Toronto Press.

Turner, V. (1967). Betwixt and between: The liminal period in rites de passage. In V. Turner (Ed.), *The forest of symbols* (pp. 93–111). Cornell University Press.

Turner, V. (1969). *The ritual process: Structure and anti-structure.* Cornell University Press.

Willett, J., & Deegan, M. (2001). Liminality and disability: Rites of passage and community in hypermodern society. *Disability Studies Quarterly, 21*(3). http://doi.org/10.18061/dsq.v21i3.300

CHAPTER 9

Tuning Goes Frig

Sid Ghosh

Resonance is
for people

with frequencies.
I am going

on without
a tuning fork.

My frequencies
go to other

zeniths. My life
is in poetic

pause.

PART III

DISAPPEARING DRAMA

EDITORS' INTRODUCTION

Part III, "DisAppearing Drama," represents disability studies work that is connected to performance studies, including theatre and dance. All chapters gathered in this part focus on the dramas of the appearances and disappearances of disability in scenes of everyday life. Dramaturgical forms of critical inquiry can be found in all cultures and throughout time. While this, of course, includes disability, the dramas of disability tend to disappear from view in Western cultures. Perhaps the drama of disability occurs more often on the stage of passing and gets folded, often seamlessly, into an enactment of appearing as a Normate participant (Thomson, 1997; see also Ware, 2020; on passing in disability studies, see Brune & Wilson, 2013; Goffman, 1963; Michalko, 1998). Or perhaps those powers and people in charge of staging what really counts do not often write the significance of disability into the script. Or maybe we simply do not notice disability's presence in all the movements of life. Carrie Sandahl and Philip Auslander characterize the drama of *Bodies in Commotion* (2005) in this way:

> First described by sociologist Erving Goffman as the "performance of everyday life" and more recently by philosopher Judith Butler as "performativity," ... the notion that disability, too, is performed (like gender, sex, sexuality, race, and ethnicity) and not a static "fact" of the body is not widely acknowledged or theorized. (p. 2)

In contrast, the chapters collected in this part *do* acknowledge and theorize the performative character of disability and bring these issues to life.

"For affective hesitation is the opening that permits attachments and events to register, to be retained and sedimented, shifting the level according to which we perceive. To see *according to* others is not to see through their eyes or to assimilate them to my vision; it is to find the perceptual field to have been reoriented by others. Here, the other is not an object in the perceptual field, but a magnetizing center, or counterweight, whose very style of being, way of seeing, and memory inflect that field. To see *with others* is hence to find one's perceptual and affective map to be redrawn through the force of attachments to others. Such a shift not only reorients the present but is accompanied by a working-through of the past."

Al-Saji, Alia. "A Phenomenology of Hesitation: Interrupting Racializing Habits of Seeing." In *Living Alterities: Phenomenology, Embodiment, and Race*, edited by Emily Lee, 133–172. Albany, NY: State University of New York Press, 2014, p. 161.

Devon Healey's chapter, "Blind Perception: DisAppearing Blindness ... with a Twist," details the movements of not seeing normally, offering a twist by re-writing "not seeing" into "blind perception." Blindness as a form of perception is one that explores the possibility of a "collective sensorium," a kind of community inclusive of blindness, not as a sometimes tolerable difference but as an essential feature of any communities' perception of the world and its people. Blind perception also brings to the fore the norms of those sighted people who are more fully ensconced in the sight/knowledge matrix. Healey reveals the power of this matrix through her narrative rendering of a medical eye examination and the ways that the various dramatic depictions, articulations, and interpretations of "eye problem" play out in her life.

Jose Miguel Esteban's chapter, "Embracing the Gesture: A Dance of the Ordinary and Its Extra," explores the meaning and movement of the "hug" as it releases ordinary and not-so-ordinary understandings of the norms of gesture. Esteban shows how our gestures convey meaning and, also, how gestures can be made to matter differently, given the social context or stage upon which they occur. This chapter represents a narrative encounter with the work necessary to understand how dance and disability are in continuous relation. Esteban speaks of this drama as *sticky*, suggesting that there is an "entangled relation between [his] gesture and its ground" and further that such entanglement is where the dance of meaning-making between disability and non-disability always occurs.

"All bodies are causes in relation to each other, and causes for each other—but causes of what?... They are causes of certain things of an entirely different nature. These effects are not bodies, but properly speaking, 'incorporeal' entities. They are not physical qualities and properties, but rather logical or dialectical attributes. They are not things or facts but events."

Kim, Eunjung. "Why Do Dolls Die? The Power of Passivity and the Embodied Interplay Between Disability and Sex Dolls." *The Review of Education/Pedagogy/Cultural Studies* 34, nos. 3–4 (2012): 94–106, p. 98.

The final chapter of this section, "Shapeshifting: Navigating the Social Construction of Multiple Disability Identities," begins with Steve Singer narrating two encounters—going to a bar and becoming a father—and doing so as a Deaf man with many other disability experiences. The assumptions of what D/deaf should look like within D/deaf communities and within hearing ones and all that lies between is dramatically represented in these two narratives and many others. As Singer explores his experiences with the dis/appearance of deafness and disability, as well as navigating these in his teaching, intimate relationships, and everyday life, he raises a further drama—that of the need for questioning. Singer writes:

> What does the social construction of disability mean for people? If disability is constructed by the environment then that tells us that its meaning can shift in various contexts. The transience of its meaning results in disability or the perception of disability appearing and disappearing.

Through the asking of these questions the meaning of d/Deaf and disability—in its many forms in the dramas of daily life—comes alive, representing the hope of an "alternative future" with "different and better disabled realities," but, in the meantime, Singer works at making "deficit-based notions of disability" disappear. This is a hope nurtured by all the chapters in this section, if not in the collection as a whole.

"DisAppearing Drama" ends with a dramatic transformation of theory and the experience of embodiment as accomplished through Diane Driedger's poems, "Charles Darwin and Me" and "Chronic Illness Dictionary."

Guiding Questions

1. Sometimes disability appears as a drama in the scenes of everyday life, in online media, film, or texts. What roles do we expect or assume disability to play or represent?
2. Adaptive arts and art therapy are ways that disabled people are included in the arts. Have you noticed other ways that disability and the arts are connected?
3. How are assumptions about non-disability included in the visual arts, performance, dance, and poetry, and how do these assumptions exclude disabled people?
4. Are the arts vital to creating alternative futures in which different dramas of disability are possible? What are the connections between the role of the arts and the role of disability within society?

REFERENCES

Brune, J. A., & Wilson, D. J. (Eds.). (2013). *Disability and passing: Blurring the lines of identity*. Temple University Press.

Goffman, E. (1963). *Stigma: Notes on the management of spoiled identity*. Simon and Schuster.

Michalko, R. (1998). *The mystery of the eye and the shadow of blindness*. University of Toronto Press.

Sandahl, C., & Auslander, P. (2005). Introduction: Disability studies in commotion with performance studies. In C. Sandahl & P. Auslander (Eds.), *Bodies in commotion: Disability & performance* (pp. 1–12). University of Michigan Press.

Thomson, G. T. (1997). *Extraordinary bodies: Figuring physical disability in American culture and literature*. Columbia University Press.

Ware, L. (2020). *Critical readings in interdisciplinary disability studies: (Dis)Assemblages*. Springer.

CHAPTER 10

Blind Perception: DisAppearing Blindness … with a Twist

Devon Healey

Key Terms: Blindness; Ethics of Seeing; Medicine; Narrative; Perception; Photography

> *"Unfortunately, the more beautiful the picture, the sadder the case."*
> —Medical Technician

This utterance harbours both an interesting and intriguing sentiment. It is not often that we hear beauty spoken of as "unfortunate" and "sad." The more "beautiful the picture," the more "unfortunate," the more "sad." Such a sentiment suggests, too, that the "picture," more beautiful or not, is indeed a sad one, a tragic depiction of … something. And, the "more beautiful" this picture becomes, the "sadder" the "case." This is an interesting sentiment, one whose intrigue invites attention.

The ways blindness is made to mean, to feel, and the ways it is seen lie buried in the picture of blindness depicted above. "Viewing" the world through blindness, "seeing" its creativity, learning from its "observations," and trusting its perceptions—all of this is lost, is disappeared in medicine's technical view of blindness, a view that sees only lack, absence, distortion, and sadness. This medical view makes implicit reference to what eyes *should* look like; it makes implicit reference, too, to the beauty of "normal" eyes, to what Rosemary Garland Thomson (1997, p. 8) refers to as the "normate"—the normal state of affairs, beautiful or not. To make appear what has been disappeared is not an easy task; it requires appearance and disappearance to collide; it requires, too, what is seen and unseen to collide. It is amid this collision, between the beauty and the sadness, that the meaning made of blindness may be revealed. The way to reveal this meaning-making may be spoken of as a narrative method, as one that requires the narration of the beauty and the sadness and the collision between the two that is blindness; a narration that resides in the various ways that blindness is lived. Let me now narrate the story of blindness as I live it.

It has been said that "seeing is believing." And, to some extent, I suppose there may be some truth in this saying. Many of us, at one time or another, may have experienced something and thought, "if I didn't see it, I wouldn't have believed it!" Better still is a picture to then share with others as proof of what you would not have believed had you not seen it. The proof in a picture lies in its capacity to support and even secure a belief in an experience or way of being in the world. This attributes the power of truth to the picture. And yet, seeing is not always believing.

My blind eyes are one of those sights that, for the medical profession, are hard to believe since they (eye doctors) cannot see what I see. They cannot see my blindness, the blind sights of my eyes, and therefore they find it difficult, if not impossible, to trust them, to believe what my eyes see. I suppose my blind eyes are among one of those things you have to see to believe. Perhaps it was this logic, this need to see in order to believe, that led me to a tiny windowless room in Sunnybrook Hospital in Toronto—a room dedicated to capturing, in the form of a picture, the illusive, almost unbelievable, sight of blindness.

My eyes were a case of sight gone blind, and the sights of my eyes were of extreme interest to the retina specialists who had referred me to that room. I stood on the threshold of the windowless room, a room made to feel tiny, almost cramped, by the massive machine it housed. This machine was a giant camera with a lens so powerful it could capture blindness in the form of a picture. This machine looked, to me, as if it were made by a children's toy company. The large bulky parts of the camera appeared to be made of hard grey plastic, akin to that of toddlers' toys made to withstand the rough treatment that can accompany children's play and movement. I am not sure why but the appearance of this machine—this camera—as a toy made me feel uneasy, almost suspicious of it.

The technician—or, as I liked to call her, the photographer—met me at the door and guided me with an open gesture of her arm toward what appeared to me to be a periscope with a plastic ledge. I wondered if, perhaps, this ledge was intended for the blind patient/subject to rest their chin on while the technician/photographer played around with the camera, adjusting and moving the lens to set up various shots, capturing blindness from all angles. She instructed me to stand facing the machine with the right side of my face pressed as close as possible to the periscope while, as I had suspected, resting my chin on the ledge. The circular hole or lens of the periscope covered half of my face from forehead to chin. I remember feeling as though I were split into two worlds, my right eye staring into the black abyss of the camera's lens while my left continued to perceive blindness. It was as though there were a split between my being and my act of perceiving. This split allowed me to notice, from my left side, the technician/photographer looking at her computer, its screen visible to both of us, while from my right, I felt the predatory lens of the camera.

The technician/photographer informed me that the lens of the camera was aligned with that of my right eye signalling that she was indeed ready to begin shooting. She counted aloud—*one, two*—and on the third count, a bright white light burst from within the dark abyss of the camera and then disappeared as quickly as it had appeared. My right eye felt as though it had been assaulted. My eyeball throbbed in its socket; water had emerged from both corners, collecting in the centre of my eye and then dripping, as if running away from the lens of the camera, down my cheek, off my chin, and onto the floor. Before I could ver-bally react to the light the technician/photographer reminded me to keep my face pressed against the periscope and my chin on the ledge; there were many more photos to take, and time—as always for medicine—was of the essence.

After what seemed like hours, I felt a hand on my left shoulder. It was the technician/photographer signalling that the photoshoot of both my eyes had come to an end. She handed me a tissue to wipe the water from my eyes and gestured, once again, with her arm to a stool where I could sit and regain my sense of being and reconnect it to my act of perception, a connection enabled largely through my blind perception. (A connection between being and perception is "normally" enabled by the sense of sight, allowing for those who see to envelop their being in visual perception.) It was as though the act of photographing my eyes intruded on my attempt to envelop being blind and the being of blindness through perception.

As did the burning from the flash of the camera, the bright white light began to fade and I noticed, once again, the screen of the computer. The technician was scrolling through the pictures of my blind eyes captured by that massive camera. I wondered—what was she seeing? Did she see what I was seeing, or something else? What was she hoping to see? What proof of blindness was she searching for in those pictures? Had she seen it? Did the pictures prove and document the truth of my blindness? Was she now believing what she saw?

"By exposing the existential-ontological dimension of the restrictions faced by disabled people, my ethico-political hope is to open up a space for re-imagining and positively re-valuing different ways of being human. To be able to do this, though, it is not enough to imagine *different individuals*—what is needed is to imagine *different worlds*."

Mladenov, Teodor. *Critical Theory and Disability: A Phenomenological Approach.* London, UK: Bloomsbury Academic, 2015, p. 7.

I remember getting up, about to leave that tiny, cramped room, when one of the pictures filled the large computer screen. I stopped, standing just behind her. The image stopped me in my tracks. What I saw, I couldn't believe. Was that my blindness? My eyes, my blind eyes, were they filling the screen in front of both of us, at that very moment? Her eyes and mine looking at blindness—I couldn't believe it.

"Are those of me, of my eyes? Are those pictures of my eyes?" The words spilled out of my mouth and filled what little space was left in that tiny, cramped room. "Yes," she replied without turning to look at me. I remember feeling as though the pictures were enveloping me. For a second, blindness was everywhere in a way different from the everywhere-ness way I usually felt it. Blindness was everywhere: in me, in the picture, in front of her, in my eyes; my blind eyes were pictures, and they were beautiful. The words formed gently on my lips—"They're beautiful," I whispered. The technician/photographer spun around on her stool to look at me. "Unfortunately, the more beautiful the picture, the sadder the case." Her words hung in the air between us once more splitting my being from my act of perceiving. I perceived beauty; my being was sad. That tiny, cramped room was now at capacity. The picture was of me, of my eyes, of my blindness. I was the case, and, unfortunately, I was a beautifully sad one. We both saw the same thing, the same picture, but I did not believe, despite the proof, what she saw.

WHAT BLINDNESS PERCEIVES

"As I examine the disabled figure, I also trouble the mutually constituting figure this study coins: the normate. This neologism names the veiled subject position of cultural self, the figure outlined by the array of deviant others whose marked bodies shore up the normate's boundaries. The term *normate* usefully designates the social figure through which people can represent themselves as definitive human beings. Normate, then, is the constructed identity of those who, by way of the bodily configurations and cultural capital they assume, can step into a position of authority and wield the power it grants them. If one attempts to define the normate position by peeling away all the marked traits within the social order at this historical moment, what emerges is a very narrowly defined profile that describes only a minority of actual people."

Garland Thomson, Rosemarie. *Extraordinary Bodies: Figuring Physical Disability in American Culture and Literature.* New York, NY: Columbia University Press, 1997, p. 8.

It is within this narrative-context that the utterance, "Unfortunately, the more beautiful the picture, the sadder the case," was spoken. And it is this context that allowed these words to be spoken. It is medicine, of course, that narrates both the context and its words. The contradictory sense of beautiful and thus sad is sensible only within the medical narration. Seeing sadness when looking at beauty is a contradictory way of perceiving an image, at least from the point of view of common sense. From medicine's view, there is no contradiction.

What is interesting, and perhaps even contradictory, is that, steeped as it is in common sense, medicine does not see the contradiction between beauty and sadness. Medicine, or the medical model (Oliver, 2009), is not only a practice of healing; it is a way of seeing. Beauty is only visible to medicine when the sadness of pathology—in this case, my blindness—is absent. Given its presence, beauty is simply not there—no contradiction, since no beauty. What is unfortunate is the "view" that sees beauty when sadness is all there is to see. Beauty, in this way, equals sadness. Thus, the medical corrective—"Unfortunately, the more beautiful the picture, the sadder the case."

But, we must now ask, what did medicine see in the picture of my eyes? This question must be paired with another question: What do *I* see when I look with my blind eyes? What is the "beautiful picture" a picture of? Is it a picture of what I see or a picture of my eyes? These questions are, of course, related to one another and, in that sense, distinct from one another. They are also inseparable from one another in that they imply pictures, a visual record, of blind perception.

What is beyond question, however, is that pictures of my eyes, blind eyes, were the subject of the medical photographs that day. Medicine "knew," and so did I, that it was taking pictures of my eyes, and both of us knew that my eyes were blind. What remained questionable was what I saw when I looked *with my blind eyes*. Medicine's answer to this question was to produce and invoke a visual record—take a picture. They did not ask me what I saw; they took a picture. My account of what I saw was not proof of what medicine believed I saw—a picture was—so, they took some.

Medicine, together with most of us, would agree that blindness generates distortion (Michalko, 1998, p. 87). It is one of the markers of a flawed sensorium. Any perception it may have is understood as necessarily flawed and distorted. In this sense, medicine and the rest of us already know what blindness perceives. This, however, is an extremely limited version of blind perception, one clearly not interested in any other blind perceptual possibilities. Blind perception is disappeared in favour of the appearance of the "correct" perception of sight—take a picture.

What, other than distortion, might blindness perceive? Sight. Blindness perceives sight. At first blush, this appears as contradictory as "Unfortunately, the more beautiful the picture, the sadder the case." What is required now is to speak of this contradiction and of how blindness might be spoken of as the perception of sight. Let me address this through the notion of "passing."[1]

My blind eyes have been diagnosed by the medical profession as "legally blind," meaning, among other things, that I have a small amount of peripheral vision remaining.[2] This peripheral vision, along with my common sense knowledge of how to "be" sighted, allows me to move through the streets of Toronto appearing to all those with sight as if I were one of them, as if I were sighted. I pass constantly, sometimes intentionally and at other times unintentionally. For example, one morning I purchased some groceries. As I was checking out, I smiled to the clerk who was assisting me, likely made eye contact and said good morning. We chatted about the snowstorm as I tapped my credit card on the machine, paying for the items, lifted my bags, made eye contact once again, said goodbye, and walked out. I gave the appearance of sight. I appeared sighted. In order to do so I had to disappear my blindness by passing or performing sight. Blindness, in all its forms and expressions,[3] makes an appearance in the world of sight; the very notion of appearance suggesting sight.

Blindness perceives the performative character of sightedness, a perception not readily seeable, let alone seen, by sight. What we, blind people, are making appear when we pass, intentionally or otherwise, is the perception of blindness; in order to pass you must know sight, you must see it, understand it. Sight is a performance, and it is this performance that blindness perceives. The performative character of sight is a blind-sight and not one of the sights of sight. Blindness perceives what is familiar in the world—sight—and makes it unfamiliar by explicitly performing it; we, blind people, make believable what is seeable by sight. In a sense, this performance is a picture of sight through the perceptual lens of blindness, a unique lens that can see sight. This blind perception has taught us, blind people, that sight is a culturally enacted "thing" or way of being in the world. In order to be understood as sighted, simply looking and seeing is not enough. You must show others that you have seen, can see, and are constantly in the act of looking and seeing. Statements such as "This place is great for people watching"; "Did you see that?"; "I will let you have a minute to read the menu"; "You look great/tired/upset/young/old"; and the like are all examples of showing, telling, and performing sight. The blind perception of sight reveals sightedness as not a biological given but rather something that is taught, done, and redone over and over again to make the familiar, at times, unfamiliar.

All perception has the potential to educate or, as Paul Gilroy (2000) says, "re-educate the sensorium" (p. 252). Re-education always means a new perception, a new way of being and of perceiving, to sense something in this way rather than that. If blindness is one of the lenses that can see sight, what might blind perception teach both sighted and blind people? How might blindness make reappear what was disappeared by a medical version of sight? How might we, blind people, re-educate the sensorium with our blind-look? I return now to the picture of blindness. I conclude this chapter by addressing these questions through engaging the connection between being and perception.

BEING AND PERCEPTION

"Perception is not a science of the world, it is not an event or an act, a deliberate taking up of a position; it is the background from which all acts stand out, and is presupposed by them. The world is not an object such that I have in my possession the law of its making; it is the natural setting of, and field for, all my thoughts and all my explicit perceptions."

Merleau-Ponty, Maurice. *Phenomenology of Perception.* London, UK: Routledge, 1962, p. xi.

The questions above do not necessarily call for a direct answer. They do, however, call for exploration. In this chapter, for example, I explored how blindness might be metaphorically depicted as a lens and how that lens is able to see sight and to re-educate the sensorium and teach it (governed by sight as it is), as well as how the sensorium disappears blindness. I will embark on this exploration further through an examination of the narrative above.

Let me start with photography, with how we determine what to photograph and what not to photograph. The work of Susan Sontag (1977) is helpful here. She says,

> [The] very insatiability of the photographing eye changes the terms of confinement in the cave, our world. In teaching us a new visual code, photographs alter and enlarge our notions of what is worth looking at and what we have a right to observe. They are ... an ethics of seeing. (p. 3)

Sontag makes use of Plato's simile of the cave (Plato, 1969). In it, Socrates introduces the cave as a simile to depict the taken-for-granted world and the Idea or Form that marks the origin of this world. He describes life in the cave as a series of images in the form of shadows cast on the walls of the cave by the Light of the

Idea. People in the cave are depicted as chained to these images, incapable of looking toward the origin, the source of the shadows.

The photograph with its "insatiable eye," Sontag tells us, changes how we are confined in our taken-for-granted world. We are confined not only to the images cast on the wall of the cave but to the production, through photography, of images of those images. We take pictures of the shadows on the wall and not of what produced them. There are two mistakes here; first, we mistake the image for the real, and second, we mistake the photograph for the image. The "terms of confinement" to our world to which Sontag refers is now changed to our confinement to the reproduction of images in that world.

The "ethics of seeing" in relation to the photograph is an ethics of looking, of what deserves our look and what we have a right to look at, to observe. Not everything is worth photographing and not everything is worth looking at. This means that we make decisions not merely about what to look at (although we do decide this); we make decisions about what deserves not only our attention but attention in general. It is culture, namely, values, customs, and the rest that form the basis of what deserves our attention and thus the basis of the "ethics of seeing." A fuller exploration of such an ethics, however, requires much more space than is availed here. I gesture toward it as a way to indicate that seeing is a decisive and thus ethical act.

For medicine, the eyes—including blind eyes—are not only worth looking at; medicine understands itself as having a right to do so. The photograph, the record, marks the insatiability of the medical eye. It also understands itself as having a right to record this looking, this gaze (Foucault, 1973 [1963]), to take a photograph. But to take a photograph of blind eyes is to take a photograph of an image, of what the photograph depicts what blind eyes see. This requires that medicine disappears what blind people see and how we experience what we see. Our seeing is disappeared in favour of making medicine's image of our blindness appear. It sees our blindness but not what we see—our blind perception. The medical picture of our blindness may be beautiful, but, "unfortunately, the more beautiful the picture, the sadder the case." In a similar way, what we see may be beautiful, but the medical image of what we see makes us a sad case.

The medical photo, like medicine itself, separates being blind from blind perception. Being blind is disappeared. For medicine, there is no being in blindness; the patient/subject/case's act of perception is gone; they are blind and this is what makes us "sad cases." The medical photo disappears blindness revealing blind perception as distortion. Any version of blind perception as perception and not distortion is disappeared in favour of a sighted perspective. When my blind eyes saw and interpreted the images of blindness on screen as beautiful, my blind perception was reduced to distortion—"the more beautiful the picture, the sadder the case"—and my being in blindness reduced to a life of adjustment. The blind sights of my eyes were nothing more than sheer distortion and the medical photograph proved it. The technician/photographer used the photograph of my blind eyes as a tool to teach me that what I saw and how I saw, my act of perception, was not perception at all; my being was not only split from my act of perceiving but also removed, severed, from my person altogether. This medical photograph of my blind eyes was "not a just image, just an image" (Barthes, 1981, p. 70).

The image of my eyes was just that—an image—and a beautiful one, but the "ethics of seeing" took beauty and turned it into sadness. The technician/photographer (medicine) consumed "just an image," the picture of my blind eyes, as "a just image" of blindness. Medicine accepted the image, the photograph as shadows on the wall of the cave, not only as the being of blindness but also what blindness perceives. They looked at the image, saw distortion, and believed what they were seeing; they believed that blindness was indeed as pictured; its image, distortion. The picture of my blind eyes, to them, was a just image of blindness thus turning me into a sad case, a representation of distortion. But, I looked at the picture and did not see distortion; I saw beauty. And this perception, my image of blindness, had to be disappeared by medicine as a way to make its own image of blindness appear and appear as just. The perception of beauty is really the perception of a sad case.

CONCLUSION

"We lean on these [social] anticipations that we have, transforming them into normative expectations, into righteously presented demands. Typically, we do not become aware that we have made these demands or aware of what they are until an active question arises as to whether or not they will be fulfilled. It is then that we are likely to realize that all along we had been making certain assumptions as to what the individual before us ought to be."

Goffman, Erving. *Stigma: Notes on the Management of Spoiled Identity.* New York, NY: Simon and Schuster, 1963, p. 2.

What the camera records or captures in the form of a picture comes alive only in the act of perceiving. An image becomes "a just image" or "just an image" depending on what we believe we are looking at. Sontag (1977) observes that "photography implies that we know about the world if we accept it as the camera records it. But this is the opposite of understanding, which starts from not accepting the world as it looks" (p. 23). *Not accepting the world as it looks is blind perception.* This perception is not a different way of seeing the world nor is it a new way. Blind perception is an outright rejection of seeing the images on the wall of the cave as Real. Blind perception is the act of "not accepting the world as it looks." It bears the beginning of understanding (Arendt, 2005). This is the beginning of understanding—not merely understanding blindness itself but rather marking one beginning, and I would say one of the major beginnings of beginning to understand. The quest to understand is not achieved when we simply accept that what we are seeing is indeed representative of the whole, the Truth. Contrary to common belief, seeing is not believing, and it is blind perception that allows for a journey of understanding, one far more dynamic and interesting than merely looking and seeing distortion. The blind journey of understanding is wrapped in beauty, a beauty so intriguing and detailed that it could never be captured on the wall of a cave. What needs to be disappeared, then, is the image of blindness as distortion. What needs to be appeared is the image of blindness as perception.

NOTES

1. Initial articulations of passing as a sociological phenomenon can be found in Goffman (1963) and in Garfinkel (1967).
2. It should be noted that all blind people, even those with no residual vision, pass. See Michalko, 1998, chapter 5, "The Gap of Adolescences."
3. I speak here not only of degrees of blindness but of how blindness is used metaphorically in expressions such as, "You are blind to the facts," etc.

REFERENCES

Arendt, H. (2005). *Essays in understanding, 1930–1954: Formation, exile, and totalitarianism.* Schocken Book.

Barthes, R. (1981). *Camera lucida: Reflections on photography.* Hill and Wang.

Foucault, M. (1973) *The birth of the clinic: An archaeology of medical perception* (A. M. Sheridan, Trans.). Tavistock Publications. (Original work published 1963)

Garfinkel, H. (1967). *Studies in ethnomethodology.* Prentice-Hall.

Gilroy, P. (2000). *Against race: Imagining political culture beyond the color line.* Harvard University Press.

Goffman, E. (1963). *Stigma: Notes on the management of spoiled identity.* Prentice-Hall.

Michalko, R. (1998). *The mystery of the eye and the shadow of blindness.* University of Toronto Press.

Oliver, M. (2009). The social model in context. In T. Titchkosky & R. Michalko (Eds.), *Rethinking normalcy: A disability studies reader.* Canadian Scholars' Press.

Plato. (1969). *The republic* (P. Shorey, Trans.). http://www.perseus.tufts.edu/hopper/text?doc=Perseus%3Atext%3A1999.01.0168%3Abook%3D7&force=y

Sontag, S. (1977). *On photography.* Penguin Books.

Thomson, R. G. (1997). *Extraordinary bodies: Figuring physical disability in American culture and literature.* Columbia University Press.

CHAPTER 11

Embracing the Gesture: A Dance of the Ordinary and Its Extra

Jose Miguel Esteban

Key Terms: Dance; Embodiment; Gesture; Ordinary

INTRODUCTION

In this chapter, I present my narrative encounters with the gesture of a hug. Attempting to enact this seemingly ordinary gesture, I release a dance that moves through the appearances and disappearances of dis/ability. I entangle myself in a creative process that simultaneously seeks and fails to embody the ordinary, revealing a choreographic task that we are always-already in the midst of interpreting.

A STORY OF DISABILITY: INTRODUCING THE DIS/APPEARANCE

I prepare to teach my dance class. I am nervous.

These nerves are not the ones that usually anticipate my dance lessons. They are not attributed to the gaze of my supervisor, nor her pen poised to record an assessment of my practice. These nerves are different. They move with uncertainty.

I look out at my students. This placement is unlike my previous ones. It is described to me as "special" not because it is the final practicum placement of my initial teacher education program but because I have been placed in a school designated as one for "exceptional" or "differently abled" students. In front of me are students who have received diagnoses through an identification of "developmental delays," "intellectual deficits," or "physical impairments." In front of me is my class of disabled students.[1] They sit in their wheelchairs accompanied by teachers or educational assistants who are ready to move them through my lesson, who are always present to support them through the ordinary gestures of everyday life at school.

> "It is through my body that I understand other people, just as it is through my body that I perceive 'things.' The meaning of a gesture thus 'understood' is not behind it, it is intermingled with the structure of the world outlined by the gesture, and which I take up on my own account."
>
> Merleau-Ponty, Maurice. *Phenomenology of Perception*. London, UK: Routledge, 1962, p. 186.

"Look, he loves to dance. He's giving my finger a hug," says one of the educational assistants. My nerves turn to confusion. I see the student's hand grasping the educational assistant's finger, squeezing it tightly, tugging it up and down, pulling it right and left. I am confused by this interpretation of the student's gesture. This is unlike any hug I have ever seen or imagined. How can this gesture be interpreted as a hug? Furthermore, how can this not-so-ordinary embodiment of a seemingly ordinary gesture be perceived as dance? It is not an ordinary hug. Perhaps it is a "special" hug. It is not an ordinary dance. Perhaps it is a "special" dance.

A DUET OF DANCE AND DIS/ABILITY: PLAYING WITH DIS/APPEARANCES

> "Disability culture: there is a fine line here, between exclusionary essentialism on the one hand, and, on the other, the desire to mark the differences that disability-focused environments (which can include both non-disabled and disabled people) offer to mainstream ways of acknowledging bodies and their needs. I do not think that disability culture is something that comes 'naturally' to people identified or identifying as disabled. And I do not think that disability culture is closed to non-disabled allies, or allies who do not wish to identify as either disabled or not. To me, disability culture is not a thing, but a process. Boundaries, norms, belongings: disability cultural environments can suspend a whole slew of rules, try to undo the history of exclusions that many of its members have experienced when they have heard or felt 'you shouldn't be like this.' At the same time, disability cultural environments have to safeguard against perpetuating or erecting other exclusions (based on racial stereotypes, class, gender, economic access, internalized ableism, etc.). This is all a lot of work, trying to think without victimization and exclusion, forgiving others and oneself when it is not yet working well, and being aware of the many different forces of privilege and power that mark how we got here."
>
> Kuppers, Petra. *Disability Culture and Community Performance: Find a Strange and Twisted Shape*. London, UK: Palgrave Macmillan, 2011, p. 4.

What must disappear for an ordinary gesture to appear? What must appear for the ordinariness of that gesture to disappear? Through the creation of choreography, dance artists constantly face the question of how a gesture conveys meaning. Yet how can a series of gestures hold the same meaning for the choreographer, the dancers, and their audience? How can we have the same experience of certain "ordinary" gestures? How can we have a common definition of such "normal" gestures? One way to encounter the meaning of a gesture is to identify an essential quality in the gesture itself, a natural and even biological intention behind the gesture's meaning. Instead, I choose to encounter the "ordinary gesture" in unexpected ways. The ordinary gesture seems simple, and it is through that appearance of simplicity that its extraordinary dance is made to disappear.

The ways in which we are asked to encounter a gesture reveal how we are expected to perform ability. We create; we observe; we embody these expectations. Through these expectations, disability disappears from our dance. Through this disappearance, disability is made to appear. We are asked to find a place for disability, implying that disability is not already dancing within the spaces through which we move. We are guided through a task of implementing accommodations that allow the disabled person access to become a dancing body. As important as these accommodations might be, the relationship between dance and disability is much more complex.

The task of accommodation is choreographic in itself. It dictates a relationship in which dance and disability cannot coexist. One must be altered for the two to come into contact. Blindness must be given sight before it can dance. Deafness must be made to hear before it can dance. Immobility must be moved before it can dance. Madness must be tempered before it can dance. Or alternatively, the dance must change to accommodate disabled peoples' access. For one to appear, the other must be made to disappear. However, this choreography fails to recognize the constant presence of disability through its absence (Titchkosky, 2011). It fails to acknowledge disability's central role as key to the un/expected embodiment of the un/expected dance.

Dance is only given the ability to choreograph, and thus govern human embodiment, when disability appears as an object to be observed, feared, fixed, pathologized, medicalized, rehabilitated, or controlled. As Rod Michalko (2002) reminds us, "Disabled people, like everyone else, bear the mark of ordinariness" (p. 153). Disability must become ordinary for the dance to continue. Dance requires that disability be encountered through the ordinary figure of a person requiring accommodation. The blind person shows us the visual medium of dance. The deaf person amplifies dance's dependence on sound. The immobile person moves us to dance through expectations of limitless mobility. The mad person rationalizes dance's control of the body and its expression. It is through the presence of disability that an expected ability is asserted. It is through an absence of disability that the expected ability can live unquestioned. Disability, however, can also guide us through an embodiment of the unexpected—if we are so moved. This is where we disrupt the gesture and its expectations. This is where we disrupt the ordinary to access the extraordinary gesture.

Disability has the ability to disrupt our dance (Albright, 1997; Kuppers, 2003). Moreover, disability provides us with a space through which to play with our embodiments of the taken-for-granted gesture. Such an invitation to play, however, should not allow us to trivialize the consequences of normalcy. We cannot forget the ways in which taken-for-granted embodiments of ability work to oppress and marginalize disabled people in violent ways. Through play, I instead gesture to Carrie Sandahl and Philip Auslander's (2005) suggestion of "*commotion.*" Understanding disability performance as commotion, they invite us to dance with disability's disturbances of normalcy while also playing through our "*co-motion*"—our movement together with disability (p. 10). Encountering this relational movement with disability, I offer another definition for this invitation to play: to take part in.

Maurice Merleau-Ponty (1958 [1945]) presents us with a provocation suggesting that we delve deeper into, and play with, our understanding of the everyday. He moves us through the everyday act of speaking by stating that "the spoken word is a gesture, and its meaning, a world" (p. 214). Through speech, our words become the gestures that interpret the choreographies through which we dance. We encounter the gestures of our dance as they become the words that allow us to speak of a world. Our words, both spoken and danced, are gestures. Our gestures, both danced and spoken, are words. We must seek to move not against or toward but rather through the world in which they come to life. We must take part in and speak with the complex world that these gestures bring forth. We must inhabit that world through which these gestures speak of the ordinary. We must embody the ordinary gestures that speak of a world.

The term *play* should also be understood with reference to its dramatic definition. Through every utterance and reading of a gesture, we are taking part in the performance of that gesture's world. Through the creation, performance, choreography, and perception of our gestures, we are constantly re-enacting a taken-for-granted world that imagines normative conceptions of ability, disability, the human, and the self. Rather than attempting to escape our entrapment in such normalcy, perhaps we could move into it and delve deeper into our complex entanglement *with* the ordinary.

In the following section I present a choreographic narrative through which I attempt to embody an ordinary gesture of everyday life. I play with the confusing gesture that my initial story of disability's appearance invites me to re-encounter. I dance with a hug. Through this narrative, I engage with contemporary dance practices while employing a method of personal, critical, and creative inquiry. In conversation with social and cultural theorists and informed by a disability studies orientation that seeks "to interrogate normalcy, to make *it* an object of study" (Titchkosky & Michalko, 2009, p. 6), I engage in the choreographic task of encountering the ordinary gesture of a hug. Through this encounter, I work to rethink the meaning of the hug. I allow myself to move through the appearances and disappearances of our dis/ability to embody the ordinary.

A CHOREOGRAPHIC NARRATIVE[2]: ENCOUNTERING THE DANCE, EMBODYING THE HUG

"What is the connection between this story of bodies missing from history and that of the aesthetic? Although any such linkage may seem tenuous, it is important to think of the role that aesthetics has played in shoring up attitudes toward the body in history, as ideas of the beautiful and sublime have relied on ideals of bodily perfection (or grotesque distortion) to legitimize a naturalized standpoint presumed to be shared by others.... Poets and performance artists seeking to situate the body in its imbricated relationship to social relations of power have developed ways ... of reclaiming missing bodies from the visual, acoustic, and legal landscapes in which they are represented and thus contained."

Davidson, Michael. "Missing Bodies: Disappearances in the Aesthetic." *Cultural Critique* 92 (Winter 2016): 1–31, p. 27.

I enter the studio with my fellow dancers, preparing for another rehearsal. I warm up and stretch my body, readying myself for whatever is asked of us. As dancers, we have trained and been trained to view our bodies as the choreographer's tools, as instruments for creating meaning. I condition my body to become a vehicle for sharing a story. I prepare my body to be manipulated as an object through which that story can emerge. I wonder though, from my body whose story will spring forth?

Through formal structures and techniques that prescribe the movements of dance, through plot and characters very distant from my own experiences, through a choreographer or a director telling me what is right and what is wrong … through the expert telling me how I can and cannot be, I constantly find myself embodying a dance that was never intended for me. In these choreographic sessions, there are expectations placed upon us dancers. I do everything I can to meet them. I do everything I can to embody these foreign narratives. My stories are excluded. My meanings disappear. Yet as the dancer, sometimes referred to as the interpreter of choreography, I am an important figure in this creative process. I am not just an object to be manipulated. I act as a subjective force in determining how my body takes part in the tasks required of me. Through *my* embodiment of the dance, can my stories and my meanings ever be excluded? With every choice I make in response to a direction or an imposed movement, I am asserting my story and perhaps embodying something unexpected.

What are the expectations of my dancing body? I am asked to engage in a process of improvisation wherein the choreographer provides us dancers with movement prompts. The movements we generate through these choreographic tasks will be manipulated and transformed into a final dance work. Through these contemporary dance practices, we are being invited to inhabit our own bodies as sites for movement discovery. Yet in this supposed freedom, I cannot help but sense an expectation moulding my dancing body. Our tasks involve my embodiment of a variety of gestures with one thing in common: they are experienced, performed, and encountered as "human" gestures.

What are the expectations of my human body? I find myself trying to meet the expectations that this dance requires of me: the expectation of my humanness. What is a human gesture? Or better yet, what is a non-human gesture if we are all tasked with being human? Perhaps there is an expectation that some of us may not be human, an expectation of a non-human presence, a non-human person. In posing the question of how a gesture can be human, a potential answer arises through an adjective often used in association with "human." This adjective seems to encapsulate an essence of the human gesture: ordinary.

Embody the ordinary gesture. How can one encounter this challenge? I start by selecting a choreographic task. I engage in my own interpretive exploration. I gesture toward what I recognize as a hug. I gesture toward what I recognize as the ordinary.

What then is an ordinary hug? The ordinary hug can be seen as an act involving two people wherein they come within close proximity to one another, each wrapping their arms around the other's body. It can take part in the routine of two friends greeting one another. It can feel like comfort from a loved one. So many images come to mind in trying to define this ordinary gesture, yet these initial attempts are incomplete. Any further attempt to define the ordinary hug would also be incomplete. Sylvia Wynter (1994) reminds me of the "fallacy" that "mistakes the representation for the reality, the map for the territory" (p. 49). Do all of my attempts at imagining a hug just result in the creation of a map for the ordinary? Can I ever discover the territory of the ordinary? Is there even a reality that is the hug? I find myself struggling to comprehend this ordinary task. But maybe comprehension will come through its embodiment. Maybe it is through the embodiment of the ordinary hug that I can approach the territory ... or maybe its embodiment will just act as another map.

There is so much to consider in my attempts to embody this arm-based wrapping action. There is so much to navigate in approaching an ability to embrace this gesture. As I reach out and take a step toward the hug, I realize that I must decide where to wrap my arms. I recognize that only the appropriate body parts may be wrapped, or else it may signal a departure from the status of the mutually agreed upon relationship between my partner and myself. Although, I cannot quite recall when or where this agreement explicitly occurred. Perhaps the decision of where to place our arms *is* the mutual agreement and the establishment of our relationship.

I move closer into the gesture. Another obstacle arises as I determine the appropriate proximity between our two bodies during this mutually agreed upon, but never discussed, wrapping of arms. Too close and there is an invasion of private space, implying that there is a private space between bodies that can be invaded. Too far and the hug becomes awkward or insincere, suggesting that a hug can be endowed with characteristics. The question then is how to determine the appropriate proximity? Perhaps the mutually agreed upon relationship, whenever it was agreed upon, can help to dictate proximal expectations.

A final variable arises as I question which two people are expected to engage in this gesture. Which other's body is my arm allowed to wrap around? Whose arms do I expect to wrap around my body? Whose arms, or other body parts, would present an unexpected encounter? Such an unexpected encounter, potentially resulting in feelings of pity, fear, disgust, or even awe and wonder, would make me fully aware that the hug is marked by the presence of something, or someone, out of the ordinary. I take a step back and drop my arms. I cannot go further. I am stuck. With every attempt to move closer toward this hug, I find it escaping my reach. With every attempt to move closer toward the ordinary, I find it escaping my embrace.

In approaching this ordinary hug, Zygmunt Bauman (2004) calls out to me. He tells me that I am stuck in the "grey zone: a kingdom of underdefinition, uncertainty—and danger" (p. 28). I am stuck in the liminal space that he describes as representing the border between those produced as "useful product" and the resulting "waste." Attempting to move within the desirable and accepted gesture, I recognize that the only way to determine my inclusion within the ordinary is through a determination of that which is relegated and even banished from the ordinary.

I gesture to Stuart Hall's (1996) assertion that "every identity has at its 'margin', an excess, something more" (p. 5), an excess that allows for an identity to be knowable. In my attempts to know the hug, to engage in its identity of ordinariness, I require a vision of inappropriate parts of the body to be wrapped. I require an ability to determine inappropriate proximity. I require a movement away from bodies that cannot engage in this gesture. I do not recognize the ordinary hug until my movements toward it are disrupted by unexpected performances of this gesture, by embodiments that fall outside of the ordinary. To recognize the ordinary, I require an appearance of the extra to the ordinary (Michalko, 2002, p. 5).

What then is the extra to the ordinary hug, or the extra-ordinary hug? It must be everything that the hug is not, everything that can be removed from the ordinary: the inappropriate wrapping, the disproportionate distances, and the unaccepted bodies. Once all traces of extra are removed, the ordinary remains. But this removal is a never-ending task. Could I ever remove all of the layers corrupting that seemingly ordinary hug? I return to the problem of determining at what point I draw the line between the ordinary and its extra. This line seems so natural and yet once I attempt to encounter it, I find myself in a limbo. This line reveals itself as more than two-dimensional. It reveals itself as "the liminal space between self and other," the liminal space through which we come to know dis/ability (Titchkosky, 2011, p. 59). Perhaps the goal then should not be to define ordinary and extra-ordinary hugs but rather to question how I am able to determine which hugs are ordinary or extra-ordinary without a capacity to define either category, without the ability to draw a line between them.

Gail Weiss (2008) presents me with a new point from which to depart. She reminds me that "it is impossible to describe even the simplest and most ordinary experiences without recourse to the horizons that contextualize them" (p. 25). My gestures seem to naturally spring forth from my body, yet they are also choreographed by the contexts and perspectives, the *ground* in which my self exists and is given meaning. What then grounds my dance? Weiss pushes me further into the entangled relation between my gesture and its ground. The ground cannot be a pure and independent object that produces and reproduces my gesture, for the two are constantly dancing together in a duet of object-hood and subject-hood; both are constantly swaying each other.

Through my inclination to find independent and fixed definitions of my gestures and the choreographies that ground them, I remain stuck. Perhaps I must delve deeper into the stickiness that holds me in this process of embodiment to "understand why the familiarity of the ordinary can always be refigured in extra-ordinary ways" (Weiss, 2008, p. 7). I must desire a moment to play with that which makes the gesture instinctively ordinary while at the same time making the gesture indescribably extraordinary. Whatever the *that* is.

I once again respond to the choreographic prompt as I gesture toward what I recognize as a hug. I once again gesture toward the ordinary. The same questions arise. I am back in the space that forces me to negotiate between a choice of body parts, between a choice of proximities, and between a choice of bodies. This time, however, I do not shy away from my question. I pause in my confusion. I take comfort in being stuck and make a choice to dwell in this liminal space. I find pleasure in the stickiness and make the choice to once again step toward my partner, toward the ordinary. This time, I embrace the hug.

I am not simply repeating my previous encounters with the ordinary, however. I invite its extra to join me. I invite that which has disappeared to be made present as together we inhabit this familiar place; together we dance within this unfamiliar space. I embrace this intra-ordinary dance, a dance of appearances. These appearances are called forth by me and for me, with me and through me. I move through an enactment and re-enactment of narratives that have come before me and will continue after me. I take part in the expectations of my humanness. Yet as Thomas King (2005 [2003]) reminds me, "The truth about stories is that that's all we are" (p. 2). My choreography of the story of humanness, which perpetuates the notion of an ordinary and its extra, must also be creating something new. In representing the ordinary, I am both *re*-presenting the ordinary while presenting *my* ordinary.

CONCLUSION

Reading back my choreographic narrative, we could easily say that disability has disappeared from my dance. We could say that neither character in my story was identified as being disabled or that there was no clear representation of disability— we could say that there was a lack of disability's embodiment moving through my story. And still, I wonder how we can utter these statements with such ease. I wonder how we could so easily make disability disappear from my encounters with a hug. This ease is expected of me as a non-disabled dancer. I am expected to partake in the ease through which disability can be made to disappear through the stories of my gestures. And it is in this space of ease that I invite us to re-read my narrative and to continue understanding how it is that we come to know the normal, the human, and the ordinary gesture through disability's disappearance.

I provoke us to reflect on the ways in which dominant imaginaries of disability allow us to embody these taken-for-granted conceptions of a gesture. I hold space for us to become aware of other imaginaries of disability, allowing us to embody different ways of relating to each other. I dare us to search for the appearances of disability that embody our expectations of the seemingly ordinary gestures of everyday life. Do we dare to make disability appear differently through the gestures of our stories? Engaging in disability studies through an interpretation of our stories, through our stories of interpretation, we might desire such different appearances of disability and such embodiments of difference to choreograph our movements through all our gestures.

My embodiment is the dis/appearance of the un/expected. My dance is the dis/appearance of my story. As I step outside the limits of defining the ordinary, I discover my extraordinary embodiment of the ordinary. Perhaps this dance has become an "extraordinary act" that, as Tanya Titchkosky (2011) suggests, "serves as a place where the stories that we are can be revealed and new narrations of ordinary lives can be told" (pp. 90–91). My repeated yet unrepeatable embodiment works to create new stories while at the same time recreate existing, naturalized expectations of how to be. This makes my embodiment powerful. This makes every embodiment powerful. As King (2005 [2003]) warns me, "once a story is told, it cannot be called back. Once told, it is loose in the world" (p. 10).

With each embodiment of my hug, each embodiment of the ordinary, it is crucial for me to enter back into the confusion and to never rest in the comfort of discovering a "truth." With an open heart, an open mind, an open body, an open spirit, and an open being, I seek to experience the expected and the unexpected;

I desire a constant movement through the entangled appearances and disappear-ances of ability and disability; I dream of the worlds through which I never stop playing with the simultaneously ordinary and extra-ordinary embodiments of meaning; and I hope to respond to the questions of my gestures not with answers but by once again reaching out and embracing the hug.

NOTES

1. Gesturing to Anne McGuire's (2016) analysis that "the person-first lexicon functions to systematically organize disabled people as 'just people'—regular, *ordinary people* [emphasis added] who happen to have a disability" (p. 188), throughout this chapter I move away from using person-first language to play with disability's disturbance of our taken-for-granted expectations of "ordinary" embodiments of personhood.

2. An initial narrative of my choreographic encounters with the extra-/ordinary gesture of a hug is published as "Embracing the Hug" (Esteban, 2020). This chapter presents new interpretations of this task, however, engaging with social and cultural theorists through a disability studies orientation.

REFERENCES

Albright, A. C. (1997). *Choreographing difference: The body and identity in contemporary dance*. Wesleyan University Press.

Bauman, Z. (2004). *Wasted lives: Modernity and its outcasts*. Polity.

Esteban, J. M. (2020). Embracing the hug. *Line bridge body: Performance across the arts, 1*, 2–7. https://www.linebridgebody.com/

Hall, S. (1996). Introduction: Who needs 'identity'? In S. Hall & P. du Gay (Eds.), *Questions of cultural identity* (pp. 1–17). SAGE.

King, T. (2005). *The truth about stories: A native narrative*. University of Minnesota Press. (Original work published 2003)

Kuppers, P. (2003). *Disability and contemporary performance: Bodies on edge*. Routledge.

McGuire, A. (2016). *War on autism: On the cultural logic of normative violence*. University of Michigan Press.

Merleau-Ponty, M. (1958). *Phenomenology of perception* (C. Smith, Trans.). Routledge and Kegan Paul. (Original work published 1945)

Michalko, R. (2002). *The difference that disability makes*. Temple University Press.

Sandahl, C., & Auslander, P. (2005). Introduction: Disability studies in commotion with performance studies. In C. Sandahl & P. Auslander (Eds.), *Bodies in commotion: Disability & performance* (pp. 1–12). University of Michigan Press.

Titchkosky, T. (2011). *The question of access: Disability, space, meaning.* University of Toronto Press.

Titchkosky, T., & Michalko, R. (2009). Introduction. In T. Titchkosky & R. Michalko (Eds.), *Rethinking normalcy: A disability studies reader* (pp. 1–14). Canadian Scholars' Press.

Weiss, G. (2008). *Refiguring the ordinary.* Indiana University Press.

Wynter, S. (1994). No humans involved: An open letter to my colleagues. *Forum N. H. I.: Knowledge for the 21st Century, 1*(1), 42–73.

CHAPTER 12

Shapeshifting: Navigating the Social Construction of Multiple Disability Identities

Steve Singer

Key Terms: Deaf; Disability; Identity; Learning Disability; Mental Illness

The bar is dingy and on the wrong side of the tracks. Outside of the place, disintegrating old cinderblocks make up the walls and more contemporary bulletproof block glass replaces plate glass likely broken years ago.

Bebe, my service dog, looks around, appearing a bit hesitant.

The middle-aged man at the door sports thick-rimmed glasses and signs in American Sign Language (ASL), "YOU NOT-MEMBER, 5$."[1]

He then looks down at Bebe and questions, "YOU BLIND?"

I respond, "ME BLIND(neg), DOG(t) SHE HEARING SERVICE DOG."

> "Humans construct the world through language. Language is a window through which we see and understand the world. Culturally, society is constructed by what the 'window' of language reveals, and this 'window' deeply influences all human action and interaction."
>
> Armstrong, Jeanette C. "Aboriginal Literatures: A Distinctive Genre within Canadian Literature." In *Hidden in Plain Sight: Contributions of Aboriginal Peoples to Canadian Identity and Culture*, edited by Jeanette C. Armstrong, Dan Beavon, David R. Newhouse, & Cora J. Voyageur, 180–186. Toronto, ON: University of Toronto Press, 2005, p. 182.

He cocks his head and looks at her for a minute and then waves us through. Walking up to the bar I wave my hand at the bartender to get her attention: "FOR ME, ONE DRAFT f.s. YUENLING PLEASE."

She looks me up and down and responds, "YOU NOT-MEMBER. DRINK ORDER(t), MEMBER MUST."

I see my friend Scott across the room and get his attention: "HEY, WHAT'S UP. DO-YOU-MIND BEER ORDER? ME NOT MEMBER."

Scott orders me a drink, and our friend Casey joins us.

Soon another man walks over. He looks to be about sixty years old and on a mission. I allow him to proceed. I know the drill. "HI, ME NAME CHRIS. WHO YOU(wh)?"

I respond, "HI, ME NAME f.s. STEVE, LAST NAME f.s. SINGER. THREE-OF-US GO COLLEGE TOGETHER."

"YOU DEAF(shift) HEARING WHICH(wh)?"

"DEAF."

"SCHOOL(t) GO WHERE(wh)?"

"HEARING SCHOOL. ME GROW-UP HEARING. DEAFHIT AGE 28. 3-YEARS-AGO. MY FAMILY(t) ME ONLY DEAF."

"YOU DEAF NOT, YOU HARD-OF-HEARING," which is not a question or even a matter related to the severity of my hearing loss but a definitive label because I am a Late-Deafened Adult and ASL is not my first language.

I counter, "ME DEAF. DEAF HAPPEN, ME NOT SAD. ME FEEL ALIVE, FEEL FREE FIRST TIME EVER. LEARN ASL, GO++ DEAF EVENTS, CHERISH DEAF COMMUNITY. ME DEAF!" My signs become more emphatic and my facial expressions, more extreme. He nods and then fingerspells an entire sentence with lightning speed. This was not the first time I have been given this kind of test. I don't catch it all, but the words "DEAF, KNOW, CALL, STUPID" inform me that if I don't act offended, I failed.

Keeping my cool, I respond, "YOU THINK ME HOH, f.s. !F-I-N-E! (spelled for emphasis) WHATEVER. ME HERE, !RIGHT!?"

He looks down at Bebe. "DOG(t) DEAF NEED NOT!" communicating that he shares a common opinion that Deaf people are not disabled and have no need of a service animal.

Growing tired of the conversation, I simply respond, "MY DECISION, NOT YOURS."

A long-time friend of my wife exclaims: "Oh, you're pregnant; congratulations!"

"Thanks," my wife responds.

Her friend pauses, looking puzzled: "I guess this means Steve will get a cochlear implant?"

Katherine, a bit mystified, responds: "Why would he do that?

She explains: "Well, don't you think it's a bit unfair to your child to have a Deaf father? Ya know, communication and all, especially if he can do something about it. He wouldn't want to be a burden."

Not knowing where to begin, Katherine simply says, "Oh, so you think it's bad for a child to be multilingual?"

> "It is not that some bodies are reducible to the same while others figure as absolute other, but rather that all resist full or final expression. The security of categories—whether of self or non-self—is undone by a radical undecidability. This issue is not one of revaluing differently embodied others, but of rethinking the nature of embodiment itself."
>
> Shildrick, Margrit. *Embodying the Monster Encounters with the Vulnerable Self.* London, UK: SAGE, 2002, p. 2.

In these two vignettes, there is little space provided where I, a Deaf man, can feel that my Deaf identity is a valued part of who I am. The prelingually Deaf man, in a valid attempt to protect his community and identity from outsiders, dismissed my membership as a complete Deaf person, choosing to assign me a marginalized label in those types of contexts as hard-of-hearing. My wife's friend was well-meaning in her concern but cast my Deafhood as a burden rather than a feature of a multicultural family. And yet, the truth is, I am still able to utter the words, "Each day of my life since I became Deaf is better than any day before it." When I became Deaf 16 years ago, I quickly came to feel that I was part of something bigger than me—a part of a cherished community that had a common experience and language. For the most part, my relationships with other Deaf people are quite positive. With the new understanding of myself as Deaf, I flourished. Without hesitation, I credit my educational, career, and family successes to the formation of my Deaf identity. These few paragraphs show how the meaning of me not being able to hear can shift depending on the context. Sometimes I am an imposter or a burden, and other times I am a proud, productive member of a culture who has much to offer to my community and profession.

How is it that something as unchanging as how much I can hear can mean so many things? There is a substantial body of literature that discusses how we, as a society, create disability (Oliver, 2013; Shakespeare, 2006). This idea that disability is socially constructed does not discredit people's experiences with pain and suffering due to illness/disability but separates these experiences from conditions artificially created by ideologies, institutions, and other social constructs (Hughes & Paterson, 2006; Swain & French, 2000). Because of how our civilizations construct disability, rooted in ideas of normalcy, it is a fairly simple task to explain to people unfamiliar with disability studies that disability is socially constructed, as I show in the narratives above.

What does the social construction of disability mean for people? If disability is constructed by the environment, then that tells us that its meaning can shift in various contexts. The transience of its meaning results in disability or the perception of disability appearing and disappearing. Sometimes this happens at the discretion of the able-bodied majority and at other times, intentionally or unintentionally by disabled individuals themselves. This chapter explores my experiences with multiple disabilities, negotiating various junctures when they appear and disappear. I juxtapose my power as a disabled individual to mediate disability narratives others create about me within a cultural landscape wherein deficit notions of disability flourish. I complicate my rhetoric by interweaving the implications of these acts on my identity, pride, and feelings of self-efficacy to show how disability(ies) can, in fact, simultaneously represent gain and social disadvantage.

It would come as a great surprise to me if my application to a tenure-track professorship in Deaf education was not bolstered by the fact that I am Deaf, because the academy should understand the importance of Deaf people contributing toward the field of Deaf education. However, I suspect that it also helped that I maintain a fairly clear speaking voice. Hearing people are accustomed to listening to people (e.g., interviews and research presentations), thus speech becomes a criterion for establishing competence (Bauman, 2008). Knowing this, I very purposefully choose when I use my voice and when I do not. I became disabled by not being "Deaf enough" in the Deaf club narrative above, but at the same time, I became "Deaf, but not too Deaf" during the hiring process for my career. Despite my distaste for the audist ideology—the supremacy of hearing and speaking as the paragon form of communication (Eckert & Rowley, 2013)—I leveraged my understanding of it to claim my place at the academic table by ensuring one of my supposed "disabilities" was not too evident.

It is easy for this shifting Deaf-focused dialogue to dominate my narrative. It is my most conspicuous identification, and it is one that is widely documented in scholarly literature. The Deaf experience is contemporarily in vogue, appearing in numerous television advertisements, shows, and social media. But what of my other disabilities that are not "feathers in my cap"? Much less is represented or written about mental illness and learning disabilities outside of educational and medical contexts, particularly in positive ways. However, these disabilities have shaped who I am and how the able-bodied world engages me in similarly monumental ways as my Deafhood. At any point, I can freely discuss Deafhood with colleagues, students, and the public, but despite the existence of my other disabilities, I feel compelled to disguise, explain away, mitigate, and otherwise make my mental illness and learning disabilities disappear. Generally, people appear afraid of mentally ill people, viewing us as unpredictable, dangerous, and incompetent, which represents one of the most tenacious stigmas (Overton & Medina, 2008). But this important part of me yearns for the same transparency, pride, and exposition as my Deaf Self. Furthermore, I feel compelled to provide my teacher candidates with authentic understandings of the students they will educate. A conservative estimate is that half of Deaf people have a disability (Guardino, 2015). I also know that Deaf students have other marginalized identifications (e.g., LGBTQA, immigrants, or experiencing poverty) that make their experiences as Deaf people more complex. Deafhood does not exist in a vacuum but is one part of intricate human experience.

"Welcome, Dr. Singer. I thought listening to his experiences becoming Deaf 11 years ago might help you in your careers as speech and language pathologists." I approach the podium and pause. I stare out to a sea of 18-year-old female faces, hoping for a lighthouse to guide me, but I only see the white caps breaking and churning. Inside I am breaking and churning too. I open my mouth and stumble over the first few words as I try to subdue the tempest seething below my surface.

They expect to hear about audiological testing and Deaf culture, but the fact that they expect these suggests there is a bigger need, and so I go with my gut. "This— paper. This paper …" I clear my throat, shift my weight a few times, and wipe the sweat trickling down my forehead. "It is an audiogram. Look at those numbers. Do you think this client might need a cochlear implant? Maybe he should go to a Deaf school? Numbers are easy. Lives are messy. This audiogram is mine, and I am messy. To be good practitioners, you must understand your clients holistically. So, let's look at my audiogram as I tell you about my 'brain weather.'" I balk, knowing that I just chose a path of conversation that outed myself—that I have mental illness and learning disabilities.

Student email: Dear Dr. Singer, I am so sorry I haven't been coming to class. I wish I could explain why, but I can't come up with the words. I'm just a mess and my anxiety is through the roof. Many days I just don't get out of bed. I am letting everyone down.

Response: I won't claim to understand what you are going through, but I want you to know that I, too, suffer. Some days, I am unsure how or why I get through the day. I think it's important that I connect you with someone who can help you access resources on campus, because despite how much I protested and still protest, I know I can't cope alone and neither should you. For now, let's not worry about class. We can talk about that later. How about coming to my office? You can come in pajamas and you need not worry about showering or anything. Please just come. I really mean it. You tell me the time and I will be there. We can meet, but don't have to talk. If you want to just sit and stare at your phone or play a game of chess, we can. I can show you funny videos of my dog. You have not let me down and if you have anxiety in or about class, we can brainstorm some ideas—I have tons of strategies I have developed over the years. I also think this is an important part of your experience that you could build on and create a project that both satisfies the course and helps you to process your emotions, but again we can talk about that at another time. For now, just be and be okay with that. We can figure it out. Please just come.

I chose to disclose my disabilities to the students and a senior faculty member in the vignettes above. In that disclosure I understood that I risked compromising my authority in the classroom and the future of my career at the institution, because the appearance of these disabilities is not often welcome. And yet, I felt empowered doing so. However, the larger implication was that I further entrenched how I internalized ableism. Internalized ableism is when disabled people come to believe the prejudices against disability are justified and that disability is inherently undesirable (Campbell, 2008). The various parts of my disability identity fought for acknowledgement. Knowing the derogatory discourses about mental illness and learning disabilities, as well as foreseeing the potential consequences of disclosure of them, created an internal dialogue every bit as destructive as someone else wielding my disabilities against me.

The first of the two narratives above highlight my unease and how I co-constructed the oppression of my disability status with the class. Based on this internal disability-as-deviance dialogue and my experience, I chose to interpret my disabilities as "more inferior" and "more provocative" than my Deaf identification. After all, it is difficult to have a different understanding of mental illness when people's language use includes the word "crazy" to mean bad. Horror movies, my favourite genre of film, also mostly centre around dangerous characters who are mentally ill. If students or faculty members sensed that I felt these subtexts of crazy and inferior about myself, they, too, might have been inclined to believe (or reinforce an existing understanding of) the hierarchy of disability I upheld. I created this hierarchy with the shame and hesitance I exhibited in the way I presented the topic. In that brief moment—in that time and space—we all constructed what Deaf and disability meant. While we had an established and anonymous general knowledge of the existence of these concepts, their appearance at that time—connected to a personality and to our respective roles at the college—defined Deaf and disability in less comfortable and tidy ways.

In the second narrative, I show a rare moment in my life when my experiences as a mentally ill adult can be interpreted as valuable through a societal lens. That I shared a common experience with my student and yet survived and thrived through mental suffering is significant. My experience demonstrates how mental illness affects a wide demographic of people and that it does not necessarily prevent individuals from achieving their goals. While it is difficult for me to conceive a world that truly values mental illness, I was able to effectively mentor my struggling student *because* my mental illness gave me the tools to read her email with compassion and pragmatism. I recalled the tortuous moments of my life when the clock ticked so slowly that I didn't feel as though time was passing at all. I remembered not being able to wash myself or be around people, though that's exactly what I needed. I remembered the shame and the burden of depression. I hoped to provide an outlet for the student and help her find a path forward, not only in her current crises but potentially in drawing from her experiences to create meaning and scholarship.

CONCLUSION

"Between me and the other world there is ever an unasked question: un-asked by some through feelings of delicacy; by others through the difficulty of rightly framing it. All, nevertheless, flutter round it. They approach me in a half-hesitant sort of way, eye me curiously or compassionately, and then, instead of saying directly, How does it feel to be a problem? they say, I know an excellent coloured man in my town; or, I fought at Mechanicsville; or, Do not these Southern outrages make your blood boil? At these I smile, or am interested, or reduce the boiling to a simmer, as the occasion may require. To the real question, How does it feel to be a problem? I answer seldom a word."

DuBois, W. E. B. *The Souls of Black Folk*. New York, NY: Penguin Books, 1903. https://www.gutenberg.org/files/408/408-h/408-h.htm

In the preceding four vignettes, being Deaf and having brain weather, my preferred label for my embodied "normal" experience with so-called mental illness, that defines who I am, shapeshifted. This shapeshifting depended on who initiated the dis/appearance of disability and in what context those dis/appearances occurred. Alteration of any of these conditions would likely have resulted in very different stories I relayed here. I show how I am acted upon by external forces and also how I participate in my own shifting, sometimes to my own detriment, and at other times claiming power. These facets of me are not simply "conditions" but how I exist and interpret the world—and I am glad for them, even when they cause me pain.

While I seem to understand my experience of shapeshifting with Deafhood and brain weather, I have a much less clear understanding of how my learning disabilities appear and disappear in similar ways. Generally speaking, people in the United States have a poor understanding of learning disabilities, what causes them, what they mean for individuals, or if they even exist at all (Cortiella & Horowitz, 2014; Jensen et al., 2004). It is difficult to situate and resolve this component of the Self when many people discredit it through skepticism, misinformation, and disregard. For younger populations, learning disabilities are the most prevalent disability (Courtney-Long et al., 2015), but despite this, at least in my life, they are given the least credence. Conversations about learning disabilities seem limited to a function-focused discourse about how to support students, and I am left feeling a gaping hole in my Self-concept. My learning disabilities manifest in ways that make retaining or using information (working memory) difficult, and I have trouble interpreting the meaning of language. When there is reason to mention my learning disabilities, such as when I begin working with a colleague on a piece of writing, it creates an end-stop in the conversation, generally resolved by changing the topic. My colleagues and students do not know what to do with this information, and I have no strong cultural model upon which I can scaffold our understanding like I do with my Deafhood. For these reasons, my learning disabilities seem to exist in a continual state of disappearance. I see how they affect the ways I interact with people, do my work, and write, but they are regarded by others as incompetence or laziness. As my learning disabilities are forced out of perceived existence, I find it impossible to integrate them into my notion of my disability identity. Instead, they become a metaphorical basket of dirty laundry that I shove into a closet so the guests don't see them. This laundry still exists, just as learning disability does in my identity, but I'm not quite sure what to do with either. The consequence is that it is difficult to affect the societal and personal narratives about this facet of me, and I am left feeling that I am indeed lazy and incompetent or, worse yet, disillusioned about who and what I really am. I feel as though my laundry should always be clean. In these acts, I write the existing derogatory narratives about learning disabilities into my own and become what I seek to avoid. What alternative is available?

With all of these convoluted, shifting, and often conflicting presences of disability in my life, I am left wondering, "When and how can all my identifications appear as equal contributors to my expertise and credentials as a disabled person and career academic?" Despite my strongest assertions and aspirations that I pilot my own course and identity, I recognize that my autonomy is constrained and enabled by the world in which I live. I try but cannot envision an existence where other people do not tell me how to feel about myself and what my value is. In part, it is this tension that has propelled me through my life, but I don't wish to define myself only in response to conflict. Instead, I wish to focus on the productive, self-efficacious, community-building, and self-defining appearances of my disabilities, so I can make life worth living.

A Life Worth Living is the title of Zaretsky's (2013) book that explores Albert Camus's philosophical quest for meaning. Zaretsky posits that it is the struggle against life's injustices that gives us worth, but a life defined by those struggles is filled with hopelessness. Instead, we must pay due attention to beauty and the general absurdity of life. We exist in an unfathomable universe for a brief century at best, and the actions we take seem inconsequential and almost silly when juxtaposed with celestial time and space. It is the significance we choose to assign phenomena that provides us a sense of meaning. Opting to find meaning in what we find beautiful is a choice. I try to create a world around me where disability neither appears nor disappears based on socially ascribed value or detriment but rather on individual preference and need. While not a realistic goal, it provides hope. There is a beauty that emerges in how my bodily and emotional characteristics have shaped me as a human. In respect to my disabilities, the meaning of my life comes from how they/I have created a man who is complex, is a bit quirky, has something to offer our variegated world population, and ultimately accepts and values how convoluted my experience is. If I can take that acceptance, understanding, and sense of value and pass it along to others, particularly other disabled people, then I will feel that I have met Zaretsky's criterion for a valuable existence. In contrast, I fear that if my response is apathy or I am complicit in further entrenching ideas of disability hierarchies through my actions, then I will have squandered my brief century. The task seems monumental, and it is, but success can be garnered through catching myself and resisting when I present internalized deficit-based ideas about my disabilities and when I affect positive change, even in barely perceptible ways. In these ways, I join fellow disabled folks and advocates in the creation of an alternative future that provides hope for different and better disabled realities. Perhaps it will be this work that will infiltrate and transform someone's notion about what disability really means to individuals, contributing toward my objective. Meanwhile, I will do my best to permit deficit-based notions of disability to disappear as I attend to the beauty I have found in my existence.

NOTE

1. The text represented in capital letters is called *gloss notation*. It is a tool used by American Sign Language (ASL) linguists and instructors to partially represent how a concept is signed. As a visual language, ASL has no written form. Various notation symbols appear (e.g., "f.s." to mean "fingerspelling" and "-" to mean "a sign that represents multiple English words"). Readers are encouraged to permit themselves to be uninformed about a language not their own and extrapolate the general meaning of what is represented.

REFERENCES

Bauman, H. (2008). Listening to phonocentrism with deaf eyes: Derrida's mute philosophy of (sign) language. *Essays in Philosophy*, *9*(1), 41–54. https://doi.org/10.5840/eip20089118

Campbell, F. (2008). Exploring internalized ableism using critical race theory. *Disability & Society*, *23*(2), 151–162. https://doi.org/10.1080/09687590701841190

Cortiella, C., & Horowitz, S. H. (2014). *The state of learning disabilities: Facts, trends and emerging issues*. National Center for Learning Disabilities.

Courtney-Long, E. A., Carroll, D. D., Zhang, Q. C., Stevens, A. C., Griffin-Blake, S., Armour, B. S., & Campbell, V. A. (2015). Prevalence of disability and disability type among adults—United States, 2013. *Morbidity and Mortality Weekly Report*, *64*(29), 777–783.

Eckert, R. C., & Rowley, A. J. (2013). Audism: A theory and practice of audiocentric privilege. *Humanity & Society*, *37*(2), 101–130. https://doi.org/10.1177/0160597613481731

Guardino, C. A. (2015). Evaluating teachers' preparedness to work with students who are deaf and hard of hearing with disabilities. *American Annals of the Deaf*, *160*(4), 415–426. https://doi.org/10.1353/aad.2015.0030

Hughes, B., & Paterson, K. (2006). The social model of disability and the disappearing body: Towards a sociology of impairment. In L. Barton (Ed.), *Overcoming disabling barriers: 18 years of disability and society* (pp. 101–117). Routledge. https://doi.org/10.4324/9780203965030

Jensen, J. M., McCrary, N., Krampe, K., & Cooper, J. (2004). Trying to do the right thing: Faculty attitudes toward accommodating students with learning disabilities. *Journal of Postsecondary Education and Disability*, *17*(2), 81–90.

Oliver, M. (2013). The social model of disability: Thirty years on. *Disability & Society*, *28*(7), 1024–1026. https://doi.org/10.1080/09687599.2013.818773

Overton, S. L., & Medina, S. L. (2008). The stigma of mental illness. *Journal of Counseling & Development*, *86*(2), 143–151. https://doi.org/10.1002/j.1556-6678.2008.tb00491.x

Shakespeare, T. (2006). The social model of disability. In L. J. Davis (Ed.), *The disability studies reader* (2nd ed., pp. 197–204). Routledge.

Swain, J., & French, S. (2000). Towards an affirmation model of disability. *Disability & Society*, *15*(4), 569–582. https://doi.org/10.1080/09687590050058189

Zaretsky, R. (2013). *A life worth living*. Harvard University Press.

CHAPTER 13

Diane Driedger

Charles Darwin and Me

we work the same
he had chronic illness
it flared in later years
after writing *On the Origin of Species*
he was overworked the doctors said
Darwin proclaimed in a letter
he was *scandalously ill and idle*

to write
he stored energy
for a pin point in time
like me
we hone in
for the task
for several hours
a flurry of thoughts
balanced on a pin head
work done
we rest on couches and beds
go back to being

in valids

survival of the fittest

Published in *Rhubarb Magazine*, Fall 2016

Chronic Illness Dictionary

1.

Uncertain

Unfurl
Unbelievable
Unwell
Unlikely
Undeterred

2.

Weak

Eek
Meek
Deke
Peak
Feat

3.

Ill

Fill
Quill
Will
Still
Hill

4.

Sick

Trick
Nick
Stick
Pick
Kick

PART IV

DISAPPEARING DEPARTURES, DIAGNOSES, AND DEATH

EDITORS' INTRODUCTION

Sometimes the way we come to disability experience or identity involves a departure from previous ways of living, feeling, and knowing. Such a departure can be very difficult and might even feel like a kind of death. However, acquiring a disability or illness designation can itself seem like a departure from a previously confusing or deadly way of being and can move a person into a more manageable place. Life-affirming, death-defying, and all that lies between, there is movement *in* disability identity, and diagnosis is part of this.

It is this movement that the chapters collected in this part narrate, describe, and theorize, and there is a unique focus on how we can and do move with diagnosis. Unlike approaches that treat diagnosis as that which arises from correct medical and social knowledge (*gnosis*) of symptoms, *diagnosis* in this part is narrated as a complicated form of interpretation that organizes some aspects of life into a set of signs that are treated as symptoms and given a label. Such labels serve not only as a description but also as an evaluation and prediction. In these ways, a diagnosis can serve like a handle that helps a person acknowledge a change, or it can be less like a handle and more like a harsh verdict suggesting that a person is not worthy of life, as when diagnosis is used to push people off a COVID-19 triage protocol or used to place people on a list for consideration for Medically Assisted Death (MAiD). Through describing processes of medical labelling, the following chapters reveal diagnosis to be a political and cultural process involved in the management of life and death. The ways in which we acquire labels and how they are used in our lives as disabled and/or ill people have much to do with how diagnosis is tied to the dis/appearance of disability.

"The redefinition of the problem of disability puts in question the whole body of research that concentrates on the biological classification of disability and the elimination of the biological condition. It also questions quality-of-life and service research premised on assumptions that bettering service systems will result in ameliorating the condition and the individual effects of disability. In this new framework, eliminating social and physical barriers that create handicaps and promoting social well-being are priorities.... This body of research challenges the position of the dominant positivist research as the only valid and legitimate source of knowledge about disadvantage resulting from disability. It also debunks the illusion that ideas and attitudes alone cause disadvantage and discrimination."

Rioux, Marcia H., and Michael Bach. *Disability Is Not Measles: New Research Paradigms in Disability.* North York, ON: Roeher Institute, 1994, p. 5.

In this part, "The Impositions of Forgotten Wor(l)ds: Rehabilitation and Memory Loss" begins with Lindsay Gravelle discussing her experiences in a rehabilitation facility. Gravelle discusses the processes of medicalization and the dis/appearances of disability throughout the rehabilitation process, reflecting on her experience of acquiring a head injury from a bicycle accident. Memory loss is a difficult diagnosis to remember, let alone understand, when in the midst of a brain trauma experience, and repeated stories become part of that with which the diagnosis puts Gravelle in touch.

In "The DisAppearances of Deafness in Early Childhood Diagnostic and Intervention Practices," Tracey Edelist shows how the province of Ontario's infant hearing screening program, aimed at catching early signs of impaired hearing, offers parents, before anything else, an abiding sense that hearing is "natural and normal." Edelist describes the ways that the literature and processes of the infant hearing screening program gives parents and caregivers a way to understand hearing, which can disappear the need for parents to more fully encounter deafness as it appears in their first few months with an infant.

Efrat Gold and Sharry Taylor's chapter, "Diagnosing Despair: Constructing Experience through Psychiatric Hegemony," combines disability studies and mad studies approaches as a way to draw out the implications of the psychiatric industry's control over the diagnosis and definition of "despair." The authors show how an "entrance into a psychiatrically disabled identity" can also be a way that "deep existential questioning and crisis become constituted as outside the range of accepted human experience" and are made to disappear.

"Alberta distinguished itself in Canadian eugenics history as having the longest and most aggressive sexual sterilization policy in the country. Its eugenics program opened with the passage of the Sexual Sterilization Act in 1928, the first such law in Canada.... Recommendations for Alberta's surgeries came from an appointed Eugenics Board and fell into five categories: psychotic patients; mental defectives, which included individuals with arrested mental development for congenital or acquired reasons before the age of eighteen; neurosyphilitic patients who did not respond to treatment; patients with epilepsy, psychosis, or mental deterioration; and individuals with Huntington's Chorea disease."

Dyck, Erika. *Facing Eugenics: Reproduction, Sterilization, and the Politics of Choice.* Toronto, ON: University of Toronto Press, 2014, p. 3.

Writing from a liberatory relation to diagnosis, Joey Tavares' chapter, "An Autist Amongst Exceptionalities," discusses his experiences with autism and medicine and his relations to others, crafting an account of the tensions and contradictions that accompany diagnosis as an adult. What a diagnosis provides; how medical people, parents, friends, and others relate to this diagnosis; and the multiple interpretations of it are all narrated by Tavares. He offers readers an opportunity to encounter the uncertainties of a certain and welcome diagnosis.

Nancy Hansen, in the final chapter of this part, "DisAppearing Disability: Disability MAiD Invisible," provides a critical discussion of the dis/appearance of disability through programs intended to offer medical assistance in dying. Hansen discusses how the space and place of disabled people is often tenuous and how disability has been defined and diagnosed as "social death" (Finkelstein, 2001). Hansen's chapter asks: Where does that leave those of us with non-conformist minds and bodies when fear of difference regularly frames disability as problematic, tragic, suffering, courageous, brave, and inspirational? Together these chapters demonstrate the intimate connection between the meaning of a diagnosis and the cultural assumptions that construct everyday conceptions of disability and illness. Disability studies and mad studies suggest that we can encounter these connections and question whether we might live them better, or in more just ways. The poem "The Pill Box Shuffle," by Leanne Toshiko Simpson, concludes this part, leading us to re-encounter how we know ourselves through what we and others perceive us to be.

"Despite the fact that the popularization of PTSD has resulted in greater awareness of the long-term harm of violence against women and children, the diagnosis itself turns the aftermath of the violence into a disorder and turns the violence itself into nothing but a preceding event. As such, it individualizes and pathologizes women's and children's expectable response to violence."

Burstow, Bonnie. "A Critique of Posttraumatic Stress Disorder and the DSM." *The Journal of Humanistic Psychology* 45, no. 4 (2005): 429–445; p. 443.

Guiding Questions

1. What are your memories of diagnosis? What is the relation between your experiences of diagnosis that signify a departure from what you expected?
2. How is disability experience both a departure and a beginning?
3. Drawing upon your embodied experiences, are there moments you would describe when a departure became a beginning, or where leaving became an arrival? Was there anything surprising about this experience?
4. How do official responses to disability orient a sense of what is possible?
5. How do diagnoses or other people's responses to disability influence the ways in which a person might experience becoming disabled?

REFERENCE

Finkelstein, V. (2001, February 7). *A personal journey into disability politics.* Leeds University Centre for Disability Studies. https://disability-studies.leeds.ac.uk/wp-content/uploads/sites/40/library/finkelstein-presentn.pdf

CHAPTER 14

The Impositions of Forgotten Wor(l)ds: Rehabilitation and Memory Loss

Lindsay Gravelle

Key Terms: Accident; Hospitalization; Memory; Nomadic Subjectivity; Occupational Therapy; Rehabilitation; Self-Understanding

> There is little I can tell you about Aglaura beyond the things its own inhabitants have always repeated: an array of proverbial virtues, of equally proverbial faults, a few eccentricities, some punctilious regard for rules ... at certain hours, in certain places along the street, you see opening before you the hint of something unmistakable, rare, perhaps magnificent; you would like to say what it is, but everything previously said ... imprisons your words and obliges you to repeat rather than say. Therefore, the inhabitants still believe they live in an Aglaura which grows only with the name Aglaura and they do not notice the Aglaura that grows on the ground. And even I, who would like to keep the two cities distinct in my memory, can speak only of the one, because the recollection of the other, in the lack of words to fix it, has been lost.
> —Calvino, *Invisible Cities*

On November 18, 2015, at around 3:00 p.m., I was riding my bicycle when my wheel caught in the streetcar track. According to the hospital record:

> She was witnessed by a bystander to have fallen on the side and hit her head. There was a brief episode lasting approximately one–two minutes of loss of consciousness according to the bystander and some convulsion type movement that was suspicious for a seizure. [Later,] she had trouble verbalizing but was following commands.... There was a laceration over her right eyebrow.... The CT scan revealed a traumatic subarachnoid haemorrhage and small intraparenchymal bleed with no mass effect. (St. Michael's Hospital, 2015)

My short-term memory disappeared in a tangle of bicycle, streetcar tracks, a trau-matic brain injury, an emergency room, and weeks of clinical assessment. From the moments leading up to the accident until one week after I have no recollection of having existed; *I* disappeared. In the hospital I couldn't remember what had happened and where I was. Nurses would try to situate me by pointing out my surroundings, trying to remind me of my accident, but I just couldn't remember to understand. I was missing my orientation points—the details that could narrate my place in the world. The hospital records state that my information process-ing was delayed: "decreased recall of new information, difficulty recalling injuries sustained during accident. Scores two/four on four-word recall." Something quite significant had happened to me, yet even now I don't recall it happening at all. I slowly began to remember again in rehabilitation, yet parts of my story will always be made up not of what I know to be my experience but of stories of me by others. I will explore this experience with short-term memory loss for what it made of me and what it revealed about everything else. Though grateful for the medical care that picked me up from that bike lane and nursed me through the worst of this accident, I am simply wondering what could be if other stories and other ways of being were invited in to complement or challenge the monologues of medicaliza-tion and rehabilitation.

These monologues shape how disability is conceived and understood even out-side of medical institutions. Titchkosky (2000) determines that "the most authori-tative representations of disabled persons arise from medical and/or therapeutic disciplines, and the social sciences" and that they have the resources, the power, and the authority to ideologically construct cultural understandings of disabil-ity that override the thoughts and opinions of the people they speak for and of (p. 198). After the accident I lost my chance to advocate for myself. Professionals stepped in to monitor and treat not only the biological consequences of my acci-dent but my very thoughts and actions. By taking away an individual's right to be themselves, others are given the reins to define and predict the lives of those living with this disability. According to Zola (1977), a medicalized society will use the metaphors of "health" and "illness" to explain a host of social problems. It locates the individual as the source of trouble as well as the place of treatment, making the origin of the trouble asocial and impersonal (Zola, 1977, p. 62). By understand-ing memory impairment as "illness," treating the individual and their material environment is presented as the best and only solution, leaving out the ways that pathology and catalogued difference carries lasting stigma in a society and culture that hungers for normalcy.

"Telling and listening to stories about the bearing of witness to suffering suggested that hospitals as institutions are filled with multiple plotlines beyond that of biomedicine. The use of the arts revealed the palimpsest of inscribed affective lines as these traversed and blurred normative binary categories such as public and private within the institution. Meeting within the space of a hospital, a place where encounters are mediated via hierarchies and protocols, the arts emerged as affectively, ontologically, corporeally, and epistemologically significant."

Davis Halifax, Nancy Viva, and Gail J. Mitchell. "(Nurse)—Writing with the Wolves." *Qualitative Inquiry* 19, no. 5 (2013): 349–352; pp. 350–351.

REHABILITATION IN PRACTICE

After my bike accident I became just such a problem in need of a solution, so I was moved into a rehabilitation program. In an effort to adjust my functionality in relation to a world that does not cope well with disability, I was assured that this specialized environment was necessary for treatment. Professionals were granted permission to remedy and sort out not only my healing body but my behaviour and my perception, affirming their prescription of what is good and right for me and for society at large. Much of this story was already written before I even began to play a part. I became a passive subject in rehabilitation. I was given a private room in a state-of-the-art facility full of amenities for health and wellness, but I couldn't leave the hospital grounds on my own. Despite being incredibly fortunate to receive the care that I did by a publicly funded health care system, this was my fate whether I wanted it or not, and at the time all I wanted was to go home. A team of specialists was introduced when I arrived at the new hospital: one occupational therapist, one speech therapist, a few nurses, and an overseeing neurologist. I was to spend weeks in their embrace, locked in an emotional dance in this modern medical palace, deprived of my community, and thrown into a world of "banal courtesies that characterize the interpersonal commerce of the customary face-to-face of disability and nondisability" (Michalko, 2002, p. 101). This team of specialists would use pathology to reintegrate their monologue back into my confused dialogue. I, the victim, was laid out at their service, ready to be saved, with no hope of healing and recovering on my own.

In *their* story, memory impairment can only be a tragedy, an unbearable "illness" (unclear as to who it was more unbearable for). As Stiker (1999) observed, "the majority of people affected by the consequences of illness or accident adhere without hesitation to the idea of rehabilitation and, as a result, to that of the empirical normality of the social state of things" (p. 144). Like the rehabilitative staff, I was wrapped up in erasing memory loss, in becoming who I was before the accident (unchanged by circumstance), as if the self is ever anything but ever-changing and always becoming. Being memoryless only had value so long as it could be cured or fit back in to cure a common sense understanding of reality. These medical practitioners and therapeutic professionals were there to help, and we were all convinced that they were the only ones who could. Zola (1977) states that "a web of political, economic, and even social psychological forces supports this system, and only with awareness can the dismantling begin" (p. 66). The health care workers who were assigned to manage my recovery were courteous and kind, and it was difficult to understand these methods as anything but. But this quest to uncover the person I had been before the accident ignored me as I was then and anything positive that I could become as a result. My changed and changing perception only mattered as a thing-to-work-on, so I was locked into their world and offered rehabilitative solutions to put me back in place. Haunted by phantoms of my past self and by things I could no longer do, there were few conceptions of me as the person I had or could become.

Rehabilitation depends on binary thinking to classify behaviours and bodies as "natural" or as dysfunctional. My self was made up of an optimal past and a dysfunctional present, and these were classified as distinct states, as if they could be handled, searched for, and traded in. After my brain began to heal, it was rare that I noticed that I was forgetting, as time and narrative began to weave together again. I rarely felt as though my memory wasn't working as it could or should, yet I had to stay and take tests that simulated, in a decontextualized environment, things that made my disability appear—a harsh reminder of how unwelcome disorder is in a world of order. The therapists invited themselves into my mind, calling on an imagined figure that they'd never met (my past, functioning self) in order to monitor my dysfunction in the hopes that my past would catch up with me. At no point was having an impaired memory ever considered to be a valid state of being, to be explored and learned from rather than suppressed and made to fit in where it doesn't belong. It was constantly called to appear and disciplined for appearing. Their tests were looking for the symptoms of a problem that is predetermined to appear in certain ways, decontextualized, making it easier for professional management.

In occupational therapy the task was to test my memory to determine my functionality in the "real" world. For example, I was brought into a room for one of our scheduled meetings. It was a stark room with cupboards along one wall and a bunch of chairs randomly assorted around a few tables pushed together in the centre. The occupational therapist sat me down and told me to watch and then copy everything that she was about to do, just as she'd done. She walked around the room touching doors, chairs, skipping some, and ending by sitting back down beside me. I had to mimic the actions of another to show that I could still copy the world around me. I couldn't. As Stiker (1999) observed, "rehabilitation marks the appearance of a culture that attempts to complete the act of identification, of making identical" (p. 128). This simple memory test would reveal if I was recovered to their satisfaction, while also revealing the importance of imitation and routine for productive citizenship. If I couldn't remember to live the same lives that society is made to live, I would be undesirably different and made redundant.

In my speech and language assessments I had to read short texts about mundane events with generic characters in order to answer questions in summary. I completed the tasks but was told I took too long. I wasn't reading like I should and once had (as if they had known), despite feeling like I had read just fine. These "failures" only appeared when someone else told me that I hadn't performed as a reader should. I could still summarize; I just did it differently than what was predetermined to be right. This task was not meant to reward my efforts; it was a test to determine how effectively I could demonstrate their already decided upon conception of memory and reading. As Titchkosky (2008) suggests, "having reading trouble may have far more to teach us about what a community values than it does about individual skill acquisition" (p. 340). Many differences are devalued even before they're called to appear and before tests were created to show what they cannot do. The therapeutic memories I do have from my time in rehabilitation are all tied to exploring, to overriding the emotional pain and confusion of being monitored and tested. By critically perceiving, interpreting, and rewriting what I read in the world, I was bypassing the need to repeat the words that write the world and trap us all in their production. But this didn't grant me my freedom, and nobody asked for my opinion.

There is a lot of redundancy in memory, yet even as redundant corrections do little to solve the redundancy of chronic forgetting, rather than dismantling an unforgiving system redundant for all, it is perpetually repeated as the humane treatment medically determined to be the only solution. Even as rehabilitation may ensure biological survival, it in no way guarantees *social* survival. Linhart (2002, as cited in Bauman, 2004) suggests those who are socially excluded "lose not only their jobs, their projects, their orientation points, the confidence of being in control of their lives; they also find themselves stripped of their dignity as workers, of self-esteem, of the feeling of being useful and having a social place of their own" (p. 13). The tests I had to take in therapy were assessing how successful I would be—or others could be—at correcting *me* in order to fit in. The solution was to make this dis/ability dis/appear instead of adapting a system that is a little bit more forgiving for nomadic minds. Those with memory impairment will always need support to understand what is taken for granted as obvious—a great burden in a world gripped by prosperity and independence. My rehabilitative tests marked me as a failure, set to be a burden, slowly eroding any hope. If rehabilitation is unsuccessful, social survival is forever marked by these impressions left behind.

> "The continued struggle to fight for small accommodations for students also ensures that perhaps we are now in the era of people with disabilities fighting to get the chance to study at all. Educators must recognize both the long history of exclusion and experimentation upon people with disabilities, as well as the more recent history of academic ableism experienced by disabled students."
>
> Dolmage, Jay T. *Academic Ableism: Disability and Higher Education.* Ann Arbor, MI: University of Michigan Press, 2017, p. 20.

NORMALCY IN REHABILITATION

Short-term memory loss leads the subject always outside of an enforced conception of reality. The dominant response (the cure) is to redundantly pull the memoryless out of their world to fit them back into a reality that no longer exists for them. One interpretation of reality is right and the other, wrong. It is socially acceptable to tell *some* people that what they see and what they know isn't real, that they're missing something, might always miss something, and cannot live without what they're missing. Enforcing these rules merely casts away perceptions lost within this socially constructed order, endorsing a typically unquestioned normalcy as if it should be obvious. It traps everyone in a world of our own construction like in Calvino's (1974) Aglaura, stuck in "an array of proverbial virtues, of equally proverbial faults, a few eccentricities, [and] some punctilious regard for rules" (p. 67). Rather than embracing life's diversity and changeability and recognizing the different worlds we all inhabit, medical rehabilitation serves to privilege normalcy and maintain the status quo. Titchkosky and Michalko (2009) discuss how "disability brings normalcy into view and allows for the possibility of wondering how normalcy came about or how it was constructed in the first place" (p. 6). When the cultural consensus is that the centre—the norm—is the only life worth living, disability or marginality become tragic, uninhabitable, and no place worth being (Titchkosky & Michalko, 2009). The appearance of short-term memory loss at the age of 27 disrupts the myth of youth and the "natural" progress of life, age, and memory. It carries such a strong stigma and is so culturally undesirable that it elicits fear in almost everyone it touches. Accompanied by the spectre of mortality, it is a looming threat to anyone involved. Despite the prevalence of memory impairment and age-related cognitive decline, most would rather run from its existence than explore and accept the lessons we may find in the forgetting. If I hadn't recovered my memory, I would have haunted everyone wishing for "normal" and "natural" lives, and this would have forever shaped the ways that I was treated by others: a tragic figure that would be at the beck and call of a "common sense" world. I caught a glimpse into a world that many people with memory impairment live every day, and I will never forget how it felt to have others expect only memory (repeated stories) when the narrative has gotten away.

Common sense is made by memory, a story echoed in repetition because it is able. By default, memory is expected to define everyone's interactions with and sensations of the world; it repeats the stories that make us all. What this shows us is that the world that we inhabit has very little to do with the present and much more to do with mutually agreed upon truths and preconceptions. The stories surging through our senses are predetermined and enforced by the monologues of education, medicalization, and nation, casting out those that cannot assimilate. If society and culture thrive and live in memory, where do those who lose access to their memories live? With memory loss, there is no sorting out the stories; there is just a void and life lived in the moment, for the moment. Letting go of the rules that confine how we build and understand place and identity frees up new ways of imagining living with and healing with memory loss. If we don't begin this work somewhere, having memory impairment will forever be something we'd all rather hope to forget. Perhaps it's as simple as looking forward rather than back. Or refusing to analyze the minds of others in order to tell them that their minds aren't enough, that they don't have what it takes to piece together *their* environment and to understand *their* place. Or simply to tell them that this place is certainly a place worth being.

"Later, I don't want this to be a record of grieving only. I don't want this to be a record only of tears…. My work is to inhabit the silences with which I have lived and fill them with myself until they have the sounds of [the] brightest day and the loudest thunder. And then there will be no room left inside of me for what has been except as memory of sweetness enhancing what can and is to be."

Lorde, Audre. *The Cancer Journals*. Argyle, NY: Aunt Lute Books, 1980, p. 40.

LEARNING FROM THE MARGINS OF MEMORY

If medicalized rehabilitation and this enforced response to impairment aren't the best or only ways to deal with this disorder, what else can be done? Although beneficial to some, this approach to rehabilitation is deemed universal at the expense of other culturally or spiritually relevant conceptions of life, rehabilitation, and recovery. Dian Million (2013) uncovers how many rehabilitative strategies are bound by capitalist realities that "produce a particular kind of knowledge, a certain kind of individual, one that works to continuously manage one's own emotional and mental hygiene" (p. 150). As my experience exemplifies, medical rehabilitation depends on the individual identifying their own errors so that they may clean up or atone for any lingering distortions in order to present a manageable self, a clean and productive body modelled from a fictitious, universal subject. Imagining differently, Million (2013) asks: "What would our governances be if they already assumed that all life, all life's 'vibrant matter,' rather than such an impossible universal subject, formed their primary responsibility?" (p. 179).

Thinking of the ways that all identities are made in relation to each other through feelings, experiences, and perceptions reveals how powerful the act of imagining and acting on these imaginations can be. From an Indigenous feminist perspective, Million (2013) writes: "The nurturing inclusiveness that is often modelled as an ideal in kinship teaches us that we form one another and create social and spiritual relations that we extend and that are extended to us in radiating bursts of affective interrelations that also include nonhuman relations" (p. 180). The ways in which we respond to others and our environment are the building blocks for the worlds that we inhabit. Simply rehabilitating the disordered body and changing the material environment does not address the social and cultural reality that would rather see dis/ability dis/appear. Rosi Braidotti's (1994) nomadic subjectivity offers another way to rethink life with memory loss. Understanding that the subject is always *becoming* rather than *being* offers a new way of understanding self and identity that is free from socially coded modes of thought and behaviour. This nomadism opens up "a creative sort of becoming ... that allows for otherwise unlikely encounters and unsuspected sources of interaction of experience and of knowledge" (Braidotti, 1994, p. 6). Nomadic subjects *live* in their body, set free from the trappings of the words and stories that define our worlds and identities. If everyone were to meet in this nomadic place, ready to *feel* rather than *correct* when faced with the disorder of memory loss, such beautiful lessons could be learned. By embracing the present, perhaps everyone can learn a little bit more about themselves and the world around them.

> "A rhizome has no beginning or end; it is always in the middle, between things, interbeing, *intermezzo*.... The middle is by no means an average; on the contrary, it is where things pick up speed. Between things does not designate a localizable relation going from one thing to the other and back again, but a perpendicular direction, a transversal movement that sweeps one and the other away, a stream without beginning or end that undermines its banks and picks up speed in the middle."
>
> Deleuze, Gilles, and Felix Guattari. *A Thousand Plateaus*. Minneapolis, MN: University of Minnesota Press, 1987, p. 25.

CONCLUSION

Returning to Calvino (1974), "nothing said of Aglaura is true, and yet these accounts create a solid and compact image of a city, whereas the haphazard opinions which might be inferred from living there have less substance" (p. 67). Those experiencing memory loss are often called out of their minds, their perceptions deemed insubstantial, forced back into the fictitious yet solid image of a world built of ever-repeated stories. It is a cruel fate to imprison those who cannot remember to know the narrative, obliging them to repeat rather than say. The imposition of forgotten wor(l)ds rejects nomadic selves in the here and now. Perhaps it is time to begin valuing and noticing the rare and magnificent moments that cannot or need not be trapped in memory but enjoyed for having happened at all. The power of rehabilitation and medicalization to manage and control the social norm is extensive because it appears in everyone repeating the words that write our worlds. These worlds that are brought into being are built to silence difference and cast deviance to the margins. They are meant to disable so that common sense can be enforced at all costs (often at the cost of those that do not/cannot fall in line). As long as binaries are defined and deviance and difference are set for optimization and assimilation against an incorporeal ideal body, nobody will ever be free to imagine new ways of reading the world. I hope for a shift away from prescribed worlds toward an affective, embodied space produced by those who cannot repeat the wor(l)ds they inhabit yet who live in the world that grows on the ground.

REFERENCES

Bauman, Z. (2004). *Wasted lives: Modernity and its outcasts.* Polity Press.

Braidotti, R. (1994). *Nomadic subjects: Embodiment and sexual difference in contemporary feminist theory.* Columbia University Press.

Calvino, I. (1974). *Invisible cities* (W. Weaver, Trans.). Harcourt Brace & Company. (Original work published 1972)

Michalko, R. (2002). *The difference that disability makes.* Temple University Press.

Million, D. (2013). *Therapeutic nations: Healing in an age of Indigenous human rights.* University of Arizona Press.

St. Michael's Hospital. (2015). *Surgery discharge summary* [Lindsay Gravelle]. Toronto.

Stiker, H.-J. (1999). *A history of disability.* University of Michigan Press.

Titchkosky, T. (2000). Disability studies: The old and the new. *The Canadian Journal of Sociology, 25*(2), 197–224. https://doi.org/10.2307/3341823

Titchkosky, T. (2008). "I got trouble with my reading": An emerging literacy. In S. Gabel (Ed.), *Disability and the politics of education: An international reader* (pp. 337–352). Peter Lang.

Titchkosky, T., & Michalko, R. (2009). Introduction. In T. Titchkosky & R. Michalko (Eds.), *Rethinking normalcy: A disability studies reader* (pp. 1–14). Canadian Scholars' Press.

Zola, I. (1977). Healthism and disabling medicalization. In I. Illich, I. K. Zola, J. McKnight, J. Caplan, & H. Shaiken (Eds.), *Disabling professions* (pp. 41–68). Marion Boyars Publishers.

CHAPTER 15

The DisAppearances of Deafness in Early Childhood Diagnostic and Intervention Practices

Tracey Edelist

Key Terms: Deaf Children; Early Hearing Detection and Intervention; Hearing Screening; Parental Worry; UNHS

INTRODUCTION

In this chapter, I examine how deafness appears and disappears in the policies and practices of Ontario's Infant Hearing Program (IHP). The IHP's mandate is to provide hearing screenings to all newborns in Ontario in order to identify babies who are or will be deaf or hard of hearing from birth or in early childhood and to provide identified infants and their families supports and services until school-age (Ontario Ministry of Health and Long-Term Care, 2002). Although the IHP's purpose is to "find" deafness, a critical interpretive analysis of IHP documents and interviews with parents of deaf and hard of hearing children who have accessed IHP services[1] demonstrates that any mention of deafness is often absent during the hearing screening process. If deafness appears after audiological assessment, the IHP works to make it disappear by supporting hearing technologies and spoken language. I frame my analysis around Judith Butler's (1993) idea that to know how something is significant, in this case deafness and its dis/appearances, we must examine how and why it matters, both as "meaning" and "materialization" (p. 32). Informed by a post-structural approach within disability studies, I examine how deafness is being made to dis/appear, from whom it is being made to dis/appear, and the cultural interpretations of deafness, disability, and language in all these dis/appearances throughout the screening and diagnostic process. How deafness matters to the IHP and parents has consequences for how deaf children access communication and language, their educational experiences and opportunities, and how they come to understand themselves in the world.

Most parents in Ontario experience the IHP's universal newborn hearing screening (UNHS) process and are presented with dis/appearances of deafness whether or not their infant becomes identified as such. As of 2019, Ontario's IHP had nearly reached its goal of screening at least 95 per cent of babies born in Ontario (Canadian Infant Hearing Task Force, 2019a; Canadian Working Group of Childhood Hearing, 2005), having screened over 130,000 babies each year since 2006–2007 (Ontario Ministry of Children and Youth Services, 2017). Although UNHS is a routine part of the birth experience for new parents in Ontario, there is inequitable access to services depending on geographic location, particularly affecting Indigenous communities in Northern Ontario.[2] As UNHS is widespread throughout the province, the IHP has a significant role in distributing meanings of deafness to parents, while minimal access to services encountered by Indigenous parents should raise concern regarding how Indigenous infants "disappear" from the IHP's radar.

Inequitable early hearing detection and intervention service delivery also occurs across Canada, as a few provinces and territories do not have fully developed programs (Canadian Infant Hearing Task Force, 2019b). UNHS is common in the Global North, and the World Health Organization promotes UNHS as a strategy to prevent and care for hearing loss in children worldwide (World Health Organization, 2016). Becoming aware of how deafness is made to matter with UNHS is important, as the meanings of deafness distributed by this widespread program have a significant role in determining the life chances of deaf children.

"Our agitation about the 'individual' and 'social' models of disability, etc., is not merely an internal discussion about the way 'disability' is understood and interventions arranged but an argument about the nature of all human beings—the essentials of being 'human.' That the discussion about models of disability has been isolated from non-disabled people is a reflection of just how disabling the boundaries of 'normal' knowledge have become.... Able-bodied people have deposited their own natural 'vulnerability' and genuine social dependency, into us [disabled people] as if this was unique to being disabled. Our 'vulnerability' is then seen as an attribute that separates us from the essentially normal—we are not quite human (the 'social death' model of disability, Finkelstein, 1991). This transference of vulnerability and consequence dependency into disabled people has not freed able-bodied people from their own dependency upon support systems to ameliorate their essential vulnerability but created a dangerous illusion about the meaning of 'normality.'"

Finkelstein, Vic. "Emancipating Disability Studies." In *The Disability Reader: Social Science Perspectives*, edited by Tom Shakespeare, 28–52. London, UK: Cassell, 1998, p. 30.

THE DIS/APPEARANCE OF DEAFNESS DURING SCREENING

For most infants born in Ontario, hearing screening happens within hours or days of birth. The possibility of deafness first appears to parents with the IHP screener's arrival and explanation of the screening test. Screeners undergo training to learn how to test using "a standardized approach" (Ontario Ministry of Children and Youth Services, 2013). In the training video "Communicating with Parents: Sample Scripts for Each Pamphlet," an actor-screener demonstrates what to tell parents about the hearing screening, how to obtain consent, how to share the infant's screening result, and how to give parents an information pamphlet about that result (Sinai Health System, 2012). My analysis includes this video as well as IHP pamphlets available online from 2014 to 2019, which have since been replaced with shorter documents. As these previous pamphlets provide insight into how the IHP has historically made deafness and language meaningful, as well as provide information consistent with the experiences of parents I interviewed, they remain important texts for analysis. The verbal and written information the screener provides to parents establishes meanings of hearing, communication, and language, which leads to dis/appearances of deafness while informing and regulating parental and professional action.

Deafness is made to matter both in textual interpretations of deafness and language and in the physical materialization of an identified "hearing loss."[3] As Judith Butler (1993) theorizes, "To know the significance of something is to know how and why it matters, where 'to matter' means at once 'to materialize' and 'to mean'" (p. 32). From the beginning of the screening process, deafness is made to matter through text as a loss and a problem (where "to matter" means "to mean") and in finding the few infants whose ears do not pass the test (where "to matter" means "to materialize") (Butler, 1993, p. 32). How the IHP makes deafness and language matter to parents, through text and with the materialization of hearing loss, reveals cultural interpretations of deafness amidst its own dis/appearances. Although deafness and accompanying developmental concerns appear as the reason behind screening, deafness disappears during screening either as something not of concern to parents whose infants "pass" or as an unexpected outcome of a "refer" result.

How Deafness Dis/Appears with a Pass Result

For babies who "pass" the hearing screening, hearing loss is presented as an irrelevant problem to their parents: "We got a pass result which means both ears are great. I'm going to give you a copy and a pamphlet, it just says everything is OK" (Sinai Health System, 2012). The possibility of deafness raised with screening disappears with the finding that "both ears are great," while babies who do not pass the screening are assumed to be not "OK." However, this disappearance is temporary as the possibility of deafness appears in the pamphlet: "Your baby has passed the newborn hearing screening." The pamphlet informs parents that although their baby "passed," the potential for hearing loss remains an ongoing concern (a problem that could materialize): "He or she is able to hear in both ears *at this time*" (Ontario Ministry of Children and Youth Services, 2014a, italics added).

The pamphlet also provides a checklist of speech and language milestones for parents to compare their infant's development with established norms, presenting hearing loss as a potential problem to future development: "A few babies may develop hearing loss as they grow older, so it is important to pay close attention to your baby's development. … Delayed language development can lead to behaviour and emotional problems and later to problems in school" (Ontario Ministry of Children and Youth Services, 2014a). Although not made to matter through the materialization of potential hearing loss, deafness is made to matter through text as a concern requiring monitoring and action if development veers away from "normal" expectations. Even within its absence, the possibility of deafness is a presence that may eventually materialize, attached to concern over negative consequences for child development.

This concern over the potential presence of deafness is stated more urgently for babies who "pass at-risk." "At-risk" babies include babies who spent over 48 hours in the Neonatal Intensive Care Unit (NICU) (Ontario Ministry of Health and Long-Term Care, 2001) and babies identified through detecting cytomegalovirus infections and genetic causes of deafness through a "risk factor screen" (Ontario Ministry of Children, Community and Social Services, 2020). Using "risk" to describe the potential of hearing loss presents it as a dangerous medical problem, and the child-at-risk "comes to represent the potential for loss" (McGuire, 2016, p. 131). The pamphlet "Your baby has passed the screening but is at risk" outlines those risk concerns as relating to language, behaviour, emotional health, and school success.

The "small chance that a hearing loss may develop over time" (Ontario Ministry of Children and Youth Services, 2014b) makes deafness ever present as a "risk" that can be mitigated by finding hearing loss early and accessing spoken language services immediately. The materialization of hearing loss is made to matter as something to be feared and something to be fixed. The desire for absence (made possible by early intervention) accompanying a deaf presence manages how parents access services for their baby, while maintaining negative conceptions of hearing loss as a risk worthy of concern.

How Deafness Dis/Appears with a Refer Result

When the outcome of hearing screening is a "refer" result, deafness appears as a possibility, but one that is made to quickly disappear amongst discourse of its un-expectedness and unlikelihood, in an effort to decrease parental anxiety. Screeners are scripted to tell parents, "We didn't get a pass today ... it doesn't mean there's a hearing loss," and to follow up with a second screening in a couple of weeks to allow fluid or debris in the ear to clear "so we can have a better chance of passing" (Sinai Health System, 2012). Presenting a "pass" result as the goal of screening discounts *any* possibility of deafness, making hearing loss an unthinkable prob-lem, while assuming a deaf diagnosis would and should be worrisome.

Parents of infants who obtain a second refer result, or who go right to audiol-ogy assessment, continue to receive messaging that deafness is unlikely. How-ever, parents are introduced to the possibility of hearing loss when their infant is referred for audiological assessment: "Most babies are found to have normal hearing. If your baby does have a hearing loss, the audiologist will direct you to the services and supports that are available to help you and your child" (Ontario Ministry of Children and Youth Services, 2014c). Hearing loss appears as an anomaly and only in reference to professional IHP services that may assist in normalization.

How the possibility of deafness briefly appears then disappears with a refer re-sult is also evident in the recollections of parents I interviewed. All the parents told me that the screener reassured them a refer result did not mean their child had hear-ing loss. For example, Rebecca[4] recalled the NICU nurse telling her, "I wouldn't worry about it; a lot of kids fail their newborn screening test, and it's not a big deal; they have embryonic fluid in their ear." When Angela's daughter did not pass her screening, the screener told her that there may have been a technical problem with the machine. Similarly, Heather recalled the screener being surprised at the refer result and repeating the test to ensure accuracy. Because of such assurances, Melissa felt unprepared for the outcome of her daughter's audiology assessment: "They just kind of tell you, 'Yeah, it's pretty common, it's usually fluid, don't worry about it.' So, we honestly didn't. I thought, 'Oh yeah, it's fluid, not a big deal' ... There was no thought in our mind[s] that she couldn't hear us." Likewise, Angela recalled, "They never really brought up the potential that, hey, this could be hearing loss."

Although identifying deafness in infancy is the IHP's primary purpose, pre-senting the possibility of hearing loss as an unthinkable, unwanted outcome of screening makes deafness appear only as an excludable type. As Titchkosky (2007) explains, "A deep provocation lies in the fact that the very ways that disability is included in everyday life are, also, part of that which structures the continued manifestation of disabled people as a non-viable type. It is, for example, provocative to think about how disability is both excluded and included simultaneously in the interstices of our lives, or included as an excludable type" (p. 5). The IHP presents the very condition that makes screening necessary as an inconceivable outcome, making deafness disappear even within a program whose purpose is to identify it.

> "If cure is a crossing from a category of otherness to that of normality, what enables that crossing? What marks the completed crossing to normality, when disability involves bodily, social, and environmental interactions and the histories that bodies carry? Cure appears as an attempt at crossing that can reveal the multiplicity of the boundaries that divide 'human' and 'inhuman' as well as 'life' and 'nonlife.'"
>
> Kim, Eunjung. *Curative Violence: Rehabilitating Disability, Gender and Sexuality in Modern Korea.* Durham, NC: Duke University Press, 2017, p. 11.

THE DIS/APPEARANCE OF DEAFNESS DURING DIAGNOSIS

The appearance of hearing loss as an excludable type throughout the screening process leads to parents being unprepared for their child's diagnosis. Parents reported being shocked with the diagnostic outcome, as during screening they had been led to believe (and wanted to believe) their child had normal hearing. Although the IHP intended to prevent parental worry during screening, these parents reported high levels of stress and anxiety when presented with an unexpected diagnosis. Deafness mattered to parents at diagnosis amidst meanings of deafness as an unwanted problem that should not have appeared.

Parents recalled understanding their child's diagnosis as something wrong, an abnormal, unfortunate, unwanted outcome, consistent with the IHP's presentation of deafness throughout screening. For example, Rebecca was not concerned about her son's hearing since she had been told there are many false positive results, and he had more pressing health issues: "We had a lot of other things to worry about, and we weren't concerned about his hearing, when apparently we should have been. So, getting that kind of misinformation and then having the audiologist tell me, 'No, this is a big deal,' I was in a little shock at that point, because I thought all the bad news we're going to get we've gotten, so we're dealing with that; but to get another 'No, this is not good,' it was like, 'Oh shit, here we go again.'" Melissa recalled being surprised and distraught upon learning of Beckie's diagnosis of permanent profound hearing loss. The audiologist responded by telling her about technology options, and Beckie's "still going to be fine." Priya shared the difficulty she and her husband had accepting her son's deaf diagnosis; they did not tell their friends until his cochlear implants were activated at one year of age. Heather recalled Wyatt's diagnostic audiology appointment being one of her most stressful times.

Parents' recollections of the materialization of deafness at diagnosis show how the disappearance of deafness as an unthinkable outcome throughout screening hindered their ability to accept the diagnosis as anything other than a tragic problem. Their stories also demonstrate how the IHP's message changed at diagnosis from the unlikelihood of deafness appearing to what could be done to help it disappear, also evident in the pamphlet "Your baby's hearing: Does your child have a hearing loss?" (Ontario Ministry of Children and Youth Services, 2014d). The section "Why is it important to identify a child's hearing loss so soon after birth?" shows how the IHP organizes hearing in terms of absence and presence.

The pamphlet presents the absence of hearing as the only factor affecting communication, making visual communication (e.g., sign language) irrelevant: "Most babies are born ready to hear their parents' voices and the sounds of the world around them. Babies with hearing loss have the same need to communicate as babies with normal hearing" (Ontario Ministry of Children and Youth Services, 2014d). These two sentences formulate the necessity of hearing for communication. The pamphlet makes hearing necessary for a baby to be ready to communicate, placing responsibility on the baby who was not "born ready" to "become ready" by conforming to hearing society's norms. What if, instead, hearing society was responsible for becoming ready to communicate in ways meaningful to a deaf baby? Putting the onus on society members to adapt communication for a deaf infant would make deafness meaningful as a valued way of being in the world. However, the IHP's ordering of hearing makes parents and infants subjects of the absence of hearing and communication and hence subjects of hearing and communication technologies.

Deafness is also made to disappear at diagnosis in the way the IHP presents information to parents about communication services. The pamphlet explains that deaf infants receive a Communication Development Plan: "Your IHP audiologist, speech-language pathologist and other professionals will provide information to help you make decisions about your child's communication development" (Ontario Ministry of Children and Youth Services, 2014d). Speech and hearing professionals are responsible for informing parents about communication options, revealing another disappearance of deafness: d/Deaf adults are not included as information providers.

Parents experienced these disappearances through the IHP's presentation of spoken language as the preferred communication option, reflective of the vast majority of Ontario parents who choose an exclusive spoken language approach, despite the IHP's option of both sign and spoken language services (Small & Cripps, 2012). For example, most parents I interviewed whose infants were diagnosed with severe to profound deafness were referred to a Cochlear Implant (CI) Program before being told about all communication options. Parents informed me that the possibility of their child learning to listen and speak with CIs eased anxiety over their child's deafness. Once their infant became a CI candidate, parents recalled being told spoken language, and therefore a "normal" life, would be possible. Lauren explained how the CI Program implants children early so that "by the time [they reach] school age, [they] will be the same as all [their] peers in hearing and spoken language. Well, that sounds fantastic as a new parent, doesn't it!" Like Lauren, Angela recalled the CI Program saying of her daughter that "because she's getting implanted so young, the neuroplasticity would be great and within five years she'd be fine." When asked what the CI Program meant by "fine," Angela elaborated: "I think that her spoken language would be fine, her auditory skills would be fine, her language skills would be fine, speech; that she would be well integrated with school and peers five years post-implantation."

These examples show that when a CI becomes possible, the problem of deafness disappears: The child is expected to become like a hearing child, making implantation an unquestionable choice and demonstrating the strong pull of normalcy. Since parents are told their child will hear and speak normally, the need to think about their child as being deaf and to consider sign language disappears, illustrative of Stiker's (1999) claim, "There is no better way to escape the fear of strangeness than by forgetting aberrancy through its dissolution into the social norm" (p. 136). However, the deaf diagnosis does not literally disappear; despite the rhetoric, a CI does not cure deafness. The IHP and CI programs tell parents not to worry about their child's diagnosis because there are interventions: "This worry is abated somewhat since it is thought that medical, rehabilitation, or other forms of professional intervention can make these abnormalities normal or, at least, as normal as possible" (Titchkosky & Michalko, 2009, p. 5). The IHP's effort to decrease parental worry during screening through the disappearance of deafness as unthinkable leads to parental worry at the appearance of deafness.

The IHP then manages this worry by shifting the focus to what can be done to help the child appear "normal."

> "The twinned developments of a system of normalizing knowledge, in which the categories of what was normal and what was not normal were to become increasingly detailed and routinized, and of a wide array of professional bodies authorized to administer the normalizing judgement had profound implications for children with intellectual differences."
>
> Malacrida, Claudia. *A Special Hell: Institutional Life in Alberta's Eugenic Years.* Toronto, ON: University of Toronto Press, 2015, p. 15.

CONCLUSION

Parental worry about the appearance of hearing loss and language delay ensures they will seek the IHP's solution of professional assistance. As Titchkosky (2007) notes: "Ordinarily it is no one's concern that the experience of worrying about embodiment *might be more* than a call for solutions to symptoms of problems" (p. 109), and indeed, the organization of parental worry does more than seek solutions. The IHP has organized worry within a medical model of hearing, speech, and language, producing meanings of hearing loss as problematic risk, while making deafness matter as an unthinkable outcome. The IHP's one positive message that professionals can help children hear and learn language turns deaf children and their families into consumers of normalizing services. There is no possibility presented that families may not want to be normalized, may not be worried about solutions, or that deafness is more than an excludable type.

At diagnosis, the materialization of deafness leads to its disappearance in the way deafness matters as something of concern and a deaf child as someone to be normalized and made to hear: Even in its materialization, deafness is made to matter as something that should be disappeared. In this case, "to matter" not only "means at once 'to materialize' and 'to mean'" (Butler, 1993, p. 32), but in the "meaning" of how deafness matters as a problem to be disappeared there is an attempt to reverse its materialization. The appearance of deafness amidst the possibility of perceived normalcy via CIs makes the need for identification an urgent concern. As Stiker (1999) explains, disabled people are "designated in order to be made to disappear, they are spoken in order to be silenced" (p. 134). The IHP presents identification (the appearance of deafness) as important, although unwanted, only for the possibility of remediation (disappearance) via professional supports and services and the use of hearing technologies.

NOTES

1. Between June and November 2016, for my doctoral research, I interviewed 12 parents of deaf and hard of hearing children, aged one to 10 years, who had used Ontario's IHP services. The University of Toronto Social Sciences, Humanities and Education Research Ethics Board approved this research in December 2015 (protocol reference #32416), renewed in November 2016. This chapter is based on findings discussed in my doctoral dissertation.

2. Although Ontario has an overall high screening rate, areas in Northern Ontario have a low screening rate, with gaps in follow-up services for First Nations newborns born and screened in hospitals but living in remote communities. In addition, there is limited access to IHP supports and services for Indigenous communities in Northern Ontario (CASLPA, 2010).

3. The IHP refers to any deviation from normal hearing as "hearing loss."

4. All names of parents and children are pseudonyms.

REFERENCES

Butler, J. (1993). *Bodies that matter: On the discursive limits of "sex."* Routledge.

Canadian Infant Hearing Task Force. (2019a). *Report card on Canadian early hearing detection and intervention programs: Ontario.* Retrieved January 4, 2021, from www.infanthearingcanada.ca/wp-content/uploads/2019/04/Report_Card_Ontario-2019_EN.pdf

Canadian Infant Hearing Task Force. (2019b). *Report card on early hearing detection and intervention programs.* Retrieved January 4, 2021, from www.infanthearingcanada.ca/wp-content/uploads/2019/04/Report%20Card-2019_FINAL_VERSION_EN.pdf

Canadian Working Group of Childhood Hearing. (2005). *Early hearing and communication development: Canadian working group of childhood hearing resource document.* Minister of Public Works and Government Services Canada.

CASLPA. (2010). *Speech, language and hearing services to First Nations, Inuit and Métis children in Canada, with a focus on children 0 to 6 years of age.* Retrieved January 4, 2021, from www.sac-oac.ca/sites/default/files/resources/Complete%20report%20-%20English.pdf

McGuire, A. (2016). *War on autism: On the cultural logic of normative violence.* University of Michigan Press.

Ontario Ministry of Children and Youth Services. (2013). *Infant Hearing Program: Hearing screening regional trainer training guide.* Government of Ontario.

Ontario Ministry of Children and Youth Services. (2014a). *Your baby has passed the newborn hearing screening* (Publication #019555). Queen's Printer for Ontario. Retrieved January 4, 2021, from www.children.gov.on.ca/htdocs/English/documents/earlychildhood/hearing/passed-screening/Passed-Screening-EN.pdf

Ontario Ministry of Children and Youth Services. (2014b). *Your baby has passed the screening but is at risk* (Publication #019609). Queen's Printer for Ontario. Retrieved January 4, 2021, from www.children.gov.on.ca/htdocs/English/documents/earlychildhood/hearing/at-risk/At-Risk-EN.pdf

Ontario Ministry of Children and Youth Services. (2014c). *Your baby needs a hearing assessment.* (Publication #019573). Queen's Printer for Ontario. Retrieved January 4, 2021, from www.children.gov.on.ca/htdocs/English/documents/earlychildhood/hearing/assessment/Assessment-EN.pdf

Ontario Ministry of Children and Youth Services. (2014d). *Your baby's hearing: Does your child have a hearing loss?* (Publication #018871). Queen's Printer for Ontario. Retrieved January 4, 2021, from www.children.gov.on.ca/htdocs/English/documents/earlychildhood/hearing/hearing/Hearing-EN.pdf

Ontario Ministry of Children and Youth Services. (2017). *Ontario Infant Hearing Program: A guidance document.* Version 2017.01. Marlene Bagatto (Ed.).

Ontario Ministry of Children, Community and Social Services. (2020). *Infant Hearing Program.* Queen's Printer for Ontario. Retrieved January 4, 2021, from www.children.gov.on.ca/htdocs/English/earlychildhood/hearing/index.aspx#results

Ontario Ministry of Health and Long-Term Care. (2001). *Infant Hearing Program: Universal infant hearing screening assessment and communication development: Local implementation support document.*

Ontario Ministry of Health and Long-Term Care. (2002). *Infant Hearing Program: Well-baby (DPOAE) screening protocol and training manual.* Retrieved January 4, 2021, from www.mountsinai.on.ca/care/infant-hearing-program/documents/midwivesprotocol.pdf

Sinai Health System. (2012). *Communicating with parents: Sample scripts for each pamphlet* [Video]. Vimeo. https://vimeo.com/61719338

Small, A., & Cripps, J. (2012). On becoming: Developing an empowering cultural identity framework for deaf youth and adults. In A. Small, J. Cripps, & J. Côté

(Eds.), *Cultural space and self/identity development among deaf youth* (pp. 29–41). Canadian Cultural Society of the Deaf.

Stiker, H.–J. (1999). *A history of disability.* University of Michigan Press.

Titchkosky, T. (2007). *Reading and writing disability differently: The textured life of embodiment.* University of Toronto Press.

Titchkosky, T., & Michalko, R. (Eds.). (2009). *Rethinking normalcy: A disability studies reader.* Canadian Scholars' Press.

World Health Organization. (2016). *Childhood hearing loss: Act now, here's how.* https://apps.who.int/iris/handle/10665/204507

CHAPTER 16

Diagnosing Despair: Constructing Experience through Psychiatric Hegemony

Efrat Gold and Sharry Taylor

Key Terms: Antipsychiatry; Diagnosis; Existentialism; Mad Studies; Medicalized Suffering; Process of Identification

> *There is something which, for lack of a better name, we will call the tragic sense of life, which carries with it a whole conception of life itself and of the universe, a whole philosophy more or less formulated, more or less conscious.... It is useless to speak of ... people who are healthy and people who are not healthy. Apart from the fact that there is no normal standard of health, nobody has proved that the human being is necessarily cheerful by nature.*
> —Miguel de Unamuno, *Tragic sense of life* (translation)[1]

> *Do I believe people have anxiety? Do I believe that people have compulsions? Of course. But I believe these feelings are a normal, human way of experiencing reality.*
> —Bonnie Burstow (quoted in Nick Arnold, "'Mental health is a myth' says anti psychiatrist Bonnie Burstow")

INTRODUCTION

We are writing this chapter against the backdrop of the COVID-19 pandemic, predicted to be the precursor to an upcoming "mental health tsunami" (Roxby, 2020). Indeed, COVID-19 is quickly highlighting the weaknesses of social, political, and economic systems worldwide, forever changing the landscape upon which we can map our meanings. Within the shifting confines of the pandemic, however, another crisis is emerging: the crisis of people's well-being in isolation. This chapter focuses on the appearances and disappearances of despair as it relates to psychiatric diagnoses within a Canadian neoliberal context.

Despair, while difficult to define, can often flow from a loss of faith or hope, where an individual might question the meaning or point of life (Jordan, 2018).[2] This experience can be deeply distressing—both to the individual and to those around them (Burstow, 2015; R, 2020). We argue that through standardizing psychiatric processes, despair, as a deeply personal and existential struggle, disappears only to be reconfigured as a psychiatric diagnosis. Pathologizing despair through psychiatry marks an entrance into a psychiatrically disabled identity, and these diagnoses become the desirable signal legitimizing human suffering. In other words, a diagnostic label becomes the validation of a person's pain through learned techniques of identifying with psychiatric concepts, while processes of deep existential questioning and crisis become constituted as outside the range of accepted human experience. This chapter is an intervention against the psychiatrization of human experiences of pain and despair.

Despite vast differences and approaches within existential philosophies, despair is generally agreed to play a central role as a catalyst for human consciousness. In this sense, despair appears as a uniquely human experience, pushing each of us to question the world, our place within it, and the meaning we can or cannot ascribe to it. While many agree that despair can be an appropriate response to some *event* (i.e., the death of a loved one, a break-up, the loss of a job, etc.), within a contemporary western context, the experience of despair is supposed to last for an *appropriate* period of time and should only present as a response to some *external* occurrence (Barsoum Raymond, 1991). Yet even a person mourning the death of a loved one can be considered "depressed" (American Psychiatric Association [cited as APA], 2013). Beyond this reactive and time-appropriate response, as framed through biological psychiatry,[3] we argue that despair comes to *appear* as pathological and *disappear* as existential struggle/crisis.

But what if we experience despair not as a response to some specific external event but in relation to the realities of ongoing injustice and oppression? Questions of despair can guide us toward developing understandings of ourselves and the world in which we are implicated and embedded. When explored, these questions and crises can help make meaning and imagine social change. In many ways, these are the explorations that allow people to knowingly practice agency, whether that practice fits into dominant social standards or rebels against them. This work explores the idea of rebellious minds in relation to appearances and disappearances of despair within capitalist frameworks of productivity. Becker's (1963) concept of a "deviant career" (pp. 25–26) will be illustrative in terms of elucidating how individuals' claims to distress can be derailed by their identification with a psychiatric label that has been applied to them.

Through the work that follows, we pose the question: What if, through psychiatric diagnoses and treatments, rebellious minds are being commodified through individuals' identification with "psychiatrically disabled" diagnostic categories? Given the current upheaval of global systems and institutions due to COVID-19, we propose that this period of flux can provide a platform upon which contextualized and relational understandings of people's well-being, including appearances of despair, can become animated.

APPEARANCES AND DISAPPEARANCES

Appearances of despair can be deeply troubling—both to ourselves and to those around us. Despair is not a singular story; it is difficult to define in part because there is so much variation in how we experience it, what we experience it in response or relation to, and how we might come to address or resolve it.[4] The point here is less about what constitutes the experience of despair than it is about the role of despair as a catalyst in the human search for meaning and in the impetus for change. In many ways, it can be the experience of hopelessness, loss of faith, and a deep search for meaning that allows each of us to consciously make choices and practice agency. Despair and how a person works through this experience can also deeply impact their insight into their lives and their feelings about themselves and their context. All of this is to say that the role of despair within human experience is of vital importance in guiding our lives and shaping our societies.

Many existential philosophers theorized about ideas of hope, meaning, faith, angst, dread, and despair in the years following WWII in Europe, deeply engaging in questions that were prescient in this era. Addressing many of these same issues through a vastly different lens, this is also the historical time frame during which the *Diagnostic and Statistical Manual of Mental Disorders* (DSM-I; APA, 1952) was first published. Faced with deep, existential questions of meaning, the dominant approach within western society has moved toward the psychiatric rhetoric of "fixing." As can be seen through advertisements for psychiatric drugs, this process has occurred as a gradual shift in meaning-making, where expectations of struggle and suffering in life have come to be challenged by discourses of drug therapies *curing* one's distress. Whether individuals find relief in psychiatric drugs or not, the fact remains that no one has a *solution* to human suffering and questioning of meaning. What disappears through psychiatric identification, then, is not despair itself but the accepted role of despair within human life.

The appearance of psychiatric diagnoses and treatments in response to despair is perhaps the most disturbing appearance addressed in this chapter. Through a process of psychiatrization,[5] an individual becomes enfolded into psychiatric language, ideology, and systems. People who are deeply distressed, questioning who they are or the world they are implicated in, become redefined through psychiatric labels, language, and treatments. When a psychiatric diagnosis is given, this supposed mental illness becomes understood as an *individual* problem, losing its connectivity with anything outside the affected individual (Cohen, 2016; Taylor & Gold, 2019). Here, the appearance of a psychiatric diagnosis works to disappear relationality and context within dominant understandings of people's distress. Importantly, this also works to further alienate people from relational, political, and philosophical approaches to their despair.

> "Thinking, as a conscious activity, is itself a form of doing, a way of *engaging* with the world ... the classic depiction of the body schema as a first person, lived experience that produces a genuine dialectic between 'the body and the world' ... is decisively interrupted and undermined by the extremely negative image of one's body that is communicated through the ongoing, oppressive look of the colonizer."
>
> Weiss, Gail. "The Normal, the Natural, and the Normative: A Merleau-Pontian Legacy to Feminist Theory, Critical Race Theory, and Disability Studies." *Continental Philosophy Review* 48, no. 1 (2015): 77–93; pp. 79, 87.

SOCIAL AND OCCUPATIONAL FUNCTIONING

Appearances and disappearances of despair and how these experiences come to be framed through biological psychiatry do not emerge out of a vacuum; this process is deeply embedded within the contemporary neoliberal context in which we exist. The move toward psychiatrizing despair simultaneously informs and is informed by the pressing issues, contingencies, context, agents, and systems of this particular historical moment.

In their chapter "The Body as the Problem of Individuality: A Phenomenological Disability Studies Approach," Titchkosky and Michalko (2012) ask: What kind of problem does contemporary society need disability to be? The authors argue that "disability can, and often does, disrupt the taken-for-granted character of the world and our life in it" (Titchkosky & Michalko, 2012, p. 132), contending that "the experience of disability ... becomes the scene where we can frame how we experience embodied existence and thus disability becomes a place where culture can be examined anew, again and again" (p. 141). When applied to the psychiatrization of despair, would the question then be: What kind of problem does contemporary society need despair to be?

Elsewhere, we have built on Nirmala Erevelles' (2011) concept of disabled bodies as "unruly" in their refusal to participate in capitalist relations through work, extending the concept to rebellious minds. We argued that through psychiatry, "a rebellious mind, a less productive mind, a non-participatory mind can be reimagined in such a way that it can itself be a site of accumulation" (Taylor & Gold, 2019, p. 138). Through this lens, the problem of despair appears as an opportunity for commodification, where those who do not or cannot participate in capitalist relations as workers become re-imagined as patients, in need of ongoing individualized care and treated with profitable psychiatric drugs (Breggin, 2007; Taylor & Gold, 2019; Whitaker, 2010).

The DSM, colloquially known as "the bible of psychiatry," is written and periodically revised by psychiatrists and psychiatric researchers who form DSM "work groups" clustered around particular diagnoses. The DSM defines pathology and disorder as it relates to so-called mental health and illness. In other words, what constitutes and can be diagnosed as a psychiatric disorder in the global north falls under the purview of the DSM. However, within the diagnostic criteria of the hundreds of psychiatric disorders listed in the current DSM-5 (APA, 2013), there is no consideration for the role of despair (or any similar process) within mentally healthy functioning. With the appearance of psychiatric commodification, we mark a disappearance of despair from having space within "normal" (read: non-pathological) human life and well-being.

Unspecified Depressive Disorder

311 (F32.9)

"This category applies to presentations in which symptoms characteristic of a depressive disorder that cause clinically significant distress or impairment in social, occupational, or other important areas of functioning predominate but do not meet the full criteria for any of the disorders in the depressive disorders diagnostic class. The unspecified depressive disorder category is used in situations in which the clinician chooses not to specify the reason that the criteria are not met for a specific depressive disorder, and includes presentations for which there is insufficient information to make a more specific diagnosis (e.g., in emergency room settings)."

American Psychiatric Association (APA). "Depressive Disorders." In *Diagnostic and Statistical Manual of Mental Disorders*. 5th ed., Washington, DC: American Psychiatric Publishing, 2013, p. 184.

What does define the majority of psychiatric disorders according to the DSM is one's ability or willingness to work and socialize *productively*, or as articulated throughout the DSM, "impairment in social or occupational functioning" (APA, 2013;[6] Cohen, 2016). This ill-defined and vague statement at the crux of what becomes labelled as a psychiatric disorder within contemporary western psychiatry can be read as a type of ultimatum—participate in society as you *should* or become a site of accumulation as a psychiatrically disabled patient requiring ongoing treatment.

Rather than presenting a laundry list of the groups most likely to receive a psychiatric diagnosis, we will emphasize that this list assumes significant overlap with groups facing marginalization.[7] Here we can pause to consider the role of despair in the context of realities of ongoing oppression. Earlier, we argued that despair can play an important role as a source from which individuals can consciously evoke their agency as a catalyst for change. Applied to the context of oppression and marginalization, despair can lead to questions and insights around one's social, political, and economic conditions. In this regard, despair can be a catalyst for realizing one's positionality and developing articulations of the systemic injustices they face. This appearance of despair is hopeful in the sense that it can lead not only to individual change but to collective shifts as well.[8]

REBELLIOUS MINDS, PRODUCTIVE ENFOLDINGS

Psychiatric disorders, defined into existence through capitalist frameworks of productivity, in many ways acknowledge that a person is struggling or is in crisis. For many, part of the relief of a psychiatric diagnosis is to have a label that acknowledges their suffering (Hande et al., 2016). However, as Scheff (1999) points out, biomedical psychiatry obscures the emotional/relational world. It has developed in a western milieu, which demands that people function as individuals, "prepar[ing] children for individual careers, enabling them to be socially and geographically mobile so that they can avail themselves of opportunities for achievement, no matter what personal and interpersonal cost" (p. 13).

While a psychiatric diagnosis might offer relief to *some* people who are suffering, it *always* simultaneously works in aid of capitalist productivity. People who have been diagnosed with a mental illness are argued to be very costly to capitalists in terms of disability and insurance claims, absenteeism, and "presenteeism" (Hemp, 2004). Yet, as Fritsch (2015) writes, disability is profitable to capitalists through treatments and forms of "capacitation," noting that "disabled bodies that are profitable, that can be marketed to, can be enhanced, or incorporated into the labour force are debilitated bodies that neoliberalism deems worthy" (p. 29). Despite this, one of the barometers of success in psychiatric treatment is a return to work and regular productivity levels. One reading of this is that psychiatry helps people, since a return to work/productivity means that a person can have a pay cheque and support themselves. Yet a radical re-reading of this same story finds rebellious minds brought into a productive fold, through treatments and drugs, where their very bodies and minds become sites of accumulation. What imaginaries could rebellious minds bring forth into reality if distress and despair were allowed to foment social change? Instead, rebellious minds disappear, reappearing as categories of deviance defined as labels and described in the DSM.

> "There is a price to be paid for the privilege of 'being in a community'—and it is inoffensive or even invisible only as long as the community stays in the dream. The price is paid in the currency of freedom, variously called 'autonomy', 'right to self-assertion', 'right to be yourself'. Whatever you choose, you gain some and lose some. Missing community means missing security; gaining community, if it happens, would soon mean missing freedom."
>
> Bauman, Zygmunt. *Community: Seeing Safety in an Insecure World.* Cambridge, UK: Polity Press, 2000, p. 4.

DEVIANT OUTSIDERS, DEVIANT INSIDERS

Howard Becker (1963) was a labelling theorist who wrote *Outsiders: Studies in the Sociology of Deviance.* Becker was interested in deviance as a social process whereby dominant groups define what is normal and what is deviant through "differences in the ability to make rules and apply them to other people" (p. 17). Using the concept of an occupational career, he developed the idea of the "deviant career" to describe the movements of people who had chosen to become "deviant outsiders" (p. 73), in particular, cannabis users and dance musicians in the 1950s. Importantly, Becker describes a breakdown in social control over the deviant as they move along in their career, noting that "important factors in the genesis of deviant behavior ... may be sought in the processes by which people are emancipated from the controls of society and become responsive to those of a smaller group" (p. 60).

The first stage in the deviant career of a cannabis user, according to Becker (1963), is that the user must learn the techniques of smoking, after which they must then "learn to perceive the effects" of the drug, to "be able to point them out to himself and consciously connect them with having smoked marihuana" (p. 49). The user must then learn to enjoy the effects, since "marihuana-produced sensations are not automatically or necessarily pleasurable ... [given] the taste for such experience is a socially acquired one, not different in kind from acquired tastes for oysters or dry martinis" (p. 53).

Here we use Becker's concept of the deviant career to develop the idea that people learn the techniques of psychiatrization, disappearing their myriad forms and subjects of despair, and through the learning of these techniques, reappear their despair as a diagnosis. We do not start off in life thinking about distress and despair in socially organized ways, much in the same way we do not start out in life desirous of or knowing how to use cannabis. Both must be learned. The organized categories of the DSM are taught within schools, perhaps something first encountered in health class, wherein we learn about mental health and illness through the lens of biological psychiatry (see, e.g., Ontario Ministry of Education, 2018). Akin to Becker's (1963) "learning to perceive the effects" (p. 49) is the idea that as people become exposed to the socially organized categories of "mental illnesses," they become able to connect their own experiences, feelings, and actions with the concepts of "mental illness" in the moment, as periods of distress occur. This encourages noticing feelings and behaviours and attributing them to something internal to themselves, taking their experience of the label's descriptive features as evidence that they are an instantiation of the label—slippage from emotional states to organized categories. Similar to Becker's (1963) idea of "learning to enjoy the effects" (p. 53), we argue that some people who become psychiatrized experience relief that their distress can be attributable to a thing that "experts" know about and can potentially fix. The identification with a psychiatric disorder provides both an explanation and hope for the end of despair.

One important difference between Becker's ideas and ours hinges on the concept of "outsider" status. Becker was studying people who had chosen a deviant outsider identity despite the negative ramifications and social consequences that accompanied that identity. A psychiatrized identity is different because it is socially sanctioned. Massive advertising expenditures by pharmaceutical companies and related anti-stigma campaigns by governments and corporations alike have normalized the concept of "mental illness" to the point that to question that there is such a thing meets with predominantly raised eyebrows. A psychiatrized person is therefore brought into insider status—still deviant but accepted by society. As a deviant outsider, Becker's cannabis user could choose to stop being a deviant outsider by ceasing to be a cannabis user. It is much more difficult for the psychiatrically deviant insider to detach from their deviant status. This is because their claims to despair have been hijacked by the application of socially acceptable labels that are endorsed and reinforced by powerful institutions like medicine, law, and education.

> "I want to introduce colonialism as a *felt*, affective relationship. Moral stigmata are produced and attached to race, gender, and sexualities as lived structures of feeling: intuited, perceived, felt, and finally, in this circuit expressed as emotions.... This might mean there is more intense affect available than there is the social means to express.... Canadian colonialism is 'felt' in that it is a broad spectrum of nuances, valences/practices with the power to generate emotionally charged meaning as *common knowledge*."
>
> Million, Dian. *Therapeutic Nations: Healing in an Age of Indigenous Human Rights.* Tucson, AZ: The University of Arizona Press, 2013, p. 46.

CONCLUSION

What is lost when people come to identify their despair as individualized mental illness? And further, what is gained through this identification? The complex web we have tried to disentangle in this chapter is only one step in unravelling, analyzing, and perhaps even building understanding around the place of despair in contemporary human experience. In this period of upheaval and flux, where the legitimacy of seemingly sedimented institutions and structures is quickly being questioned and excavated, we invite a non-pathologized relation to despair, a collective vision of despair, in hopes of creating new imaginaries of what our world might look like.

NOTES

1. Although cited from its translation, we found this quote in Dianne Barsoum Raymond's 1991 introductory book *Existentialism and the Philosophical Tradition*, an engaging and informative book exploring existentialism and its key concepts, including despair.

2. Our discussion on despair is not meant to be comprehensive but to focus on the importance of despair as an experience, catalyst for change, and analytic framework rather than on the experience of despair itself. For existential discussions on despair, see Kierkegaard (1985 [1843]) *Fear and Trembling*, Sartre (1944) *No Exit*, or Camus (1991 [1955]) *The Myth of Sisyphus*, to name only a few.

3. Biological psychiatry "involves the search for physiological, genetic and chemical bases" for psychiatric disorders (Kirk & Kutchins, 1992, p. 10). Importantly, it should be noted that the DSM-I and DSM-II defined psychiatric disorders through the concepts and theories of psychoanalysis, not biological psychiatry. For further reading on the history and changes throughout DSM editions, see Kirk and Kutchins (1992), Whitaker (2010), and Burstow (2015).

4. Consider the approaches of Kierkegaard (1985 [1843]) and Camus (1991 [1955]), resolving despair through faith in a higher power versus acceptance of meaninglessness and the complete indifference of the world toward humans.

5. There is no unified definition for psychiatrization. Generally, this entails a process where an individual becomes enfolded into the psychiatric system through diagnoses or institutionalization. For a discussion of this term, see Mills (2014) and Rose (2006).

6. P. 124, Bipolar I Disorder criteria C; p. 161, Major Depressive Disorder criteria B; p. 222, Generalized Anxiety Disorder criteria D; p. 237, Obsessive-Compulsive Disorder criteria B; p. 272, Posttraumatic Stress Disorder criteria G, to name only a few common diagnoses where "impairment in social or occupational functioning" are necessary criteria for diagnosis.

7. See Metzl (2009) *The Protest Psychosis: How Schizophrenia Became a Black Disease*; Burstow (2015) *Psychiatry and the Business of Madness: An Ethical and Epistemological Accounting*; Hansen et al. (2014) *Pathologizing Poverty: New Forms of Diagnosis, Disability, and Structural Stigma under Welfare Reform*; and Million (2014) *Therapeutic Nations: Healing in an Age of Indigenous Human Rights*.

8. Consider the role of radical Black and Indigenous thought, borne of ongoing injustice, oppression, and—one might argue—despair, in uncovering the deep, multi-layered systems and ideologies of oppression that lead to the conditions of marginalization. For example, see Fanon (1952) *Black Skin, White Masks*, Simpson (2017) *As We Have Always Done: Indigenous Freedom through Radical Resistance*, and Lorde (1984) *Sister Outsider: Essays and Speeches*.

REFERENCES

American Psychiatric Association (APA). (1952). *Diagnostic and statistical manual: Mental disorders*. American Psychiatric Association Mental Hospital Service.

American Psychiatric Association (APA). (2013). *Diagnostic and statistical manual of mental disorders* (5th ed.). American Psychiatric Publishing.

Barsoum Raymond, D. (1991). *Existentialism and the philosophical tradition*. Prentice Hall.

Becker, H. S. (1963). *Outsiders: Studies in the sociology of deviance*. The Free Press.

Breggin, P. (2007). *Brain-disabling treatments in psychiatry.* Springer.

Burstow, B. (2015). *Psychiatry and the business of madness: An ethical and epistemological accounting.* Palgrave Macmillan.

Camus, A. (1991). *The myth of Sisyphus, and other essays* (J. O'Brien, Trans.). Vintage Books. (Original work published 1955)

Cohen, B. (2016). *Psychiatric hegemony.* Palgrave Macmillan.

Erevelles, N. (2011). *Disability and difference in global contexts: Enabling a transformative body politic.* Palgrave Macmillan.

Fanon, F. (1952). *Black skin, white masks.* Grove Press.

Fritsch, K. (2015). Gradations of debility and capacity: Biocapitalism and the neoliberalization of disability relations. *Canadian Journal of Disability Studies, 4*(2), 12–48. https://doi.org/10.15353/cjds.v4i2.208

Hande, M. J., Taylor, S. A., & Zorn, E. (2016). Operation ASD: Philanthrocapitalism, spectrumization, and the role of the parent. In B. Burstow (Ed.), *Psychiatry interrogated.* Palgrave Macmillan.

Hansen, H., Bourgois, P., & Drucker, E. (2014). Pathologizing poverty: New forms of diagnosis, disability, and structural stigma under welfare reform. *Social Science & Medicine, 103,* 76–83. https://doi.org/10.1016/j.socscimed.2013.06.033

Hemp, P. (2004, October 1). *Presenteeism: At work—but out of it.* Harvard Business Review. https://hbr.org/2004/10/presenteeism-at-work-but-out-of-it

Jordan, J. (2018, March 15). *Pragmatic arguments and belief in God.* Stanford Encyclopedia of Philosophy. https://plato.stanford.edu/entries/pragmatic-belief-god/

Kierkegaard, S. (1985). *Fear and trembling* (A. Hannay, Trans.). Penguin Books. (Original work published 1843)

Kirk, S. A., & Kutchins, H. (1992). *The selling of DSM: The rhetoric of science in psychiatry.* Walter de Gruyter.

Lorde, A. (1984). *Sister outsider: Essays and speeches.* Crossing Press.

Metzl, J. M. (2009). *The protest psychosis: How schizophrenia became a black disease.* Beacon Press.

Million, D. (2014). *Therapeutic nations: Healing in an age of Indigenous human rights.* University of Arizona Press.

Mills, C. (2014). *Decolonizing global mental health: The psychiatrization of the majority world.* Routledge.

Ontario Ministry of Education. (2018). *The Ontario curriculum grades 9 to 12: Health and physical education, 2018.* http://www.edu.gov.on.ca/eng/curriculum/secondary/health9to12.pdf

R, E. (2020, May 6). *Awakening: Shedding the "mentally ill" identity and reclaiming my life.* Mad in America. https://www.madinamerica.com/2020/05/awakening-shedding-mentally-ill-identity-reclaiming-life/?fbclid=IwAR1z3hKaO6NfhP7cziRbpLH30DKXoA0gg6b9OOfsZtyJFFvRztZWndlP1Jc

Rose, N. (2006). Disorders without borders? The expanding scope of psychiatric practice. *BioSocieties, 1,* 465–484. https://doi.org/10.1017/S1745855206004078

Roxby, P. (2020, May 16). *Psychiatrists fear 'tsunami' of mental illness after lockdown.* BBC News. https://www.bbc.com/news/health-52676981

Sartre, J. P. (1944). *No exit and three other plays.* Vintage Books.

Scheff, T. J. (1999). *Being mentally ill: A sociological theory* (3rd ed.). Aldine de Gruyter.

Simpson, L. B. (2017). *As we have always done: Indigenous freedom through radical resistance.* University of Minnesota Press.

Taylor, S., & Gold, E. (2019). Madness and individualism: Unravelling in crazy times. In D. Honorato, M. A. Gonzalez Valerio, M. de Menezes, & A. Giannakoulopoulos (Eds.), *Taboo transgression transcendence in art and science 2018* (pp. 135–143). Ionian University Publications.

Titchkosky, T., and Michalko, R. (2012). The body as the problem of individuality: A phenomenological disability studies approach. In D. Goodley, B. Hughes, & L. Davis (Eds.), *Disability and social theory* (pp. 127–142). Palgrave Macmillan.

Whitaker, R. (2010). *Anatomy of an epidemic: Magic bullets, psychiatric drugs, and the astonishing rise of mental illness in America.* Crown Publishers.

CHAPTER 17

An Autist Amongst Exceptionalities[1]

Joey Tavares

Key Terms: Antipsychiatry; Autistic; Coalition Against Psychiatric Assault; Diagnosis; Identity-Formation; Medicalization; Representation; Theory of Mind

---

Lexicon

ASD: Autism Spectrum Disorder

Autist or Autie: autistics' self-moniker

Cognitive Liberty: medical or professional altering of consciousness is the antithesis of cognitive liberty; "interference with our right to our own awareness constitutes nothing less than a violation of our humanity" (Burstow, 2019a)

Commons: "All the things that we (at whatever level) decide have to become a common. This is part of the building of a political community cooperating in the definition of the common and in establishing the rules by which it can be used" (Dardot & Laval, 2014, cited in Mestrum, 2015). A fundamental characteristic of the "common" is that it never is inherent in the nature of the thing but always is the result of a social co-activity. Commons are created by cooperating people who decide how this common can be made available to all. It is a fundamental critique of private appropriation and ownership (Mestrum, 2015).

Neurodiversity: the variety of configurations of the brain, especially with regard to autism (Blume, 1998)

Neurodivergent: neuroatypical, or the opposite of neurotypical

Neurotypical: a human being not besot by neurological disorder

The Majority: used instead of the potentially diminutive "neurotypical"

Theory of Mind (ToM): where one has, or has not, the ability to "mind read" social cues, "the ability to attribute mental states to oneself and other people as a way of making sense of and predicting behaviour" (Tager-Flusberg et al., 1993)

INTRODUCTION[2]

I begin with my relationship to disability,[3] to autism, and to its representations. These relationships are a lifelong buffeting between others and their conceptions, caught and informed by representations of me. Disability and diagnosis have appeared as liberating yet also have been limiting, largely through medical orientations. Those and other contradictory assumptions, expectations, and representations of autism surround us, akin to a storm—a storm of depiction that informs the self and our relationships to others. For the purposes of this chapter, I turn to the metaphor of a tree, the trunk of which represents our collective imaginaries. Striations and breaks found along the trunk's surface represent moments where our collective imaginaries *seem* to conflict. The many leaves of the tree represent the myriad representations of ability and "dis"ability. This chapter is concerned mostly with two of these representations: (1) medical renderings of autism and (2) autism and identity. Both representations lead me into a discussion of how autism can be a journey into selfhood, our interconnected relations, and the complexities of being.

"Naming a disease, disorder, or syndrome carries with it significant cultural baggage and no small amount of controversy."

Wright, David. *Downs: The History of a Disability.* New York, NY: Oxford University Press, 2011, p. 10.

MEDICAL REPRESENTATIONS OF AUTISM

The DSM-5 describes Autism Spectrum Disorder (ASD) as a series of criteria, including "deficits in social-emotional reciprocity, non-verbal communicative behaviours, and in developing and maintaining relationships; stereotyped repetitive motor movements, inflexibility, fixated interests, ritualized behavioural patterns, and hyper- or hypo-reactivity to sensory inputs" (American Psychiatric Association, 2013, pp. 50–51). Autism is pathologized with extreme treatments, including psychiatric medications and electroshock therapy. Counselling and behavioural therapy are available prior to a certain age, yet there remains a dearth of social services for adults (Lai & Weiss, 2017). In all of these, allopathic medicine represents autism as a disease, a disorder, and a debilitating condition.

When first diagnosed, I was thrilled. I eagerly allowed myself to be quoted in a clinical work titled *Asperger Syndrome in Adulthood: A Comprehensive Guide for Clinicians* (Stoddart et al., 2012), in a chapter detailing how liberating an adult, or late, diagnosis could be:

> I just got home, and I burst into tears. Thank you both so much. When you are on your rocking chairs, look up and remember me amongst so many others I am certain that you've helped so much. I "knew," however, objective naming is paramount to actualization. So much of my life makes SENSE now, where before, I was hemming and hawing and rowing my boat over that mountain right behind the Little Engine … that can. I can. Your work is important. It has, in no small feat, changed my life; my perspective newly enabled, I go onwards. Although, I guess I have to accept now that regular humans were indeed my parents, and no one is coming to pick me up. Ah well. One fantasy let go, a new dream realized. I'm allowed. Thank you. (pp. 76–77)

As yet, growing into my acceptance of this assigned identity, I realized that I was limiting my understanding of myself to a terminology and modality that, although adding to my understanding of self, took away from my wholeness and localized me socially as *less than*. However, my disability, as it is presented when I identify myself as autistic, is more than that to me and to others. I consider autism as sometimes bearing illness and, many other times, bearing fruits of unique perspectives, senses, and efforts that are oft coined as thinking outside of the box by the majority, intrinsic, on the other hand, to me and mine. As an illness, autism can manifest itself troubling my ability to use public transport or take part in long duration activities that require me to be online and electronically engaged. At the same time, my desire to be a part of the academic discourse regarding invisible disabilities, or differences, is furthered by those instances where I cannot participate as the majority do; a determination to overcome. In this way, my disability causes me difficulties, yet those difficulties allow, encourage, and at times force me to contribute to a conversation that may allow my differences to be understood as part of a community that has broadened its umbrella of normal to include a wider spectrum of abilities. That my differences allow me to be outside the box, in physical and mental modalities, an "outlier," as it were, is an opportunity to provoke the priority that psychiatry and allopathic medicine take in defining autism as a disease.

Through my studies and work as an activist with the Coalition Against Psychiatric Assault, I researched the etymology of this descriptor, "autism," first coined in 1912 by Swiss psychiatrist Eugen Bleuler. From the Greek word *autos*, the self (autism = self-ism), Bleuler used the referent as a descriptor of a schizophrenic-like disorder where fantasy dominates reality in the mind of the self-absorbed sufferer (Fusar-Poli & Politi, 2008; Kuhn & Cahn, 2004). As I invested myself in an antipsychiatry stance, I realized that there is more to whom it is that I am as an autistic than the detractions or difficulties that can arise in and from my interactions with the greater collective.

I do not suffer who I am. Why, then, was it so crucial for me to have an identity accepted by the majority? My relation to disability has been a lifelong buffeting between others and their conceptions of me, from parents in my early years who refused diagnoses they considered dangerous at the time to an adulthood and the same late diagnosis that at one point I found liberating. In emancipating myself from medical renderings of autism, I disappeared as a man with limitations and emerged in myself and society as a being who has much to add to our greater collective. In seeking to critique psychiatry's domain over the labelling and identifying of the exceptional as less than, I began with myself and then took my efforts into my academic aims. As a burgeoning activist taking an antipsychiatry stance, *I* identify *myself* as a highly sensitive intuitive empath (HISE, pronounced "hissy"; pun intended), and the freedom from self-oppression I have experienced is an enlightening motivator for presence, praxis, and contribution. I do not *have* autism; I *am* autistic.

All of our unique branches lead to the same lofty treetop: our Commons, our community, our *intersticiary imaginaries*. Interstices are connections, where meetings are made. Imaginaries are things, events, actions, or dreams imagined before they are enacted, and yet every action gives rise to ways of imagining. For example, I envisage getting a glass of water before I actually do it. If our interstices are our oppositions, as with puzzle pieces fitting together where they are different, then our interstitial imaginary is that collective framework we create together.

Our interstitial imaginary is, then, in this rendering, our collective latticework of intersectionalities. And yet, psychiatry and medicine are worrying. There is no argument that many disabilities are aided by allopathic medicine and scientific research, but how much is too much? Have we strayed into a corner where we position disability as only a loss, limit, or lack (Titchkosky, 2018)? What about disability as identity?

> "Labelled people described the ways in which they are 'not allowed to love'—prevented from having friendships, from having relationships and from bringing up their children.... While some labelled people spoke of loving their families—their parents, their partners and their children—others spoke to the ways in which these relationships are incommensurate ... 'love' can morph into violence and control of their bodies ... revealing the urgent need to re-imagine parenting, partnerships and friendships in the lives of labelled people."
>
> Ignagni, Esther, Ann Fudge Schormans, Kirsty Liddiard, and Katherine Runswick-Cole. "'Some People Are Not Allowed to Love': Intimate Citizenship in the Lives of People Labelled with Intellectual Disabilities." *Disability & Society* 31, no. 1 (2016): 131–135; p. 133.

AUTISM AND IDENTITY

How do autistics differentiate themselves, not only from medicalized identities but from each other on a spectrum? Below is a short series of pictorial gradients from an article by C. L. Lynch (2019) at neuroclastic.com, which present an answer in their framing to the conundrum "whose autism?" and how its effects express themselves.

Here, first, is the way autistics perceive the majority's view of the spectrum:

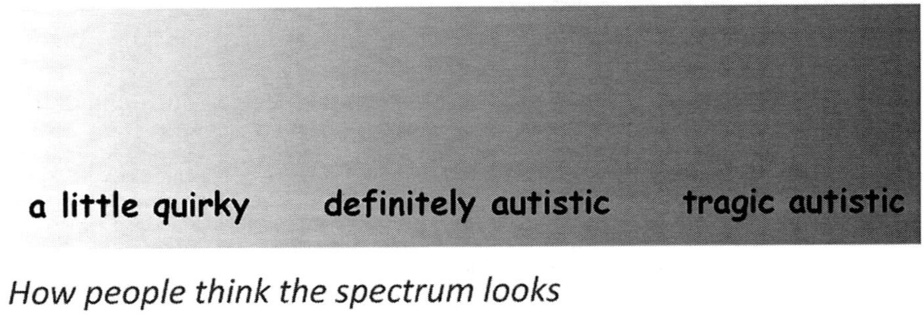

a little quirky   definitely autistic   tragic autistic

How people think the spectrum looks

Figure 17.1: A graphic representation of a spectrum meant to indicate how people commonly understand the autism spectrum

Lynch, C. L. (2019, May 4). *"Autism is a spectrum" doesn't mean what you think.* NeuroClastic. https://neuroclastic.com/its-a-spectrum-doesnt-mean-what-you-think/

What follows is a common appearance of the autism spectrum, with seven measures of capacity, followed by three different examples of how an autist might score, or how they end up being seemingly disparate outliers on a singular spectrum. Please note: Other autists constructed this exemplifier, and this work and I are in their debt.

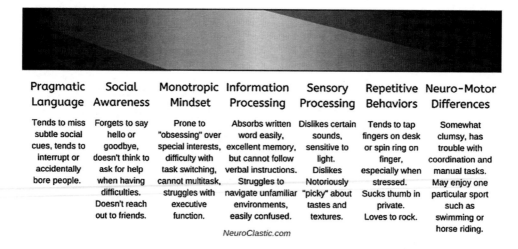

Pragmatic Language	Social Awareness	Monotropic Mindset	Information Processing	Sensory Processing	Repetitive Behaviors	Neuro-Motor Differences
Social communication including body language, eye contact, small talk, and turn-taking in conversation.	Ability to pick up on etiquette, social norms, taboos. Ability to form and maintain relationships.	Narrow but intense ability to focus, resulting in "obsessive" interests and difficulty task-switching.	Ability to assimilate and apply new information quickly or to adapt to new environments or situations.	Challenges interpreting sensory information, hypersensitivity or hyposensitivity to stimuli.	Tendency to "stim" in response to varying emotions. Can be beneficial or harmful in nature.	Ability to control body movements. Ranges from clumsiness to complete loss of ability to move with intention.

www.theaspergian.com

Figure 17.2: A graphic representation of a gradient meant to indicate one way that autism actually appears in a person

Lynch, C. L. (2019, May 19). In stigmaphrenia [Author], *Update: Detailed what is autism?* So, You're Autistic. https://soyoureautistic.com/2019/05/09/update-what-is-autism/

Pragmatic Language	Social Awareness	Monotropic Mindset	Information Processing	Sensory Processing	Repetitive Behaviors	Neuro-Motor Differences
Tends to miss subtle social cues, tends to interrupt or accidentally bore people.	Forgets to say hello or goodbye, doesn't think to ask for help when having difficulties. Doesn't reach out to friends.	Prone to "obsessing" over special interests, difficulty with task switching, cannot multitask, struggles with executive function.	Absorbs written word easily, excellent memory, but cannot follow verbal instructions. Struggles to navigate unfamiliar environments, easily confused.	Dislikes certain sounds, sensitive to light. Dislikes Notoriously "picky" about tastes and textures.	Tends to tap fingers on desk or spin ring on finger, especially when stressed. Sucks thumb in private. Loves to rock.	Somewhat clumsy, has trouble with coordination and manual tasks. May enjoy one particular sport such as swimming or horse riding.

NeuroClastic.com

Figure 17.3: A graphic representation of a gradient meant to indicate one way that autism actually appears in a person (high functioning)

Lynch, C. L. (2019, May 4). *"Autism is a spectrum" doesn't mean what you think.* NeuroClastic. https://neuroclastic.com/its-a-spectrum-doesnt-mean-what-you-think/

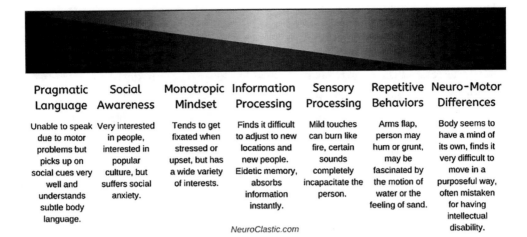

Pragmatic Language	Social Awareness	Monotropic Mindset	Information Processing	Sensory Processing	Repetitive Behaviors	Neuro-Motor Differences
Unable to speak due to motor problems but picks up on social cues very well and understands subtle body language.	Very interested in people, interested in popular culture, but suffers social anxiety.	Tends to get fixated when stressed or upset, but has a wide variety of interests.	Finds it difficult to adjust to new locations and new people. Eidetic memory, absorbs information instantly.	Mild touches can burn like fire, certain sounds completely incapacitate the person.	Arms flap, person may hum or grunt, may be fascinated by the motion of water or the feeling of sand.	Body seems to have a mind of its own, finds it very difficult to move in a purposeful way, often mistaken for having intellectual disability.

NeuroClastic.com

Figure 17.4: A graphic representation of a gradient meant to indicate one way that autism actually appears in a person (severely autistic)

Lynch, C. L. (2019, May 4). "*Autism is a spectrum*" doesn't mean what you think. NeuroClastic. https://neuroclastic.com/its-a-spectrum-doesnt-mean-what-you-think/

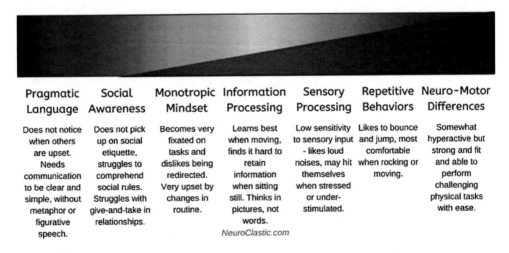

Pragmatic Language	Social Awareness	Monotropic Mindset	Information Processing	Sensory Processing	Repetitive Behaviors	Neuro-Motor Differences
Does not notice when others are upset. Needs communication to be clear and simple, without metaphor or figurative speech.	Does not pick up on social etiquette, struggles to comprehend social rules. Struggles with give-and-take in relationships.	Becomes very fixated on tasks and dislikes being redirected. Very upset by changes in routine.	Learns best when moving, finds it hard to retain information when sitting still. Thinks in pictures, not words.	Low sensitivity to sensory input - likes loud noises, may hit themselves when stressed or under-stimulated.	Likes to bounce and jump, most comfortable when rocking or moving.	Somewhat hyperactive but strong and fit and able to perform challenging physical tasks with ease.

NeuroClastic.com

Figure 17.5: A graphic representation of a gradient meant to indicate one way that autism actually appears in a person (independent)

Lynch, C. L. (2019, May 4). "*Autism is a spectrum*" doesn't mean what you think. NeuroClastic. https://neuroclastic.com/its-a-spectrum-doesnt-mean-what-you-think/

As can be seen in these figures, in the more social dissection of autism behavioural patterns, the medical markers are describing various outcomes in performance vectors (Lynch, 2019). Which of these is the high-function autist in relation to the first example I presented? In my relationships, uttering the word *autism* can mean an instant judgement of less abled. However, autistics are a palette of traits, intermingled, which manifest uniquely in each individual. There is, to my mind, no such thing as being "a little autistic" (Lynch, 2019). A spectral measure of autism, such as the one in the DSM-5 could allow one to interpret an autist as less autistic or more autistic than another. This is a troubling take. The measures as explicated in the diagrams *created by other autists* show that autism is a spectrum with different outcomes on the same set of measures. Another contrasting antagonization, again from allopathy, is that autism is a psychiatric illness, a condition one must have. I repeat: As an autist identifying myself, I do not *have* autism—I *am* autistic. Autism exists as a singular expression of the human collective condition, along a spectrum of measures that indicate its presence amongst others.

That said, there are those who take an antipsychiatry stance questioning whether autism exists at all, either as an outcome of genetic traits or ill-assigned diminutive social constructs. Nick Walker (2014), a proponent of the neuro-diversity movement, believes that autists are neurodivergent from the majority and that "autism and other neurocognitive variants are simply part of the natural spectrum of human biodiversity." Child psychologist Sami Timimi, along with two "ex-autistics" (Neil Gardner and Brian McCabe), co-authoured a critique (2011) of the psychiatrization of children through autism, in their contribution to Richard Melling's "The Myth of Autism" (2011), and concluded that this divergence (autism) does not factually exist but in the minds of medical professionals.

Then there are the mid-liners. Majia Nadesan (2013), the mother of an autistic child and a researcher, believes autism is as much a social construct as it is pathological and that a societal understanding of this interstice, rather than a collective ignoring of it, would promote an understanding between both social and medical practitioners in respective fields of service to autism. Dr. Bonnie Burstow (2019a, b), the late prominent antipsychiatrist and a proponent of the psychiatric construction of autism versus its social or physical reality, brought up the historical notion of cognitive liberty, an umbrella under which proponents of these different modalities (genetic, neurodiverse, neurodivergent, non-existent, etc.) could come together to seek recourse for their various autist communities. Burstow's positioning was supported in an interview with the aforementioned neurodiversity advocate Nick Walker in the same work. Much as with Majia Nadesan's position, Dr. Burstow felt that we needed to find similarities in our differences—and needed to come together to find common ground. In so doing, divergent idealists might challenge the anti-autistic position. Autism appears as a contested identity, and frankly, other than Nadesan as a mother of an autistic and Walker as a neuro-diverse being on the autism spectrum, it is of note to this author that non-autistics are doing a lot of this contending.

Identity is incredibly complex and beautifully nuanced. At the same time, as this chapter has so far shown, we have encountered different representations of aut-ism, which implicate the self, identity, and relationships. I wonder, then, about the following: How do autistics differentiate themselves, not only from psychiatrized or other allopathic identities but also from each other on a spectrum that is not as far stretched as it may seem? How do autists feel about themselves? I have no idea what autism is. I know what I am *told* it is. What *I* know about me is that I Am. In general, I have found that the cultural understandings of autism here in the Western world, although it allows those of us who are able to live for the most part without patronizing and sometimes damaging pathology, isolation, and insti-tutionalization, also force us to live as outsiders, where everybody already knows what is best for us, pats us on our heads, and tells us, "You don't seem autistic," as if that were a compliment. Whose autism is autism? Medicine's? The Majority's? Mine and other autists as our own self-identifying interstice?

"Be honest. Look at me when I'm talking to you. Do you really see all that you say? Or is it a convenience of language to ascribe to my eyes those qualities, emotions, messages you derive from the rest of my face, our surroundings, or the words I speak? Aren't you projecting your own expectations, interpreta-tions, or desires onto my blank eyes? And if you're really being honest, really looking closely, my eyes are no more vacant than a sighted person's eyes. My eyes and your eyes send back only reflections. Of course this hypothesis comes full circle. If I see your eyes as blank, it is only because I am projecting what I see (or don't see) onto you. But only you can say for sure. Go ahead. Take a good look. Pull the wool off your eyes. Tell me what you see."

Kleege, Georgina. *Sight Unseen*. New Haven, CT: Yale University Press, 1999, p. 138.

AUTISM AS A JOURNEY INTO SELFHOOD, RELATIONS, AND BEING

In this final section, I comment on how various representations of autism can allow us to enter into other imaginaries, different meanings of the self, our relations, and what it means to *be*.

"You seem so normal" is a habitually shared perception I field from members of the majority, as well as "You're exaggerating your behaviourisms." My disability appears in a particular way, already rooted within individualistic and medical orientations to normalcy that precede me. What is more, I am expected to accept such an assignment of myself, *told* who I am, as either "too much" or "not enough" (Michalko, 2009, p. 71). Perhaps, if we allow ourselves to be together, to live, to experience together, to thrive from investing in each other's interstices—perhaps then we can come to imagine the collective in a different way, that is, a way that is far, far away from the spectrum of individualistic, medicalized, or majoritized orientations. Perhaps we can come to a praxis of practice in which the ways of selfhood, identity, and all of our relations are *made*, co-created—collectivized. We co-create our interstitial lattice together, and we can *change* it together, too.

Interestingly enough, as with the knowledge producers who define autism for the autistic, these and other assignments of identifiers are often expounded upon, questioned, interrogated, or dismissed in the personal social sphere. The only demand appears to be that I accept the other's assignment. Again, as with professional or scientific research, I am not (yet) permitted to define myself in the social arena—it is someone else telling me who I am. Again (ad nauseam?), I am defined as either "too much" or "not enough" (Michalko, 2009), according to this Other's scope of the reality I live in. My lived experience is invalidated almost immediately. As disability appears as a defective element, I *dis*appear ...

A different disappearance lies in this process: My disability disappears when the scope of a given other holds ideals regarding the phenomenon of autism as a gift. This is a fetishization of my disability, my identity—my being as an autist. To these others, I am not disabled; rather, I am enabled with their conceptions of autism: spiritually connected, an honest person, granted a gift of empathy, a savant with the secret to life. These positionalities are expectations that, indeed, make my differences and their realities disappear for the sake of imagined affluences. It is unfortunate that many characterizations of the autistic in popular culture perpetuate these fetishes, these myths: the savant gambler, the empathic doctor, or the insular expert computer hacker. These ideations idealize a popular majority cultural consensus of autism, creating tensions between understandings of autism as a state of being at times requiring accommodations for the sake of participation and daily living and that of the imagined keeper of the unknown—an almost super-human being. I recall seeing an episode of a musical television series some years ago, by the name of *Glee* (Murphy et al. 2011), where a character with Asperger's (ASD) was introduced; it was a shit-show of offense to behold. An autistic friend and I were so incensed at the inaccuracies that we wrote the producers and asked if they had even consulted an autistic before creating the character. Of note, there was no reply to our well-thought-out query. Much like the protestations of Majia Nadesan (2013), the social constructs of autism by the majority impede a holistic balancing of cognitive liberty with the sometimes-necessary intervention, be it prophylaxis or other accommodations to allopathy that can come with coping as a being who is an outlier on the severe side of the spectrum.

Along the lines of disappearances, discourse surrounding autism and disability often centres on the question of "What is missing?" McGuire and Michalko (2011) suggest that it is examining ourselves and how we enjoin either as the majority or outliers that can inform or elucidate "the missing pieces" (p. 163). Their exquisite example of a developmental psychological test, called the "Sally Anne Test," is interesting in that, in the test scenario, normal children pass the test by answering that Sally will look for the marble she left in her box and not in Anne's box where it was placed by naughty Anne whilst Sally was out for a walk. Autistic children fail this test by stating that Sally will look for the marble where it actually is, in Anne's box (McGuire & Michalko, 2011). As obviously antagonized in my presentation of this test scenario, the literally correct answer is, to my autistic mind, *given* to the respondent in the very question! What other answer is there but the one that is actually true? I must then antagonize further: Is this a measure that positively indicates (diagnoses) social mind-blindness, as with Baron-Cohen's "Theory of Mind" (ToM), where one has, or has not, the ability to "mind read" social cues, the ability to "attribute mental states to oneself and other people as a way of making sense of and predicting behaviour" (Tager-Flusberg et al., 1993, p. 3)? Or rather, is this a measure, scientific if indeed it is, indicative of a literal answer to a question where the location of the marble in question is made obvious in the test itself, where the subject is given the answer in Anne's described actions? I am in amazement that the correct answer is, for the purposes of this test, the wrong one. Puzzling, indeed. My efforts in this deconstruction of the "Sally Anne Test" are inspired by the positing of autists as beings with *different* minds than the majority, which comes from autistic researcher Melanie Yergeau's (2013) exhaustive refutation of ToM and its premise of autistics as other than human. Here is their succinct syllogism:

- The whole point of ToM is that autistic people do not have it.
- The whole point of ToM is that humans do have it.
- The whole point of ToM is that *autistics are not human.*

This poignant obviation of the intrinsic flaw of ToM by Yergeau is complimented by a revolutionary study by Eliane Deschrijver and Colin Palmer, who reassessed findings from decades of ToM research related to autism. Their challenge to the status quo disputes the notion that autists cannot grasp what others may or may not think (as in the case of the "Sally Anne Test"), rather focusing on the issues autists have with assessing the level of disparity between their own cognition method and that of a given control—namely, the majority modal framing (latticing) of cognition, or ToM (Deschrijver & Palmer, 2020).

It is our differences that lend to our greater commonality, and the fomenting and formation of our community, that imagined, interstice lattice of our Collective that is the completed interlocking puzzle—our Commons. As with a puzzle, our variances on the spectrum of humanness fit together where we are different, *not* where we are the same. We must exult in similitude as we enjoin at the interstices of our myriad uniqueness. It is our consciousness of the Other that is key, and our commitment to finding ourselves in that other, in those variances where we make each other whole.

CONCLUSION

I have provided a way, a framing, into autism and its representations in such a way that allows us to reimagine normalcy (Titchkosky & Michalko, 2009), to make the certain uncertain (Titchkosky, 2011), and to comment upon how we are, together, constantly shaping our relationships. I see a common and enduring connection between all humans. What a wonderful lens to imagine through, combined with the leaves of the tree analogy, where we come together celebrating, enjoined in our differences, the interstice by which our greatest puzzle, our Commons, comes together and comes alive. As with the allegory of our Collective as a Tree, our leaves may vary in shape and size, yet our aims are the same, and our shared roots firmly planted as our striations toward a socially just society come into fruition.

NOTES

1. My sincere thanks to Dr. Kevin Stoddart for his gracious permission to utilize an extract from his work; the inherent disclosure of my anonymity is made of my own free will. Thanks go out as well to the web-producers and author C. L. Lynch at neuroclastic.com, for their granting my use of their efforts in my own. Thanks go out as well to wiktionary.org for some of the finer definitions in my lexicon and to Canadian Scholars and Women's Press for this deeply appreciated opportunity to contribute to our Collective. For this honour, my humble appreciation is boundless.
    Note: The file images from www.neuroclastic.com originated before their domain name change from www.theaspergian.com.

2. I give thanks to the First Nations, Métis, and Inuit Nations for sharing the land that I live, love, and learn on. I honour my commitment to my duty and ancestry with this acknowledgement. Let us remember always where we stand, why we are fortunate, and the promises we did, do, and *will* keep. Even though we are under the auspices of dark times, there is a bright future ahead of us; all we have to do is look up and our grandmother moon is showing us those days to come.

3. I invite the reader to take into consideration my use of words relating to disability; these are my choices and at times creations, or neologisms as the linguists call those words we make up on the spot that can be understood … *our* language, growing and changing as *we* shape it … another allegory for our Collective framing of our interstitially imagined lattice. Let any errors in grace make for great discussion, as we collectively evolve how we respectfully refer to one another together. With love, eh? ;-)

REFERENCES

American Psychiatric Association. (2013). *Diagnostic and statistical manual of mental disorders* (5th ed.). American Psychiatric Publishing.

Blume, H. (1998, September). *Neurodiversity: On the neurological underpinnings of geekdom*. The Atlantic. https://www.theatlantic.com/magazine/archive/1998/09/neurodiversity/305909/

Burstow, B. (2019a, July 14). *On cognitive liberty: A principle to rally behind*. Mad in America. https://www.madinamerica.com/2019/07/cognitive-liberty-principle-rally-behind/

Burstow, B. (2019b). *The revolt against psychiatry: A counterhegemonic dialogue*. Springer Nature.

Deschrijver, E., & Palmer, C. (2020, August 27). *New theory suggests autism may not be tied to mindblindness*. Medical Xpress. https://medicalxpress.com/news/2020-09-theory-autism-tied-mindblindness.html

Fusar-Poli, P., & Politi, P. (2008). Paul Eugen Bleuler and the birth of schizophrenia (1908). *American Journal of Psychiatry*, *165*(11), 1407–1407. https://doi.org/10.1176/appi.ajp.2008.08050714

Kuhn, R., & Cahn, C. H. (2004). Eugen Bleuler's concepts of psychopathology. *History of Psychiatry*, *15*(3), 361–366. https://doi.org/10.1177/0957154X04044603

Lai, J. K., & Weiss, J. A. (2017). Priority service needs and receipt across the lifespan for individuals with autism spectrum disorder. *Autism Research*, *10*(8), 1436–1447. https://doi.org/10.1002/aur.1786

Lynch, C. L. (2019, May 4). *"Autism is a spectrum" doesn't mean what you think*. NeuroClastic. https://neuroclastic.com/2019/05/04/its-a-spectrum-doesnt-mean-what-you-think/

McGuire, A. E., & Michalko, R. (2011). Minds between us: Autism, mindblindness and the uncertainty of communication. *Educational Philosophy and Theory*, *43*(2), 162–177. https://doi.org/10.1111/j.1469-5812.2009.00537.x

Mestrum, F. (2015, August 27). *Social commons: A new alternative to neoliberalism*. Russia in Global Affairs. https://eng.globalaffairs.ru/articles/social-commons-a-new-alternative-to-neoliberalism/

Michalko, R. (2009). The excessive appearance of disability. *International Journal of Qualitative Studies in Education*, *22*(1), 65–74. https://doi.org/10.1080/09518390802581885

Murphy, R., Falchuck, B., Brennan, I. (Writers), & Stoltz, E. (Director). (2011, September 20). The purple piano project (Season 3, Episode 1) [TV series episode]. In I. Brennan, B. Falchuk, & R. Murphy (Executive Producers), *Glee*. 20th Century Fox; Brad Falchuk Teley-Vision; Ryan Murphy Productions.

Nadesan, M. H. (2013). *Constructing autism: Unravelling the 'truth' and understanding the social*. Routledge.

Stoddart, K., Burke, L., & King, R. (2012). *Asperger syndrome in adulthood: A comprehensive guide for clinicians*. W. W. Norton & Company.

Tager-Flusberg, H., Baron-Cohen, S., & Cohen, D. J. (1993). An introduction to the debate. In S. Baron-Cohen, H. Tager-Flusberg, & D. J. Cohen (Eds.), *Understanding other minds: Perspectives from autism* (pp. 3–9). Oxford University Press.

Timimi, S., Gardner, N., & McCabe, B. (2011). *The myth of autism: Medicalising men's and boys' social and emotional competence*. Palgrave Macmillan.

Titchkosky, T. (2011). *The question of access: Disability, space, meaning*. University of Toronto Press.

Titchkosky, T. (2018). Language. In T. Heller, S. Parker Harris, C. J. Gill, & R. Gould (Eds.), *Disability in American life [2 volumes]: An encyclopedia of concepts, policies, and controversies* (pp. 406–410). ABC-CLIO.

Titchkosky, T., & Michalko, R. (2009). Introduction. In T. Tichkosky & R. Michalko (Eds.), *Rethinking normalcy: A disability studies reader* (pp. 1–14). Canadian Scholars' Press.

Walker, N. (2014, April 1). *What is autism?* Neuroqueer: The writings of Dr. Nick Walker. https://neuroqueer.com/what-is-autism/

Yergeau, M. (2013). Clinically significant disturbance: On theorists who theorize theory of mind. *Disability Studies Quarterly, 33*(4).

CHAPTER 18

DisAppearing Disability: Disability MAiD Invisible

Nancy Hansen

Key Terms: Ableism; Absence; Discrimination; Eugenics; Invisibility

Medical Assistance in Dying (MaiD) is a contentious social issue and particularly so for disabled people in the wake of recent judicial decisions requiring broadened access to the process (CanLii, 2019; SCC, 2015). The changes to MaiD legislation have greatly increased eligibility and decreased restrictions in that death need no longer be at hand and individuals may want to die after a three-month waiting period (Inclusion Canada, 2020). As a disabled woman, using crutches for mobility, this subject—the medical and bureaucratic organization of an individual's death—quite literally impacts my life. Disability-led organizations are raising serious concerns regarding how these changes may directly affect disabled people (Institute for Research and Development on Inclusion and Society, 2017). We (disabled people) are the world's largest minority—over one billion people worldwide and more than 20 per cent of the working-age population in Canada (Statistics Canada, 2018; World Health Organization, 2020). Yet, we are rarely present when these polarizing discussions take place (Wolbring, 2003). Perhaps most disturbing is that many times our absence remains unnoticed and unremarkable (Capurri, 2020). The arbitrary privileging of certain forms of physicality is largely unrecognized (Scuro, 2018).

Historically, our presence has been seen as disruptive to public sensibilities (Saltes, 2018). It is only since the 1970s that the so-called "ugly laws" barring "the disfigured" from public space were repealed in North America (Schweik, 2010). When social discomfort equates difference—in this case, disability—with weakness and deficit, this can result in unplanned encounters with strangers projecting sympathy, difficulty, pity, pain, and "fixes" (such as assistive devices or some form of medical intervention measures) onto those individuals defined as "different." Our space and place are tenuous in that it is perceived that the space we occupy would be better used by non-disabled people (Kitchin, 1998). At times, we seem to be moving toward tolerance rather than acceptance (Scuro, 2018). Unlike acceptance, tolerance is in effect putting up with something while maintaining a position of assumed superiority. Indeed, disabled people's perspectives are routinely dismissed (Hansen, 2015). Individuals who raise concerns are frequently discounted as activists (Capurri, 2020), in much the same way as members of other marginalized groups (racialized, gender, or sexual) have experienced.

Where does this leave disabled people when we find ourselves chronically othered or invisible in the midst of selective social inclusion?

> "We focus on th[e] less-privileged narrative that nevertheless continues to 'haunt' not just the text but also the historical and contemporary contexts that connect to other narratives of exploitation (the middle passage and slavery), racial segregation (Jim Crow), incarceration (institutionalization of disabled people), sterilization (eugenics), and the more contemporary practice of the trade in human organs in poor communities across the globe (transnational capitalism) ... we offer a crip re-reading of Immortal Life to foreground the complexity of how disability as a central organizing logic intersects with race, class, and gender to animate a 'haunting' narrative."
>
> Gill, Michael, and Nirmala Erevelles. "The Absent Presence of Elsie Lacks: Hauntings at the Intersection of Race, Class, Gender, and Disability." *African American Review* 50, no. 2 (2017): 124–125.

In what follows, I illustrate these seemingly contradictory frames that I experienced when I was contacted in June 2019 by an academic colleague asking if I would participate in a conference on Medical Assistance in Dying (MAiD). She felt that the experience and perspectives of disabled people were absent from the event and needed to be addressed. I accepted the invitation as I had been studying this subject of assisted death for more than a decade. My first research study was travelling to Germany as part of a select international group of disabled academics studying the various disability killing sites in Germany, utilized during the Nazi period. Since then, I have followed how the lives of disabled people are so readily dismissed. I am troubled by the lack of critical analysis that often accompanies discussions on medically assisted death.

With my lifelong experience with disability—in scholarship, activism, and as I go about my daily activity—I am well acquainted with regular, random encounters with strangers in public spaces (shopping malls, building lobbies, and conference centres) who, with no prior warning, tell me that I am "inspirational," "brave," or "courageous"; exclaim, "that looks painful/difficult"; or ask, "why don't you use a wheelchair?" or "can't they fix that?" It would seem that the bar is set very low regarding the expectations of disabled people's participation in daily life.

Disabled people find themselves occupying an interesting duality. "People with unconventional bodies like ours must always choose, when entering the public arena, between invisibility and spectacle" (Frazee, 2019). How and when we become visible and how that visibility is interpreted may not, however, be of our choosing. It seems that Western society retains a palpable level of indecision in relation to the worth and validity of nonconformist minds and bodies (Evans, 2004; Nario-Redmond, 2020). I often wonder who benefits from these unsolicited comments and how they originate. Cultural understandings of disability are, for the most part, not based on actual encounters with disabled people. Rather, they tend to be drawn from outdated beliefs focused on correction, cure, or elimination (Scuro, 2018).

This excerpt from the UN Special Rapporteur on the Rights of Persons with Disabilities (2019) clearly articulates what is at stake here:

> Despite the significant advances in the recognition of the rights of persons with disabilities at international and national levels, the deeply rooted negative perceptions about the value of their lives continue to be a prevalent obstacle in all societies. Those perceptions are ingrained in ableism—a value system that considers certain typical characteristics of body and mind as essential for living a life of value. Based on strict standards of appearance, function and behaviour, ableist ways of thinking consider the disability experience as a misfortune that leads to suffering and disadvantage, and invariably devalues human life. As a result, it is generally assumed that the quality of life of persons with disabilities is very low, that they have no future to look forward to and that they will never live happy and fulfilling lives. (p. 3)

Preparing for the MAiD conference, I began to examine the latest writings and configuration of eugenics and euthanasia by numerous disability groups. For example, the Council of Canadians with Disabilities and the Canadian Association for Community Living have raised serious concerns for disabled people with increased access to MAiD (Council of Canadians with Disabilities, 2018). There are numerous examples nationwide where disabled people have been offered medically assisted death as an option rather than access to necessary programs and services (Enns, 2019).

There were numerous telephone meetings with other panel members—I was the only visibly disabled person on our panel. During our teleconferences, I raised disability issues related to possible unconscious bias, access to support services, vulnerability, and quality of life. The other panel participants, though not dismissive, seemed largely oblivious to my concerns.

Five months after the initial invitation, the conference was on the horizon. The night before the event, a lovely speakers' dinner was held. Good food and interesting conversation ensued. As I was leaving the venue an employee approached me and said,

"You need a wheelchair?"
"No, that's okay," I replied.
"You should have a wheelchair."
"No thanks, I've been doing this [using crutches] my entire life."
She turns to my colleague and says, "Poor thing."

On conference day, I arrive, and I am told it is the largest ever number of delegates attending the event, with over 200 people. They appear largely white, male, upper-middle-aged, and (at least visibly) non-disabled. All the MAiD subject panels are in the afternoon. Mine is the last of the day—three members, three questions, forty minutes in length. However, there are numerous panels in the interim. Throughout the afternoon I learn that the evocative language and terminology—assisted suicide, euthanasia—have been removed from MAiD legislation. Words are selectively revised, and the residual elements of eugenic history are neutralized, in much the same way as Evans (2004), analyzing the Nazi T4 program, has noted the power of discourse to neutralize difficult or uncomfortable language. The focus was on ease of access, process, and availability of MAiD. A series of upbeat videos are presented with testimonials from prospective MAiD candidates. The option is presented as providing control, dignity, and human rights. There is often a tendency to conflate these concepts with ultimate individual responsibility and control (Capurri, 2020). There is no discussion of disability, vulnerability, power differentials, or privilege.

"Catherine Frazee says, 'through Bill C-7—the government is making it possible for people with disability to kill themselves.... Now this amendment proposes opening up an entire new approach to assisted death, where it's now an alternative not to a painful death, but to a painful life—to a life that is considered intolerable or not worth living.'"

'Cold Comfort to Be Offered the Choice to Die' When Not Offered Support to Live, Says Disability Advocate." *The Current*. CBC, November 19, 2020. https://www.cbc.ca/radio/thecurrent/the-current-for-nov-19-2020-1.5807944/cold-comfort-to-be-offered-the-choice-to-die-when-not-offered-support-to-live-says-disability-advocate-1.5808541

ECHOES FROM THE PAST

It is as if everyone in the room is of the same mind. I feel increasingly uncomfortable, to the point that it is almost visceral. I have not felt like this in quite some time. It reminds me all too strongly of the Aktion T4 "research" projects in Germany in the early 1930s. The T4 experiments were a pilot program for the Holocaust where at least 400,000 disabled people were murdered—before Jews, queers, and other marginalized population groups (Evans, 2004).

Almost 80 years on from the extreme proponents of eugenics and the final solution, and what have we learned? Discussions are led and programs and policies are developed by individuals who remain distant from the real quality of life and actual lived experience of disabled people (Capurri, 2020).

So much silence and so many selective appearances and disappearances. There are no concerns or difficulties articulated. No one mentions disability. Finally, the last panel of the day is underway. It is my turn to speak, and I ask, "How many people here are comfortable with disability?" In a room of well over 200 people, perhaps 20 people raise their hands. I am not surprised. I follow up with basic information concerning the barriers disabled people face on a regular basis to access goods and services. The audience appears unfamiliar with these circumstances. There is a vigorous discussion following my presentation, and my comments are greeted with significant applause. The panel is completed, and I exit the stage. I am emotionally exhausted. Afterward, I am approached by several delegates thanking me for my important contribution.

The following day I telephoned my academic colleague who initiated the conference invitation. I wanted to give her an update on how it went. I tell her that it was the most difficult but most important thing that I have ever done in my academic life—sitting in a room reiterating the value of my existence and quality of life. She says that she is so sorry that I went through that. "Oh no, please don't feel that way," I respond, because it was very important that I took part. I told her that it was crucial that I attended. She tells me that she is sitting in the shopping mall with tears running down her face. Months later, I still think about that conference.

TOGETHER IN TENSION

Inclusion and exclusion are not a simple duality: they exist in concert (Mascareño & Carvajal, 2015), and they exist in tension. This subtle but collective aversion manifests itself in many ways and on several macro and micro levels together (Scuro, 2018).

> Over the last 50 years, the disability rights movement has been challenging these deeply rooted negative perceptions, stating that the real problem is the failure of society to eliminate barriers, provide the required support and embrace the disability experience as part of human diversity. However, the claims of persons with disabilities to have their rights recognized are often dismissed and the underlying power imbalance invalidates their lived experiences. Their narratives are considered to be subjective and ill-suited to decision-making and thus are not given the space to be genuinely weighed or to challenge ableism. Access to the platforms on which discussions are taking place is limited, rendering the disability movement unable to share information on an equal basis with others. (Special Rapporteur on the Rights of Persons with Disabilities, 2019, p. 4)

Internally, at my very core, I almost feel the need to justify my existence. Lack of critical engagement with difficult histories may have serious consequences for the disability community in the 21st century. There are disturbing similarities between arguments found in Nazi documentation concerning "quality of life," "useless eaters," or "lives less worthy" and mainstream genetics and medical ethics discussions concerning disability taking place today (Evans, 2004; Mansfield et al., 1999). "There is often a tendency to conflate quality of life with worthiness to live" (Hansen & Janz, 2009, p. 30). Killing people who suffered from congenital mental or physical "malformations … is made to appear justified," because such "creatures" required long-term care, aroused "horror" in other people, and represented the "lowest animal level" (Evans, 2004, pp. 24–25). Strikingly similar arguments have been put forward by medical ethicist Peter Singer (1994) who proposes "to embrace a social ethic where some human lives are valued and others are not" (p. 121).

I find it interesting that Singer's reputation as an animal rights activist is far better known than his stance on disability. Animal rights at times appear to outweigh human rights for disabled people in some quarters (Herzog, 2018). Furthermore, there is a tendency to present an oversimplified, reductionist, and in some instances dehumanizing version of disability (Herzog, 2018; McPherson & Sobsey, 2003). Additionally, disability scholar William Armer (2005) cautions against "entering into an era of *eugenics* – the practice of human genetics within a societal atmosphere, or cultural field, which is informed by eugenic ideology" (p. 3).

As we strive for social perfection on many levels, the range of what is considered acceptable has narrowed considerably (Capurri, 2020). The arbitrary nature of inclusion and exclusion continues to manifest itself in the most disturbing ways: "The enduring barriers that Canadians face in living how, where, and with whom they want means that giving people with disabilities assistance in dying in lieu of assistance to live is ableism, not equality" (Janz, as quoted in Tait, 2020).

> "The question of the entrepreneurial nation remained, what to do with the 'unproductive,' those not exploitable as laborers? And ultimately, how can disabled people be made of use to the economic order? The solution has been to make disablement big business. Under the Money Model of disability, the disabled human being is a commodity around which social policies are created or rejected based on their market value. The corporate 'solution' to disablement—institutionalization in a nursing home—evolved from the cold realization that disabled people could be commodified."
>
> Russell, Marta. *Beyond Ramps: Disability at the End of the Social Contract: A Warning from an Uppity Crip*. Monroe, ME: Common Courage Press, 1998, p. 127.

DISABILITY IN THE TIME OF COVID-19

Airbrushing disability from the historical narrative reinforces the status quo (Capurri, 2020). Such an approach keeps the social discomfort level at arm's length and maintains the belief that we need not revisit this difficult and/or disturbing history in a modern context (Bauman, 2000). However, it would seem that history is indeed repeating itself. During the COVID-19 pandemic, I read the following headlines from various respected news outlets postulating whether or not providing medical care to disabled people is feasible during a period of medical rationing.

> People with Down Syndrome Could Be Left to Die of Coronavirus to 'Save' Medical Supplies (McCloskey, 2020)
>
> What Is a Ventilator and Who Gets One If COVID-19 Turns Catastrophic in Canada? (Zafar, 2020)
>
> Rationing Care Is a Surrender to Death: Limiting Treatment for the Old or Chronically Ill May Also Violate Civil-Rights Law (Guelzo, 2020)
>
> Americans with Disabilities Are Terrified: They Fear They Could Be Denied Lifesaving Treatment If They End Up in the Hospital with COVID-19 (Godfrey, 2020)

These media headlines show just how quickly we move from valuing diversity and inclusion to questioning social worthiness in times of adversity. What happens when the modern state characterizes disability as structurally flawed minds and bodies (Mostert, 2002)?

Unfortunately, this has become all too clear in recent months. In a suburb of Toronto, care workers left an institution en masse—some were ill, others said they no longer felt safe, thus abandoning the disabled people inside (Tsekouras, 2020). In a Montreal suburb, elderly occupants of an old age home were discovered in conditions of profound neglect and squalor (Henriques et al., 2020). These are not simply actions of a few frightened or self-absorbed employees. Rather it is symptomatic of a much larger systemic abandonment of a segment of the population (disabled and/or elderly) that is deemed to be expendable. Relatedly, Jean Truchon, one of the individuals who petitioned the Quebec Court for wider access to MAiD, chose to expedite assisted death rather than endure the deteriorating conditions in his nursing home (Ha, 2020).

As Inclusion Canada (2020) explained in their news release:

> It is not disability that causes people's suffering, just like it is not a person's indignity or sexual orientation that causes suffering in Canadian society, though there are higher than average suicide rates for Indigenous persons and the LGBTQ2S community. Suffering comes from living in a society where the conditions of your inclusion and dignity are denied because of your personal characteristics.

"The social, political, and cultural analysis undertaken by disability studies form a prism through which one can gain a broader understanding of society and human experience, and the significance of human variation.... Scholarship in this field addresses such fundamental ideas as who is considered a burden and who a resource, who is expendable and who is esteemed, who should engage in the activities that might lead to reproduction and who should not, and, if reproduction is not the aim, who can engage in erotic pleasures and who should not."

Linton, Simi. *Claiming Disability: Knowledge and Identity*. New York, NY: New York University Press, 1998, pp. 117–118.

CONCLUSION

There are many layers of complexity in regards to disability and MAiD. What is of importance is that policies are often (although unrecognized) infused with ableism. This discussion is not about numbers, politics, or rhetoric. It is about policies that excuse killing people. It is dangerous to think that one is always in control or that there is no risk of displacement or removal (Z. Lutfiyya, personal communication, February 1, 2005).

The situations of profound disadvantage and neglect that we (disabled people) find ourselves in through disaster or public policy have been naturalized over decades, as Catherine Frazee (2005) explained in the aftermath of Hurricane Katrina:

> As a consequence of generations of exclusion, impoverishment and overlooking, disabled people's experience of disaster is more acute, more long-lasting, more catastrophic. While calamity may be random, its impacts never are. For the most part, catastrophe stalks by category, and disabled people figure prominently on its radar. (p. 120)

With this in mind, we must begin to confront and address the disordered, complex distinctiveness at the very essence of humankind (Mostert, 2002). As technology is given ever greater prominence in almost every aspect of daily life, we must ask ourselves a crucial question: Is the belief in the objective safety of science reinforcing long-established social practices (Bauman, 2000; Burleigh, 1997; Mostert, 2002)? This may well be disruptive to the established social–cultural comfort zone. However, we must ask ourselves who is really uncomfortable, how are they uncomfortable, and why? "Today, if granted a comparable moment of attention, other disabled Canadians should call upon our leaders to make good on the fundamental promises of citizenship: equal protection of the law, equal opportunity to live with dignity, and equal recognition in governance and culture" (Frazee, 2019).

Our future depends on a robust yet balanced discussion that finds disabled people and their allies at the centre. Without such a discussion, we run the risk of disappearance.

REFERENCES

Armer, W. (2005). *In the shadow of genetics: An analysis of eugenic influences on twentieth century social policy for disabled people in European and North American societies* [Unpublished doctoral dissertation, Leeds University]. The Disability Archive. https://disability-studies.leeds.ac.uk/library/author/armer.williamgeorgebill/

Bauman, Z. (2000). *Modernity and the Holocaust.* Cornell University Press.

Burleigh, M. (1997). *Ethics and extermination: Reflections on Nazi genocide.* Cambridge University Press.

CanLii. (2019). *Truchon c. Procureur général du Canada, 2019 QCCS 3792.* https://www.canlii.org/fr/qc/qccs/doc/2019/2019qccs3792/2019qccs3792.html

Capurri, V. (2020). *Not good enough for Canada: Canadian public discourse around issues of inadmissibility for potential immigrants with diseases and/or disabilities, 1902–2002.* University of Toronto Press.

Council of Canadians with Disabilities. (2018, September 4). *Canada's medical assistance in dying regulations fall short.* http://www.ccdonline.ca/en/humanrights/endoflife/Media-Release-4Sept2018-MAiD-Regulations-Fall-Short

Enns, R. (2019, October 12). *Liberty or equality? Unrestricted access to medically assisted death endangers vulnerable people.* CBC News. https://www.cbc.ca/news/canada/manitoba/opinion-ruth-enns-maid-disability-1.5318540

Evans, S. (2004). *Forgotten crimes: The Holocaust and disabled people.* Ivan R. Dee.

Frazee, C. (2005). Disability in dangerous times. *Journal on Developmental Disabilities, 15*(3), 118–124.

Frazee, C. (2019). *Canadian leaders should defend human dignity in life—not just death.* CBC News. https://www.cbc.ca/news/opinion/assisted-dying-1.5330654

Godfrey, E. (2020, April 3). *Americans with disabilities are terrified.* The Atlantic. https://www.theatlantic.com/politics/archive/2020/04/people-disabilities-worry-they-wont-get-treatment/609355/

Guelzo, A. (2020, March 26). *Rationing care is a surrender to death.* Wall Street Journal. https://www.wsj.com/articles/rationing-care-is-a-surrender-to-death-11585262558?reflink=share_mobilewebshare

Ha, T. T. (2020, April 8). *Jean Truchon, MAiD advocate, receives assisted death early because of coronavirus fears.* Globe and Mail. https://www.theglobeandmail.com/canada/article-jean-truchon-maid-advocate-receives-assisted-death-early-due-to/

Hansen, N. (2015). *Better dead than disabled, I don't think so!* UM Today. https://news.umanitoba.ca/better-dead-than-disabled-i-dont-think-so/

Hansen, N., & Janz, H. (2009). The ethics of making space for non-conformist minds and bodies in healthcare. *Developmental Disabilities Bulletin, 37*(1&2), 29–43.

Henriques, B., De Souza, M., & Spector, D. (2020, April 11). *Coronavirus: 31 dead, elderly covered in feces at Dorval long-term care facility.* Global News. https://globalnews.ca/news/6807585/coronavirus-dorval-residence/

Herzog, D. (2018). *Unlearning eugenics: Sexuality, reproduction, and disability in post-Nazi Europe.* University of Wisconsin Press.

Inclusion Canada. (2020). *Safeguards in medical assistance in dying.* https://inclusioncanada.ca/campaign/safeguards-in-medical-assistance-in-dying/

Institute for Research and Development on Inclusion and Society. (2017). *Concerns with expanding access to medical assistance in dying: A review of evidence.* https://irisinstitute.ca/wp-content/uploads/sites/2/2017/11/Expanding-Access-to-MAiD-Literature-Review-Oct-2017.pdf

Kitchin, R. (1998). "Out of place," "knowing one's place": Space, power and the exclusion of disabled people. *Disability & Society, 13*(3), 343–356.

Mansfield, C., Hopfer, S., & Marteau, T. (1999). Termination rates after prenatal diagnosis of Down syndrome, spina bifida, anencephaly, and Turner and Klinefelter syndromes: A systematic literature review. *Prenatal Diagnosis, 19*(2), 808–812.

Mascareño, A., & Carvajal, F. (2015). The different faces of inclusion and exclusion. *CEPAL Review, 116,* 127–141. https://www.cepal.org/en/publications/39616-different-faces-inclusion-and-exclusion

McCloskey, J. (2020, March 26). *People with Down syndrome could be left to die of coronavirus to 'save' medical supplies.* The Metro UK. https://metro.co.uk/2020/03/27/people-syndrome-may-lower-priority-live-saving-coronavirus-care-12466194/

McPherson, G. W., & Sobsey, D. (2003). Rehabilitation: Disability ethics versus Peter Singer. *Archives of Physical Medicine and Rehabilitation, 84,* 1246–1248. https://doi.org/10.1016/S0003-9993(03)00107-2

Mostert, M. (2002). Useless eaters: Disability as genocidal marker in Nazi Germany. *The Journal of Special Education, 36*(3), 155–168. https://doi.org/10.1177/00224669020360030601

Nario-Redmond, M. (2020). *Ableism: The causes and consequences of disability prejudice.* Wiley-Blackwell.

Saltes, N. (2018). Navigating disabling spaces: Challenging ontological norms and the spatialization of difference through 'Embodied Practices of Mobility. *Mobilities, 13*(1), 81–95. https://doi.org/10.1080/17450101.2017.1333279

Schweik, S. (2010). *The ugly laws disability in public.* New York University Press.

Scuro, J. (2018). *Addressing ableism: Philosophical questions via disability studies.* Lexington Books.

Singer, P. (1994). *Rethinking life and death: The collapse of our traditional ethics.* St. Martin's Press.

Special Rapporteur on the Rights of Persons with Disabilities. (2019, December 17). *Report on the impact of ableism in medical and scientific practice.* United Nations Human Rights Office of the High Commissioner. https://www.ohchr.org/EN/Issues/Disability/SRDisabilities/Pages/BioethicsDisabilities.aspx

Statistics Canada. (2018). *New data on disability in Canada, 2017.* https://www150.statcan.gc.ca/n1/pub/11-627-m/11-627-m2018035-eng.htm

Supreme Court of Canada (SCC). (2015). Carter v. Canada (Attorney General), 2015 SCC 5. https://scc-csc.lexum.com/scc-csc/scc-csc/en/item/14637/index.do

Tait, C. (2020, January 27). *Edmonton woman makes national appeal for people with disabilities.* Edmonton Sun. https://edmontonsun.com/opinion/columnists/tait-edmonton-woman-makes-national-appeal

Tsekouras, P. (2020, April 10). *Staff at Ontario facility for vulnerable adults walks out following COVID-19 outbreak.* CTV News. https://toronto.ctvnews.ca/staff-at-ontario-facility-for-vulnerable-adults-walks-out-following-covid-19-outbreak-1.4891552

Wolbring, G. (2003). Disability rights approach toward bioethics? *Journal of Disability Policy Studies, 14*(3), 174–180. https://doi.org/10.1177/10442073030140030701

World Health Organization. (2020). *Better health for disabled people.* https://www.who.int/france/multi-media/details/better-health-for-people-with-disabilities

Zafar, A. (2020, March 31). *What is a ventilator and who gets one if COVID-19 turns catastrophic in Canada?* CBC News. https://www.cbc.ca/news/health/covid19-ventilators-1.5515550

CHAPTER 19

The Pill Box Shuffle

Leanne Toshiko Simpson

It barely weighs anything but holds all my heaviness inside it. Clasped in the palm of my hand, I inhale its chalky, sour scent and breathe out fear—of what it does to me and what I have done to myself, in days unremembered. It is oblong in shape, white like porcelain, and almost impossible to break in half when I need less of it. I dream of needing less of it. The engraving in its dull and smooth surface measures its mass, 120 mg of *do not break, chew, or crush. In fact, you may want to stop fragmenting yourself at all.* It is a substance with many labels—chemical, molecular, name-brand, or generic. Some might call it atypical, but to me it's a constant. When I consume it, I become weighty and clouded, tethered to the earth by the churning of my liver. It brings a drought to my mouth until I wash it away with a swill of cold water. There are nights when my body regrets this unholy partnership, wakes up at 3 a.m. so I can clutch the toilet. There are others when my dreams are beguiling and innocent, like I've never known any pain at all. But in the palm of my hand, I and it live in a world of possibility. In the moment before I choose it (or not), two roads diverge in a yellow wood. On one path, I follow it toward a promise it cannot keep, and down the other, I mourn a long-time friend and foe. We rehearse this dance every night, but somehow it always feels brand new. How odd it is to hold what has become a part of yourself in this way and wonder who you are without it—if what's keeping you alive is also keeping you contained, and whether you could be embraced without the clutch of a pill.

PART V

DISAPPEARING DREAMS

EDITORS' INTRODUCTION

"DisAppearing Dreams," the final part of this collection, brings together chapters that nurture the possibilities of interpretation, imagination, narrative, and hope—all the stuff of dreams.

One reason that the meaning of disability is never certain and never fully settled is because there is an intimate provocation between disability and dreams. Not only does disability enter our dreams, but we can dream of places and encounters where disability matters in new and unexpected ways. Different dreams are always possible in the face of disability insofar as embodiment of any sort is never free from cultural interpretations and material structures.

> Leroy Moore: "The National Black Disability Coalition (NBDC) has been working on creating a working theory and practice of Black DS [disability studies]. Once again we continue the conversation about disability identity from a Black perspective. We agree it is different from dominant culture disability, but the questions are—What are the differences? How does the Black community display those differences? And how do Black disabled people, family members, and loved ones sit within their disability in their communities? It is the intent of Black DS to examine many questions and experiences, provide research, and engage Black disabled scholars. The range from history, culture, arts, sciences, leadership, and politics from the experience of Black people with disabilities must have a home that is Afro-centric, most importantly to engage Black disabled pride and knowledge."
>
> Dunhamn, Jane, Jerome Harris, Shancia Jarrett, Leroy Moore, Akemi Nishida, Margaret Price, Britney Robinson, and Sami Schalk. "Developing and Reflecting on a Black Disability Studies Pedagogy: Work from the National Black Disability Coalition." *Disability Studies Quarterly* 35, no. 2 (2015).

In the first chapter of this final part, "The Infinity of the Encounter: Deafness, Disability, Race, and the Sound of Story," Elaine Cagulada introduces the promise of the unfinished story. Her chapter demonstrates a way of attending to single stories about deafness, disability, race, and truth in such a way that digs out the hidden meanings of their interwoven multiplicity. Cagulada makes use of a news media account of being Black, playing ball, hanging out at a bus stop, and being suspected of robbery as the material to which she applies a method characterized by her as "story ... influenced by interpretive disability studies, a pedagogy for reading disability and blackness (Pickens, 2017), and the Anishinaabe ontology of mnidoo-worlding (Manning, 2017)." Following through on the promise that there is always another story, even within powerful police stories, Cagulada allows the dream of respect for the fluidity of human life's complexity to be dreamed again.

Chelsea Temple Jones in her chapter, "'Where Are the Goddamn Pens?': And Other DisAppearances in Writing Intellectual Disability," is also engaged in storying tied to dreams. Jones says, "I spin memories into words in order to recall the end of this vestigial inquiry with a group of triple-labelled writers. By triple-labelled I mean people whose lives are eclipsed by labels of intellectual disability, incompetence, and vulnerability." This vulnerability intersects with her own as she comes to know of and process the death of one of her dissertation research participants. Jones engages with "creative analytic practice (CAP), a way of using writing as a method of discovery," and through this method and these experiences, Jones re-writes her understanding of her research, herself, and people understood as having an intellectual disability. The dream of mattering, where people who have acquired the label of intellectual disability are encountered as meaning makers and whose thoughts, feelings, and existence *matters*, is palpable throughout this chapter.

Maya Chacaby, an Anishinaabe teacher and autistic scholar—"Indigen-autie" in Chacaby's terms—attends to the movement of Anishinaabemowin, especially the active sense of words as a doing, as a way to story the post-colonial theorizing of Homi K. Bhabha. Chacaby's play, or dialogic narrative, is a unique engagement with theorizing, transposed into script form and infused with sharp wit and humour— including writing a script about social scripts! Here we witness a discussion between three characters, Friendly, Encounter, and In-Between, all three of whom bring us in touch with the dream of making meaning through theory in new ways. Chacaby's script allows for the life of disability and Indigenous ways of knowing to thrive by remaking norms of social interactions into moments to theorize our unexpected forms of interrelation and their meanings.

We end this part with the late Lynn Manning's (2009) poem "The Magic Wand," a part of his spoken word play *Weights* narrating the meaning and movements of being a young Black man who is shot in the head, survives, and re-encounters himself, his friends, and his artistic practices as profoundly blind. This poem represents the dreams that grow from self-reflection on the eyes of the world. Manning is sometimes seen by others as blind, sometimes as Black; Manning perceives both ways of seeing himself and in so doing dreams his unique rejoinder—this poem.

"The Magic Wand" can be read as our dream as editors of this collection, to imagine a "restless, reflexive return" (Titchkosky, 2011) to the ways disability already appears and disappears in our lives and to orient us to a possible encounter with disability as full of unexpected meanings. Working with a plethora of disability experience, *DisAppearing: Encounters in Disability Studies* is oriented toward making disability appear in its complexity, a complexity that resists being explained. Our hope is that this collection provokes readers to seek out new relations on the borders of appearance and disappearance of our bodies, minds, senses, and emotions.

"Throughout, I highlight what black liberation struggles might critically cull and ethically adapt from mad time. This emphasis reflects my belief that black freedom movements can gain much by foregrounding madness in their accounts of black life and agendas for black liberation. The fact is that some freedom-loving and freedom-fighting black people *get mad* and *go mad* amid onslaughts of antiblack violence, terror, degradation, and hurt. Too often, however, mad people are treated as casualties, and madness as mere liability, in revolutionary struggles. I insist that we honor the mad among our ranks, remembering that madness is "loaded with information and energy" that can inform and invigorate liberation movements. I do not mean to romanticize mania, depression, schizophrenia, and melancholia. Nor do I recommend that revolutionary thinkers or liberation movements aspire to psychiatric disorder. I know that these conditions, at the level of lived symptoms and psychosocial stigmas, are painful for many. However, a condition can be a source of pain *and* a recourse for revolution."

Bruce, Le Marr Jurelle. *How to Go Mad without Losing Your Mind: Madness and Black Radical Creativity*. Durham, NC: Duke University Press, 2021, p. 207.

Guiding Questions

1. How is disability included in your dreams?
2. Do your dreams allow you to imagine your life, experiences, and relations in different ways, ways that might be unexpected?
3. How might dreams, both literal and figurative, and their many complexities allow us to engage with the appearances and disappearances of disability in new, unforeseen, and even wondrous ways?
4. Why might it be important to attend to the ways that disability is dreamed as part of, or excluded from, collective life?
5. How might disability touch our dreams and shape our hopes for the future?
6. If we dreamed a world where disability experience was welcomed and expected, what sort of world might it be? What social awareness would it require? What would need to become obsolete?

REFERENCES

Manning, D. T. (2017). The murmuration of birds: An Anishinaabe ontology of mnidoo-worlding. In H. A. Fielding & D. E. Olkowski (Eds.), *Feminist phenomenology futures* (pp. 154–182). Indiana University Press.

Manning, L. (2009). The magic wand. *International Journal of Inclusive Education*, *13*(7), 785. https://doi.org/10.1080/13603110903046069

Titchkosky, T. (2011). *The question of access: Disability, space, meaning*. University of Toronto Press.

CHAPTER 20

The Infinity of the Encounter: Deafness, Disability, Race, and the Sound of Story[1]

Elaine Cagulada

Key Terms: Fact; Mnidoo-Worlding; Policing; Story; Truth

> *"So much of the work of oppression is policing the imagination."*
> —Saidiya Hartman, "Under the Blacklight: Storytelling While Black and
> Female: Conjuring Beautiful Experiments in Past and Future Worlds,"
> African American Policy Forum

INTRODUCTION

In this chapter, I introduce a different way of attending to single stories about deafness, disability, race, and truth. My approach to story is influenced by interpretive disability studies, a pedagogy for reading disability and blackness (Pickens, 2017), and the Anishinaabe ontology of mnidoo-worlding (Manning, 2017). I treat disability not as a fixed single phenomenon but as always appearing in the fluidity of human life's complexity (Titchkosky, 2007, p. 37). The appearance of disability, together with its dis/appearance, always tumbles in both the flows and throes of conflicting interpretations. A pedagogy for reading disability and blackness alongside the Anshinaabe ontology of mnidoo-worlding teaches us that disability, while relegated to and perceived as the margin, is always already everywhere, including in the place we call the margins. Disability, therefore, not only makes normalcy possible since it, too, is everywhere; it also exceeds single stories and definitions.

On the danger of single stories, storyteller Chimamanda Adichie (2009) says, "The single story creates stereotypes. And the problem with stereotypes is not that they are untrue but that they are incomplete. They make one story become the only story." My work, following Adichie (2009), speaks of the necessity of storying single stories of encounters between deaf people and police. It seeks not only to dispute the truth but to contribute to the completion of the story of the relation between deaf people and law enforcement, in particular the police. This storying makes it possible for us to hear more than one story about deafness, race, and truth; storying shifts how we listen for deafness, for disability. Through storying, we might experience the sound of story. I begin my analysis with an account of two news articles regarding an encounter among deafness, race, the police, and the truth. I then return to the stories presented in the news articles and story my encounter with them as a way to open up the possibility of alternate interpretations and counternarratives. My analysis is guided by the following questions: How is the appearance of police as a feature of everyday life continuously sustained through single stories of what it means to be deaf, disabled, and/or racialized? What single stories of truth are required to manage the everyday dis/appearance of some people as problems and the institution of police as solvers of problems—that is, what I understand as the normalcy of police? Does storying relations between deaf people and the police disrupt the normal ways this relation is storied?

CHECKING FACTS

I turn now to two texts, where text, as Tanya Titchkosky (2007) writes, "is a social location and organizer for the accomplishment of meaning, making text count as a form of social action" (p. 27), and examine the social action located in two 2004 news media articles, one in the *Inclusion Daily Express* and another in *The Globe and Mail*. The news media, including print and electronic, report events within the framework of what has come to be known as "fact." However, facts, or what is understood as what "actually" happened, are often disputed, and this is the ground upon which phenomena such as justice and injustice are based. Note the headline in the article from *Inclusion Daily Express* (Reynolds, 2004), which reads: "Advocacy Groups Support Deaf Man Who Accuses Police of Assault." Thrown into the middle of things, we learn in this article that the story begins on a late evening in September 2002. The police questioned and subsequently detained Peter Owusu-Ansah, a 25-year-old deaf Black man (Reynolds, 2004). In the *Inclusion Daily Express* article it is reported:

> According to Owusu-Ansah, he was talking with friends on a street corner on the evening of September 13, 2002, when Toronto police constable Wayne Taylor approached him and asked to see his identification. When Owusu-Ansah was not able to show identification, the officer asked for

his name, birth date and address. He gave his first name, but not his last, he said, because he was tired of being stopped by police—more than 17 times in the past few years. (Reynolds, 2004)

The story refers to the experience of racism: "tired of being stopped by police—more than 17 times in the past few years." Clearly, we can infer that Owusu-Ansah was not arrested on each of these 17 times; we can infer that he was not engaged in criminal behaviour each of these 17 times. Based on what we know about the institution of police being a symptom of systemic racism and colonial violence (Stelkia, 2020), we may also infer that the number of times he has been stopped by police in the last few years has something to do with how racialized people come to be Othered in encounters of policing.

Consider as well the following 2004 headline from *The Globe and Mail* (Abbate, 2004): "Two Constables Found Not Guilty of Assaulting Deaf Man in 2002." This headline represents the conclusion of a story but not the story itself. *The Globe and Mail* article goes on to say that the two police constables accused of assaulting Owusu-Ansah are found not guilty by the presiding judge, Judge Robertson. Owusu-Ansah's account of events is inconsistent at various points, according to Judge Robertson, and he showed no signs of having endured physical assault. The story of Owusu-Ansah's encounter with police becomes a story of whether the law, represented in the character of a judge, believes Owusu-Ansah's story of events to be true. In *The Globe and Mail* article, the final decision from Judge Robertson is reported as follows:

Police legally stopped and detained Mr. Owusu-Ansah for a brief time, the judge concluded. The group was stopped at the intersection of Eglinton and Bayview Avenues because of a reported robbery nearby that involved a large number of black males. Bias or racism played no part, the judge said. (Abbate, 2004)

This excerpt might be read in a straightforward and simple way; Owusu-Ansah was legally stopped and detained due to a robbery reported nearby that involved a large number of Black males—as simple as that. But, while the judge concludes that bias or racism did not play a part in the encounter between police and Owusu-Ansah, we question the truth of this claim. After all, a robbery was committed nearby and committed by "a large number of black males." We also know that Owusu-Ansah is Black and that he had been stopped by police 17 times in the past few years. This makes it difficult, if not *impossible*, to agree with Judge Robertson that "bias or racism played no part." To say that bias or racism are *not* at work when the credibility of a deaf Black man is up for question and when two police constables are found not guilty of assaulting him is to say something more than bias was not involved. To say with certainty that bias or racism is there but not here is to inhabit a space of certainty that convinces us that we can objectively know where bias as well as racism begin and end. Indeed, to locate bias or racism in some places and not others is to believe that policing can be non-biased and non-racist when, time and time again, more harm to marginalized populations caused by police officers tells us that racism and bias play a *pivotal* part in policing in Canada. Far from straightforward, then, this story is complicated and made evermore so by the law's practice of diluting complexities into facts, evidence, and bias-free conclusions.

Two headlines, two different parts of a story. In one story, we are thrown into the middle as we learn of Owusu-Ansah's encounter with police. In another, we learn that the two police constables charged with assaulting Owusu-Ansah are found not guilty. The first story acts as the middle, the second acts as the end. How did the events of the September evening lead up to this middle and end? These media accounts produce a story not only about a person who is arrested but of relations among police, deaf people, and Black people. And even if it is difficult to imagine deafness playing a role in Owusu-Ansah's experience with policing, to imagine deafness tied to racialization, his deafness is nevertheless part of who he is and, therefore, part of these stories. These relations among police, deaf people, and Black people are framed within the parameters of deafness, blackness, policing and are all geared to the production of the Truth. However, we can imagine another set of facts based on interpretations of "what happened" from these two news media articles. We can imagine how different facts can be borne from the way that events are interpreted, events that already arrive before us as themselves interpretations, as stories. Of course, many possibilities can arise from facts, even while facts might appear as closed containers. Facts, too, are constructed, interpreted, and shaped by perception. Facts, we can say, cannot escape interpretation nor can they escape bias. I take these facts, the stories presented as facts in these news media accounts, and tell yet another story, a story impossible to tell without their first telling. My story, then, stories the story of the news accounts.

THE SOUNDS OF STORY

What follows is a different story from the news media accounts. This story, another story of the events told in the news media accounts, is not meant to replace the actual events of what happened that evening as the *truth*. Rather than become a stand-in for the truth of that evening, what I have narrated below is only meant to draw our attention to the *life* and *possibility* that deafness, disability, and race can represent when narrated with more caution. There is an urgent import to attend to the life of deafness, disability, and race when policing has threatened and continues to threaten to disappear the life of deafness, disability, and race as undesirable and disposable. Hearing another story living within the stories told in the news accounts of Owusu-Ansah and the police constables, my listening is inspirited by the will to bring a different face of a single story of deafness, disability, and race to view. I imagine how such a story, arising from another, might be shared and experienced. Lost in thought, I wonder, how might such a story—another story—sound?

Some Time Then and Now

On a late night in September, Officer Taylor from the Toronto Police Service is called to midtown Toronto after reports of a robbery. The neighbourhood is asleep when he arrives, with just the quiet hum of his patrol vehicle keeping him company. *Hum*, it goes, as they pass a deserted school and empty playground. *Hum*, again it murmurs, prodding past expensive European vehicles parked in parallel, sitting calm and confident along paved sidewalks in the grey of the night. Large brick homes, divided by shrubs aglow with daily maintenance, follow neatly one after another as Officer Taylor drives through block after block. *Hum*, it continues, until he happens upon a bus stop.

Enjoying the comfort of a sheltered bus stop in a stylish part of town, Peter Owusu-Ansah and his friends are waiting for their ride home. After playing basketball at the Bob Rumball Centre for the Deaf, they are both satisfied and exhausted from the recreation of the evening. Some rub their shoulders and stretch their necks to reduce tension that had built up after a friendly game of ball among competitive friends. Some instinctively put their hands on their bellies, wondering if the post-game McDonald's was the best idea. Everyone takes a moment to flex their fingers in an attempt to prevent the cramps that can arrive after an intense evening of hoops. And as they all take a moment to stretch their fingers and hula their wrists, they take a break from discussion and enter into their version of silence for the umpteenth time this evening. Stretch first, sign after.

The *hum* of the police vehicle halts near the bus stop, leaving the resounding buzz of streetlights to take centre stage as the evening's soundtrack. Maybe it is the look of deafness—their fast-moving fingers and the emotive expressions on their faces as they converse and discuss next week's plans; maybe it's the way the concrete refracts the orange hues of a nearby streetlight, painting the street in varying shades of shadows; maybe it's their casual presence juxtaposed with a cop who has been called to an affluent neighbourhood to address stolen goods, called because there were approximately 20 Black males involved in a robbery nearby. Whatever the reason, the appearance of Owusu-Ansah and friends does not go unnoticed that evening. Their appearance, in some ways, is timely for Officer Taylor. For Taylor, things seem to be checking out.

The buzzing of the streetlight only becomes louder as Taylor approaches Owusu-Ansah and his friends in order to ask for their identification. The evening seems to take a breath, as if preparing for an encounter that is always beginning, across time and geographies. This interaction is not as clean as the police-policed relation is perhaps made out to be; what unfolds is messy. Taylor has approached, with all his expectations, including perhaps those about blackness, race, deafness, and disability, a group of friends who, too, have all their expectations, including perhaps about being approached by the cops. This encounter of expectations unfolds in rhizomatic fashion, though mostly in retrogression, it seems, for Owusu-Ansah. No stranger to a cop's suspicions, Owusu-Ansah wonders if he will be wrong about what comes next.

As the night watches, worlds draw nearer, unasked questions hover like stars. Is Officer Taylor thinking about how he might be an unwelcome guest to an otherwise friendly gathering? As he saunters over, badge gleaming like it was polished earlier that evening, is Taylor brought to think about how his presence is emblematic of an institution that requires the extinguishing of Black life? Like the concrete thoroughfare just beyond the bus stop, these questions help carry the scene while absently lingering in the background.

Beneath the orange glow of the street, the slight tremor of an autumn breeze borrows everyone's attention. For a moment, as the breeze comes and goes, Owusu-Ansah's and Taylor's worlds overlap. And yet, Taylor's demands on Owusu-Ansah's deafness sets them worlds apart. The supposed straightforward exchange of being asked for identification and then being shown identification is always already steeped in complexity. There are interlocking expressions of race, disability, gender, authority, and more at work, ebbing, flowing, and making meaning of encounters between the police and the policed. Identification must already occur, it seems, in order for the question of "Can I see identification?" to be made possible.

Appearances, overdetermined on all sides, continue to move messily in the encounter between Taylor and Owusu-Ansah. Questions of identification posed amid the backdrop of Taylor's certainty that trouble *is* present at this bus stop only tighten the knots tangled by ways-of-knowing clashing into one another. Only the night can really listen, really take in the feel of institutional expectations of compliance struggling in the face of deaf, Black life. Again, the officer insists on identification. Again, Owusu-Ansah tells Taylor that he is deaf and waiting for the bus. Taylor, alert as ever at the uneasy turn of the evening, calls for back-up in the name of Officer Moosvi. And just as swiftly as this part of the telling goes, Moosvi appears and Owusu-Ansah is arrested. Thrown into the back seat of a police vehicle, Owusu-Ansah is then taken to a deserted school yard where, according to Owusu-Ansah, "he [Moosvi] started to punch my face ... he kept punching my face and he kneed me and he slapped me and he took off his vest and asked me if I wanted to fight him" (Reynolds, 2004). Moosvi, when asked why he drove Owusu-Ansah to an abandoned school yard after arresting him, explained that "it would be a safer place to talk and his cruiser would not interfere with traffic" (Abbate, 2004). These are two ways to regard the same moment, two ways that challenge singular notions of fact and truth; these are two very different stories.

As if old news, both police officers are found not guilty of their assault against Owusu-Ansah. Swiftly came the officers to interrupt the calmness of an evening, to disrupt a moment of togetherness among members of a community, and just as swiftly, accountability for the violence they inflicted disappeared. Online, the main news report of these events is now archived (Abbate, 2004). The outcome, it seems, is almost as mundane as waiting for a bus ride home.

> "Policing as an institution remains rooted not only in the violence of the plantation, but in an even older violence: the violence of the logic that allowed Black people to be justifiably enslaved in the first place, which flows from the violence of ranking and valuing human lives in a radically unequal fashion. These forms of violence continue to underwrite policing, and its own violence, regardless of the community or country in which the policing is taking place; indeed, regardless of who is doing the policing."
>
> Walcott, Rinaldo. *On Property*. Windsor, ON: Biblioasis, 2021, pp. 31–32.

ESSENTIAL DIS/APPEARANCES

Every story told is itself storied by language. The language used in the article from *The Globe and Mail* rings differently than the language used in the article from *Inclusion Access Daily*. Distinct from these is a language that invites a different orientation to a story already told. *Listen*—deafness and disability beyond their adjectival use. *Look*—disability in motion. Then—what and how do we hear and see, differently?

At first blush, due to the links between policing and anti-blackness that have survived over time and across geographies, it may seem that deafness and disability do not matter to the story of Owusu-Ansah and to the encounters of deaf people with police. And yet, as Theri Pickens (2017) reminds us, "one never has to justify a black disability reading. Both have consistently been present, intertwined" (p. 96). Part of a pedagogy for reading blackness and disability, according to Pickens, is resisting the urge to do the detective work of finding disability where our search for what we consider "disability" often relies on our own single stories of how disability appears, moves, and behaves. Black deafness—phraseology influenced by Pickens' (2017) analysis of "Black blindness" in Tyehimba Jess's character of Blind Lemon Jefferson (p. 94)—creates the circumstances for the encounter between Owusu-Ansah and the police officers. Black deafness complicates the appearance of enforcement's demand for compliance where officers combine mouth, teeth, tongue, and lips to *speak* in full expectation that those to whom they speak *hear* so as to *understand* so as to *obey*.

Alongside lessons from Pickens on a pedagogy for reading blackness and disability, we might turn to mnidoo-worlding to deepen our understanding of how we sense the world and how we are already sensed by the world in relation to each other. Mnidoo-worlding influences all stories, including Owusu-Ansah's encounter with the police constables, by showing us how to hear and see differently. By influencing all stories, mnidoo-worlding may guide our reading so that we may fully understand Black deafness and Black disability as never needing justification and as always present together. Binding Anishinaabe ontology and phenomenology together, Dolleen Manning (2017) says that mnidoo-worlding is "a condition of being attuned to what is there in the world in a particular way" (p. 157). In the world, we have deafness, disability, policing, race, and truth. Mnidoo-worlding asks us to tune our listening and look to these various things, already in and of the world, differently. We are called to move into the single story of what it means to be deaf, racialized, and policed. Manning (2017) speaks of mnidoo consciousness as part of mnidoo-worlding. She writes,

> This infinite mnidoo consciousness conditions finitude, not merely as a "life-sustaining" interpenetration (as with oxygen molecules that fill our lungs in a shared biological process). But more enigmatically it is an integral fusion that is always already there. We might think of this

undifferentiated "consciousnessing" as akin to black matter flowing through us. It allows for other experiences to emerge and challenge the presentation of empirical "truth" (consequently, it is often overwritten by an acute presence of objective reality). I am part of this tumultuous unified body. (p. 169)

There is an essential disappearance surfacing here, one where the infinitude of mnidoo consciousness arises and conditions the finite mnidoo consciousness. This conditioning takes place from within a disappearance that, as Manning (2017) says, "is always already there" (p. 169). In the story, the encounter between Owusu-Ansah and Officer Taylor begins on a finite night in September, where infinite stories of policing, normalcy, and anti-blackness are already playing into how their meeting will unfold. And through the art of story, this encounter is always beginning. The infinite mnidoo-consciousness that conditioned their meeting teaches us that there is an integral fusion that always already exists between people, worlds, and differences. The art of story arranges us in the infinity of the encounter.

When examining how singular stories of truth are maintained through the infinity of the encounter, mnidoo-consciousness presents an entry point into understanding ourselves as part of the "tumultuous unified body [of infinitude and finitude]" (Manning, 2017, p. 169). Manning (2017) writes of the relationship between infinitude and finitude, which is then followed by the example of oxygen filling our lungs—again, an integral fusion always already there. It is difficult to imagine the stories in the *Inclusion Daily Express,* the *Globe and Mail,* and this chapter as fused. Perhaps even more challenging is comprehending the worlds of Owusu-Ansah, the police constables, and Judge Robertson as already part of a tumultuous unified body. Understanding worlds in relation to an image of a unified body, of something akin to a tapestry of narratives that weave together to tell the colours and textures of a grander fabric, indeed allows for "other experiences to emerge and challenge the presentation of empirical 'truth'" (Manning, 2017, p. 169). In my story of Owusu-Ansah's encounter with the police constables, from the hum of a police vehicle to the flicker of a streetlight, we are thrust into another narrative, registering some parts of the story as familiar and encountering others as less familiar. We have the finite, what we can reach out and grasp, that is, an outline of an encounter we can be certain happened on a September evening in 2002. And we have the infinite, the faces of a story that slip through the spaces between letters and words, sliding sides to a tale that may never manifest in the form of a palatable single story. Nonetheless, the faces of a story look back at us.

The same mnidoo-worlding that influences my story guides our reading, where we might ask, how does the sound of story invite us to tune to deafness, disability, and race differently? To truth differently?

In tandem with the "presentation of objective reality" that mnidoo-worlding promises to surface, disability studies proposes to, as Tanya Titchkosky and Rod Michalko (2009) say, "complicate our taken-for-granted relations to normal conceptions of body and mind, of impairment and disability, of nature and culture, and of non-person and person" (p. 10). For mnidoo-consciousness and disability studies, then, there is nothing satisfactory about the untroubled single story. Indeed, guided by mnidoo-worlding and disability studies, we can trouble the single story of Owusu-Ansah and the police constables portrayed in news media accounts so as to discover its complexity, its many faces, and so that we might also rupture normal conceptions of deafness and disability, of fact and truth, of the police and the policed. Together with this rupturing, mnidoo-worlding and disability studies might also rupture the normalcy of silence—to hear for who and what lives in the deep recesses of a story's pauses. It might be said that narratives linger there, waiting to be heard and reborn again as the stories once hidden to hold a single story in place.

> "In today's society, storytelling is separated from day-to-day living.... But when I was a kid, storytelling was something that happened while you were cooking food in the fire pits. You might roast a moose under the sand with rocks, and that was eight hours of waiting—and so, storytelling."
>
> Meshake, Rene. *Injichaag My Soul in Story: Anishinaabe Poetics in Arts and Words.* Winnipeg, MB: University of Manitoba Press, 2019, p. 23.

INTO THE TUMULT/CONCLUSION

Influenced by Pickens' (2017) pedagogy for reading disability and blackness and by Manning's (2017) Anishinaabe ontology of mnidoo-worlding, re-story becomes a way for us to rest with the waywardness, the tumult of being part of a tumultuous unified body. Indeed, a re-imagining of more radical futures, where deafness, disability, race, and truth are made to matter differently, finds its possibility when fused with the disability studies' call to disrupt normalcy. Deafness and disability resist capture by the single story of policing and policing's expectations of compliant bodies. The resistance to being fixed in one place resides at the core of story. Disability need not appear *only* upon the human body and race need not rest *only* upon the skin we're in. Through storying, we might find them in the rhythmic flicker of an orange streetlight, in the slow stretching of fingers, or in the way utterances can dance between worlds, both far and fused. In my story of the encounter between Owusu-Ansah and the Toronto Police Service constables, the focus on telling a single story about police found not guilty of assault necessarily disappears through the story so that different possibilities of that evening might arrive before us. Story encourages us to engage reading as living and lived, thereby prompting an attention to the ways our reading and our orientation to what we read might activate and conjure the possibility of perceiving many faces to a single story. Alongside these many faces, we might find that deafness, disability, and race live in all places. From the horizon of one narrative, we interpret the horizons of many more. Diving into how we make sense of what appears commonplace, such as a judge's decision to deem two police constables not guilty of assault, is a journey of making the known unknown again. In this journey, we forswear singularities as the only way to know the world and each other. Abandoning our knowns through the art of story is perhaps one way to reveal the tumultuous unified body that stories, ever so slightly, speak of.

"How can there be accountability to 19-year-old Ashley Smith, who died in her isolation cell in Kitchener just a few years ago? How can there be accountability to 'Emily no. 049' who died in the Kuper Island Residential School and wasn't grieved by the White adults running the school because she was Indigenous, deaf, and 'quasi-dumb'?... How can there be accountability to children who are born tomorrow or ten years from now—especially those who, because of disability, race, or class, are born disproportionately likely to live all or part of their lives in the terrible spaces of the carceral/ institutional archipelago? This future 'yet to come'—that of the Ashleys and the Emilys of tomorrow—is a looming presence that has to be lived with, that has to be contended with, today."

Ben-Moshe, Liat, Chris Chapman, and Allison C. Carey. (Eds.). *Disability Incarcerated: Imprisonment and Disability in the United States and Canada.* New York, NY: Palgrave Macmillan US, 2014, p. 18.

NOTE

1. A sincere thank you to Peter Owusu-Ansah for being open to reading this chapter prior to publication and for the words we exchanged over email.

REFERENCES

Abbate, G. (2004, October 14). Two constables found not guilty of assaulting deaf man in 2002. *The Globe and Mail*. https://www.theglobeandmail.com/news/national/two-constables-found-not-guilty-of-assaulting-deaf-man-in-2002/article1005205/

Adichie, C. (2009). *Chimamanda Ngozi Adichie: The danger of a single story* [Video]. TED. https://www.ted.com/talks/chimamanda_ngozi_adichie_the_danger_of_a_single_story

Manning, D. T. (2017). The murmuration of birds: An Anishinaabe ontology of mnidoo-worlding. In H. A. Fielding & D. E. Olkowski (Eds.), *Feminist phenomenology futures* (pp. 154–182). Indiana University Press.

Pickens, T. (2017). Blue blackness, black blueness: Making sense of blackness and disability. *African American Review, 50*(2), 93–103. https://doi.org/10.1353/afa.2017.0015

Reynolds, D. (2004, July 22). Advocacy groups support Deaf man who accuses police of assault. *Inclusion Daily Express*. https://mn.gov/mnddc/news/inclusion-daily/2004/07/072204onadvabuse.htm

Stelkia, K. (2020, July 15). Police brutality in Canada: A symptom of structural racism and colonial violence. *Yellowhead Institute*. https://yellowheadinstitute.org/2020/07/15/police-brutality-in-canada-a-symptom-of-structural-racism-and-colonial-violence/

Titchkosky, T. (2007). *Reading and writing disability differently: The textured life of embodiment*. University of Toronto Press.

Titchkosky, T., & Michalko, R. (Eds.). (2009). *Rethinking normalcy: A disability studies reader*. Canadian Scholars' Press.

CHAPTER 21

"Where Are the Goddamn Pens?": And Other DisAppearances in Writing Intellectual Disability

Chelsea Temple Jones

Key Terms: Intellectual Disability; Research; Writing Group

INTRODUCTION

As it turns out, Richard was dead. I hadn't seen him for three or four weeks, which isn't unusual in our drop-in writing group; people come and people go. But I'd been missing him. He liked to copy words out of tabloid magazines whose headlines, at the time, exclaimed the news of another British royal baby. I stumbled into my final writing group session with arms full of notebooks and pens. There were never enough of these items, it seemed. Each Friday morning research session over the last five years had begun with a scramble to dig up materials—*Does anyone mind using a green crayon? Where is the staff? Will they lend us a pen?*—followed by an hour of dry quietness as we wrote. Five years of writing. Five years of trying to make space, be present, and reject normalcy through writing.

Sometimes I wished to step out of my body, observe, and pen some proper field notes. Instead, I settled for knowing that witnessing often means being in a moment as it flits by, if I'm lucky, and working from memory later. Even now, I spin memories into words in order to recall the end of this vestigial inquiry with a group of triple-labelled writers. By triple-labelled I mean people whose lives are eclipsed by labels of intellectual disability, incompetence, and vulnerability—especially under the guise of paternalistic institutional research ethics protocol (Thompson, 2002). These people, sometimes considered "too risky" for research, are often excluded from knowledge production about themselves (Martino & Schormans, 2018). When they're included, it can be a lengthy and ethically precarious process to gain access to them (Jones, 2021). Yet, our group met weekly.

Sometimes we wrote as a pod of three or four people; other times all 10 research participants (plus some stragglers) showed up.

I kept glancing at the door, expecting Richard to fly into the room. Earlier, I'd asked the staff where he'd been lately. He'd been sick, they said. He died a couple of weeks ago. They hadn't told me because his health status was confidential. I ripped open a package of pens and let them spill into the middle of our writing table. One of the writers glanced up at me and looked away quickly. I tried to soften into a smile.

So, Richard had disappeared. He was the first to go. As it turns out, intellectual disability can disappear from research.

WRITING INTELLECTUAL DISABILITY AS RESEARCH

My participant observation called on me to write alongside the triple-labelled writers in this research group as part of my doctoral research. The group was called "Once Upon a Time." We were an understated but recalcitrant bunch—ignoring writing prompts, ripping pages from notebooks, copying words from other books, drawing tattoo designs, gingerly shredding poetry into confetti.

Writing is ultimately a way of getting to the crux of action research, a method of both inquiry and representation (Richardson, 2000). Here, writing represented the queer gesture of "finding a use" for something that is often deemed to have no use—that is, writing with people too often considered non-writers (Ahmed, 2019, p. 218). Writing alongside people who are supposed to be ineligible to narrate their own lives was a "less-used [path]" into writing that required us to create our own support systems because, as Sara Ahmed (2019) writes, the world is often described not by oppressed people but by those who have been accommodated (pp. 218–220). Or, as Catherine Prendergast (2001) puts it, writing itself is a question of "rhetoricability"—that is to say, it has little to do with syntax, grammar, or vocabulary but is something someone is *granted*. To write otherwise, from the perspective of those who are neither accommodated nor granted rhetoric, is not to "give voice" but to dwell in a new space and hope for a different world to appear, even if you do not quite understand it.

Part of the work involved convincing outsiders that our writing offered something substantial to knowledge production—not only for what was on the page but for the affective movements that emerged from writing. As Judi Marshall (2016) explains, "Apprehending when form and content are congruent is likely to be as much felt as an intellectual process" (p. 111). This chapter focuses on the "felt" side of writing—the situational ethics that deals with the unpredictable, sometimes un-understandable moments that crop up in the field (Ellis, 2007), the stuff that remains hard to explain—that eventually led to my own hesitation to write at all.

> "We often say that our ancestors and those who have died are resting in peace, but many of our disabled ancestors cannot do so because their stories are incomplete. How can our disabled ancestors rest in peace when many of them, especially those who lived before the disability rights/arts movements, did not have the opportunity to talk openly or act creatively with their disabilities in an open and free environment? Even in death, our ancestors' disabilities are erased.... My Black disabled ancestors want to come out to speak their stories. They want me to write these stories through short stories, poetry, and songs. They want to speak to disabled youth and to the general public. They tease me regularly—more than ten times a year. They check in, and if I have not written anything, then they sit on my shoulders keeping me awake at night—like tonight. They are diverse: from slaves to blind Blues artists to Black disabled boys and men who were lynched and shot and caged by the state, and women who were also musicians or activists."
>
> Moore, Leroy F. "Black Disabled Ancestors Can't Rest in Peace Until We Write the Whole Story." *Peace Review* 31, no. 4 (2019): 515–519; pp. 514–515.

WRITING INTELLECTUAL DISABILITY AS CREATIVE ANALYTIC PRACTICE

The overlap of non-normative writing and situational ethics in the field left me searching for a form that shows respect and curiosity toward its given shape (Marshall, 2016). I turned to creative analytic practice (CAP), a way of using writing as a method of discovery (Richardson, 2000). CAP writing is circular and unpredictable, using narrative and poetic representation, among other devices, to analyze the world when normative, linear language is not enough. CAP is used to support "ethical sensibility" by emphasizing the affective ebbs and flows of writing (Done et al., 2011) and has recently been used to favour unfinished stories that draw attention to those missing from research (Wright, 2019). This writing style relies on the struggle and crystallization of mixed methods and the researcher's skill in weaving "a fleshed out, embodied sense of lived experience" (Richardson, 2000, p. 937) in ways that align with Hélène Cixous's (1976) and Julia Kristeva's

(1984) writings against rigid, rational, masculinist (and I'll add ableist) prose that dominates research.

Through CAP, the "Once Upon a Time" writers and I stretched into new, semiotic forms of writing, where we located ourselves outside of normative language. Following creative expression experiences described elsewhere as "fabulation" (halifax et al., 2018), "musicking" (Small, as cited in Carlson, 2015), and "mad devising" (Kuppers et al., 2016), writing disability through CAP taught me that the "space between" (Dolmage, 2014) myself and triple-labelled people is one created by moments of mis- and un-understanding in writing, which are often glazed over as "untranslatable" gaps in research. These are fleeting moments that there isn't always time to address (halifax, 2009), but whose potential has not yet been exhausted (Ahmed, 2019). These "untranslatable" moments were the sparks I wished to explore, knowing that I would not always have the language with which to take them up—finally realizing that I could only ever fail to signify in my attempt to engage with difference (Dolmage, 2014, p. 106).

MOMENTS OF DIFFERENCE: A POEM

One such "in-between" moment emerged when a participant named Prince Diana handed me a piece of paper filled edge-to-edge with "+" and "o" symbols in blue-inked scrawl. The text was indecipherable to me. I asked Prince Diana if they would help me understand the writing. They simply pointed at the page, shrugged, and said, "It's a poem about my grandmother riding a bicycle."

This piece of writing was one of many that cracked open the situational ethics hovering around this project.

Here's what happened: On the same day that Prince Diana (PD) wrote a poem about their grandmother riding a bicycle, they encountered a staff person:

Staff: What are you guys doing here?
PD: I'm writing something.
Staff: I'm talking to Chelsea. Did you forget? [Looks over the participant's shoulder at their notebook.] You're writing somethin', that's for sure.
PD: Thank you for coming.
Staff: Wow, I'm being thrown out.

In this moment, I didn't know quite what to do. I looked up at the staff person and stammered a response: "We're writing." And then, according to my audio recording, the seemingly more urgent question came to my mind: "Do you know where the pens are?" The staff person shook her head and walked away. My opportunity

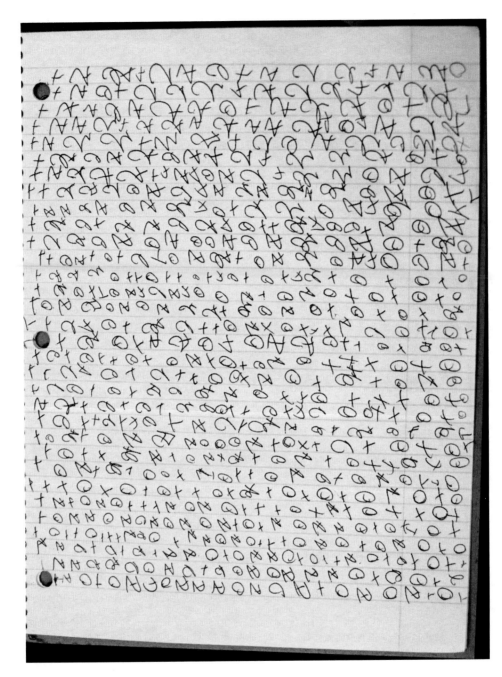

Figure 21.1: A photograph of a full page of writing in a spiral notebook

Chelsea Temple Jones

to advocate for Prince Diana's work—and our collective work, given that some people were without pens—seemed to dissolve. I felt deflated by my own shitty allyship. I remember thinking: *Where are the goddamn pens?*

There are more ways to read into this encounter than there is space to recount here. Triple-labelled people have life experiences that are routinely disavowed as abnormal and invalid because of their untranslatability. James Berger (2014) describes these people as "dys-/disarticulated"—people who are routinely identified as figures "outside of language" (p. 32). From this vantage point, disability is "that place" that exists "beyond all discourse that would provide a final affirmation or negation to the social-symbolic world" (p. 13). Yet, as Susan Wendell (1996) explains, collectively people with disabilities have accumulated a significant body of knowledge (a "cultural corporeality") that could be—and is being—further developed (p. 73), such as through the upswelling of disability, mad, and Deaf art in Canada and elsewhere (Chandler, 2019). Still, triple-labelled people remain sorely underrepresented in art, solidifying their place "outside of language" (Berger, 2014, p. 32)—a cultural location well established by ableist microaggressions such as the one that flashed over our writing group that day.

I began working on the premise that our bodies are not separate from our text. And one's understanding of the text is also an ethical orientation toward it. In other words, how Prince Diana's text is read is also how Prince Diana is read. To interpret the text as un-understandable is to interpret the person in the same discounting way.

At one point, Prince Diana stopped showing up to "Once Upon a Time" writing sessions. When I asked a staffer where they had been lately, the staff person, who was new and had been recruited to help me dig up some pens, said she simply didn't know.

"Bodies are ... shaped by contact with objects and others, with 'what' is near enough to be reached. They may even take shape through such contact or take the shape of that contact. What gets near is both shaped by what bodies do and in turn affects what bodies can do. The nearness of the philosopher to his paper, his ink, and his table is not simply about where he does his work, and the spaces he inhabits, as if the 'where' could be separated from what he does. The 'what' that he does is what puts certain objects within reach. Orientations are about the directions we take that put some things and not others in our reach."

Ahmed, Sara. "Orientations: Toward a Queer Phenomenology." *GLQ* 12, no. 4 (2006): 543–574; p. 552.

WRITING INTELLECTUAL DISABILITY AS EXPRESSIVE WRITING

In a research landscape where the un-understandable lacks value, it is imperative to find use for "dys-articulate" matter that has been designated to have little use, to paraphrase Ahmed (2019, p. 218). For many triple-labelled people, writing is a eugenic tool of research, rehabilitation, or therapy, if it is something they get to experience at all (Pollard, 2012). In the context of Western neoliberal-ableism (Goodley et al., 2014), writing too often attempts to make sense of disability and to make people with disabilities make sense both in narratives that aim to character- ize intellectual disability and by moving labelled people away from "circumstances in which it is safe to be absent-minded" and toward literacy training (Freud, 1987, p. xiv). Indeed, a post-structuralist argument suggests that it is through condi- tioning of normative, logocentric language structures that writers—even abstract, creative, expressive writers—remain safe in circumstances where translatability and understandability are highly valued. In my experience, day centres for disabled folks are not those kinds of places.

The encounter between Prince Diana and the staff person was no anomaly. Writers' works were belittled outside of our group boundaries. Advocating be- came exhausting. Part of this exhaustion stemmed from the ground-level material challenges that nagged at my post-structuralist feminist sensibilities: The research took a hesitant, interpretive, phenomenological approach to confronting the ques- tion of what it means to encounter intellectual disability as *presence* rather than as *problem*. Meanwhile, there were never enough pens for writing. Where did the pens go, anyway? Every week we stored them in the same cubby hole. Every week they were gone.

The situational ethics at hand called on me to later advocate for an epistemo- logical shift away from understanding disability as bodily absence, and toward newfound "bodily presences" (Abram, 1996, p. 89)—moments where the body is meant not necessarily to be known as understandable but to be felt and *present* through such gestures as writing (Vernon, 1979). In other words, our praxis pushed into moments where foibles are not meant to be corrected, hidden, or dis- avowed but are instead intended to be re-understood as part of the unknown, but inventive, fabric that makes up our lived experiences. In moments where we were made vulnerable, we also resisted (Sabsay, 2016). We layered "expressive writing" into our CAP approach, naming it as our main method. For us, "expressive writ- ing" meant reflecting on the "untranslatable," pre-verbal sensations present in the lifeworld (van Manen, 2014; Vernon, 1979). This is a type of writing that doesn't buy into ideological calls to "better" ourselves through correct use of language. "Expressive writing" broadens the gesture of writing to include making shapes in the air with our fingers, whispering, drawing images on paper, folding paper, and other ways of usurping normative language as the grand organizer of the logo-centric world, including writing a poem about your grandmother riding a bicycle (Derrida, 1976).

What followed, then, was an unconventional analysis of "expressive writing" as situational, relational, and embodied. Consider, for example, bracketing any normative perception of Prince Diana's writing. Whereas intellectual disability is presented to us as an always-already set, familiar object—as a flat, ahistorical, un-deniable diagnosis or an unchangeable way of being (Carlson, 2010)—bracketing calls us to segregate our ideas of this apparent "reality" of embodiment impair-ment, as well as our acts that follow its meta-narrative, such as triple-labelling (Titchkosky, 2007). Bracketing Prince Diana's expressive writing led me to re-position myself in order to understand the text for what it is: a series of pen strokes across a page, carrying unknown—but *present*—meaning. There is a dis-juncture between what I know about the text and what Prince Diana knows about the text—this in-betweenness that too easily evaporates with time opens questions about the validity of Prince Diana's writing and knowledge and its eligibility to be counted in knowledge production about disability, even after they disappeared. We were writing *somethin'*, that's for sure.

NO LONGER WRITING INTELLECTUAL DISABILITY

Just as intellectual disability can disappear, so too can one's capacity to write. After five years, I knew it was time to call off the research; it had become exhausting to live as a rookie "entangled academic"—someone compelled to apply thinking and action and to develop ideas through experiencing (Marshall, 2016, p. xvii).

My entanglement began early in the process, long before Richard and Prince Diana entered the scene. In August 2013 I wrote to my university's Research Ethics Board (REB) with an idea. I wrote up my application to the university querulously, arguing for a participatory research approach that would position triple-labelled people to analyze their own texts "as human creators of knowledge." The word *human* was a small but key piece of advocacy here. As Bill Hughes (2007) points out, "for most people 'it goes without saying' that they are human beings. For dis-abled people in many historical contexts 'it has to be said'" (p. 677). I also made my research position clear: "I want to write with people who aren't looked at as writ-ers, people who aren't allowed to try writing because you think they *can't*." To sell the idea, I found myself proposing a participatory research-based writing group that resolved to produce transformative text.

I never *actually* bought into the idea that the research would reach its resolution. Research is never innocent nor does it come with any expectation of a happy, transformative ending—even if one can be imagined at the proposal stage. Even though I was not following an emancipation formula, the work included a reading of participants' cultural history, understood participants as "knowers" involved in knowledge creation (Goodley & Moore, 2000; Ignagni & Church, 2008); acknowledged that disabled people are *not* "perpetually available" for research (Snyder & Mitchell, 2006, p. 28); allowed as-autonomous-as-possible writing processes for people involved (Mertens, 2010); adopted feminist instruction that knowledge is culturally derived and therefore critical self-reflection is necessary (Davies, 2000); and, finally, worked with the inclusion of multiple, evolving methodologies that are open to improvisation (Price, 2012).

I don't believe we are at a place where research with triple-labelled people is any of these things. After all, only I would eventually be granted a PhD for this project, while the writers—all diligently writing—would be recorded as participants, collaborators, or subjects to/of knowledge even while the research's impact on their lives went on unknown. The writers would disappear, ground up into the academic industrial complex's knowledge production machine, their availability moot due to lost memories and confidentiality agreements that would have them not exist outside of fieldwork.

"Disability activism and art, the shape of which is difficult to predict, not only present unique opportunities to explore questions that have animated the field of social movement studies for decades, but also hold potential promise as sites for asking questions about the expanding affective worlds of activism, some of which escape the state-focused lens privileged by social movement scholars and moreover, the role of emotions in generating social change ... this includes a reappraisal of artistic, radical, and affective practices as interventions in their own right, as well as a greater appreciation for how disabled bodies and minds figure in these interventions."

Kelly, Christin, and Michael Orsini. *Mobilizing Metaphor: Art, Culture and Disability Activism in Canada*. Vancouver, BC: UBC Press, 2016, p. 17.

CONCLUSION

On my final day with these people, staff and writers held a party for me in the day centre's lunchroom. I handed over the bundle of gifts: notebooks and pens dressed in rainbow-print giftwrap. Writers served cupcakes and coffee. I thanked the group for their presence and for their self-advocacy both on and off the page. I said aloud and clearly that the party shouldn't be for me; it should be for all of us and for our hard work. The celebration was fitted in between programming and lasted exactly 30 minutes. As we left the lunchroom, I saw a staff person gathering the notebooks and pens to be locked away for safekeeping, she said. I protested, but to what end? This discouragement is, in no uncertain terms, the exhausting work of writing alongside intellectually disabled people, whose writing is, so often and so tragically, disappeared.

Ahmed (2019) assures us that a queer way of working is "to start with the weighty, the heavy, the weary, and the worn" (p. 227). The exhaustion at the root of this writing stems in part from my own queer sensibilities but also from knowing that writing intellectual disability involves grieving the disappearance of its people and their work. On one end of the project, this writing necessarily reminds me of the long, dark reach of transinstitutionalization and the policing of triple-labelled people's expression (Haley & Jones, 2020). On the other end, the paradoxical work of research-based writing is the willingness to sign on to institutional violence, including that which is reproduced each time I am sole author—neither "giving voice" nor doing anything radical.

Yet, in a research climate where ethics are precarious and where people are strategically placed as both vulnerable and subject, I sensed a responsibility to take part in experiences as "bodily presences" to be felt and present—and to remind us of triple-labelled presences that are overlooked (Abram, 1996, p. 89) and designated "not much use" (Ahmed, 2019, p. 218). Maurice Merleau-Ponty (1964 [1948]) suggests there must be a place for "the confused beginnings of scientific knowledge" if we want to picture the world "as it really is" (pp. 41, 40).

If we are to take on intellectual disability in research, we must take the action of writing to encompass the untranslatable, memory/remembering, silence/silencing, and disappearance/disappearing moments as observable and notable as part of our praxis (Jones & Cheuk, 2021). Such gestures demand a different type of methodological exploration, rigour, and ethics in the field—new orientations that honour the possibility and *presence* of triple-labelled people as those who must be invested in knowledge production about themselves. I left this project knowing that research involving triple-labelled people is limited and not clean-cut. And once our work—our writing—is intermingling, there is a great deal of labour ahead in demanding its validity in a field that participates in the limiting institutionalization of the body (Snyder & Mitchell, 2006). Yet, our task, as Patti Lather (2007) writes, "is to meet the limit, to open to it as the very vitality and force that propels the change to come" (p. 37).

REFERENCES

Abram, D. (1996). *The spell of the sensuous*. Vintage.

Ahmed, S. (2019). *What's the use?* Duke University Press.

Berger, J. (2014). *The disarticulate*. New York University Press.

Carlson, L. (2010). *The faces of intellectual disability: Philosophical reflections*. Indiana University Press.

Carlson, L. (2015). Music, intellectual disability, and human flourishing. In B. Howe, S. Jensen-Moulton, N. Lerner, & J. Straus (Eds.), *The Oxford handbook of music and disability studies* (pp. 37–53). Oxford University Press.

Chandler, E. (2019). Introduction: Cripping the arts in Canada. *Canadian Journal of Disability Studies, 8*(1), 1–14. https://doi.org/10.15353/cjds.v8i1.468

Cixous, H. (1976). The laugh of the medusa. *Signs, 1*(4), 875–893.

Davies, B. (2000). *A body of writing, 1990–1999*. AltaMira Press.

Derrida, J. (1976). Linguistics and grammatology. In *Of grammatology* (pp. 27–65). The Johns Hopkins University Press.

Dolmage. J. T. (2014). Prosthesis. In *Disability rhetoric* (pp. 1–19). Syracuse University Press.

Done, E., Knowler, H., Murphy, M., Rea, T., & Gale, K. (2011). (Re)writing CPD: Creative analytical practices and the 'continuing professional development' of teachers. *Reflective Practice, 12*(3), 389–399. https://doi.org/10.1080/14623943.2011 .571869

Ellis, C. (2007). Telling secrets, revealing lives: Relational ethics in research with intimate others. *Qualitative Inquiry, 13*(1), 3–29. https://doi. org/10.1177/1077800406294947

Freud, A. (1987). Foreword. In M. Milner (Ed.), *On not being able to paint* (2nd ed., pp. xii–xv). International Universities Press.

Goodley, D., Lawthom, R., & Runswick-Cole, K. (2014). Dis/ability and austerity: Beyond work and slow death. *Disability & Society, 29*(6), 980–984. https://doi.org/ 10.1080/09687599.2014.920125

Goodley, D., & Moore, M. (2000). Doing disability research: Activist lives and academy. *Disability & Society, 15*(6), 861–882. https://doi.org/10.1080/713662013

Haley, T. L., & Jones, C. T. (2020). Introduction: Sites and shapes of transinstitutionalization. *Canadian Journal of Disability Studies, 9*(3), 1–16. https://doi.org/10.15353/cjds.v9i3.643

halifax, n. v. d. (2009). *Disability and illness in arts-informed research: Moving toward postconventional representations*. Cambria Press.

halifax, n. v. d., Fancy, D., Rinaldi, J., Rossiter, K., & Tigchelaar, A. (2018). Recounting Huronia faithfully: Attenuating our methodology to the "fabulation" of truths-telling. *Cultural Studies ↔ Critical Methodologies, 18*(3), 216–227. https://doi.org/10.1177/1532708617746421

Hughes, B. (2007). Being disabled: Towards a critical social ontology for disability studies. *Disability & Society, 22*(7), 673–684. https://doi.org/10.1080/09687590701659527

Ignagni, E., & Church, K. (2008). One more reason to look away? Ties and tensions between arts-informed inquiry and disability studies. In A. Cole & J. G. Knowles (Eds.), *Handbook of the arts in qualitative social science research* (pp. 625–638). SAGE.

Jones, C. T., & Cheuk, F. (2021). Something is happening: Encountering silence in disability research. *Qualitative Research Journal, 21*(1), 1–14. https://doi.org/10.1108/QRJ-10-2019-0078

Jones, C. T. (2021). "Wounds of regret": Critical reflections on competence, "professional intuition," and informed consent in research with intellectually disabled people. *Disability Studies Quarterly, 41*(2). https://doi.org/10.18061/dsq.v41i2.6869

Kristeva, J. (1984). The semiotic and the symbolic. In *Revolution in poetic language* (M. Waller, Trans.) (pp. 19–90). Columbia University Press.

Kuppers, P., Heit, S., Sizemore-Barber, A., Preston, V. K., Hickey, A., & Wille, A. (2016). Mad methodologies and community performance: The Asylum Project at Bedlam. *Theatre Topics, 26*(2), 221–237. https://doi.org/10.1353/tt.2016.0032

Lather, P. A. (2007). *Getting lost: Feminist efforts toward a double(d) science*. State University of New York Press.

Marshall, J. (2016). *First person action research: Living life as inquiry*. SAGE.

Martino, S. A., & Schormans, A. F. (2018). When good intentions backfire: Research ethics review and the intimate lives of people labelled with intellectual disabilities. *Qualitative Research Forum, 19*(3). https://doi.org/10.17169/fqs-19.3.3090

Merleau-Ponty, M. (1964). *The world of perception* (O. Davis, Trans.). Routledge. (Original work published 1948)

Mertens, D. M. (2010). *Research and evaluation in education and psychology: Integrating diversity with quantitative, qualitative, and mixed methods* (3rd ed.). SAGE.

Pollard, N. (2012). Communities of writing. In N. Pollard & D. Sakellariou (Eds.), *Politics of occupation-centred practice: Reflections on occupational engagement across cultures* (pp. 146–161). Wiley-Blackwell.

Prendergast, C. (2001). On the rhetorics of mental disability. In J. Wilson & C. Lewiecki-Wilson (Eds.), *Embodied rhetorics: Disability and language in culture* (pp. 45–60). Southern Illinois University Press.

Price, M. (2012). Disability studies methodology: Explaining ourselves to ourselves. In K. M. Powell & P. Takayoshi (Eds.), *Practicing research in writing studies: Reflexive and ethically responsible research* (pp. 159–186). Hampton Press.

Richardson, L. (2000). Writing: A method of inquiry. In N. Denzin & Y. Lincoln (Eds.), *Handbook of qualitative research* (2nd ed., pp. 923–948). SAGE.

Sabsay, L. (2016). Permeable bodies: Vulnerability, affective powers, hegemony. In J. Butler, Z. Gambetti, & L. Sabsay (Eds.), *Vulnerability in resistance* (pp. 278–302). Duke University Press.

Snyder, S., & Mitchell, D. (2006). *Cultural locations of disability*. University of Chicago Press.

Thompson, S. A. (2002). My researcher friend? My friend the researcher? My friend, my researcher? Mis/informed consent and people with developmental disabilities. In W. van den Hoonaard (Ed.), *Walking the tightrope: Ethical issues for qualitative researchers* (pp. 95–106). University of Toronto Press.

Titchkosky, T. (2007). *Reading and writing disability differently: The textured life of embodiment*. University of Toronto Press.

van Manen, M. (2014). *Phenomenology of practice: Meaning-giving methods in phenomenological research and writing*. Left Coast Press.

Vernon, J. (1979). *Poetry and the body*. University of Illinois Press.

Wendell, S. (1996). *The rejected body: Feminist philosophical reflections on disability*. Routledge.

Wright, R. K. (2019). 'All the lonely people': Embracing autoethnographic creative analytical practice at the 2017 World Masters Games. *Annals of Leisure Research, 22*(3), 342–361. https://doi.org/10.1080/11745398.2018.1503087

CHAPTER 22

Are You My Homi? Close (Autistic) Encounters of the Third Kind

Maya Chacaby

Key Terms: Autistic Encounters; Betweenness; Cards; Dialogue; Go Fish; Homi K. Bhabha; IndiginAutie; Liminal; Play; Script

Are You My Homi? Close (Autistic) Encounters of the ("not a third term that resolves the tension between two cultures, or the two scenes of the book, in a dialectical play of recognition" [Bhabha, 1994, p. 162]) Third Kind: a play on the interstitial spaces between autistic encounters with the imposed meaning-making interactions of socially normative humans and the reactive fear of ambivalence this often causes, that is itself a "neurotic orientation" (Bhabha, p. 162, 1994).

Scene 1, Act 1

University classroom. Thursday afternoon. First day of class. With a familiar teacher.

ENCOUNTER sips her coffee, conversing intently with the diffused sunlight that glances off taupe walls in a grey–yellow spectrum of thoughts. She is triumphal in her positioning: a room with no direct air vents, sunlight, sharp angles, scents, traffic noises, or humans sitting behind or in front of her. She is just about to relax when FRIENDLY enters. As they intersect, two signs appear fixed above their heads. IN-BETWEEN appears out of the wall to narrate the encounter:

FRIENDLY enters.

"Within feminist disability studies, the suggestion that 'woman' is disabled by compulsory heterosexuality and patriarchy is met with ambivalence. While the claim establishes an important conceptual connection between disability and gender, it also reflects (and risks perpetuating) dominant conceptions of disability as lack and deficiency, to the extent that disability is unjust to women. This association leaves in place, albeit unintentionally, the idea that disability is inherently contaminating and that certain bodily conditions themselves are disabling.... Within feminist disability studies, exploring conceptual and lived connections between gender and disability helps to make visible the historical and ongoing interrelationship between all forms of oppression."

Hall, Kim Q. *Feminist Disabiltiy Studies*. Bloomington, IN: Indiana University Press, 2011, pp. 4–5.

IN-BETWEEN

Normative social encounters give the sign of identity its integrity, an assumption of stability and unity. Both signs, "Friendly" and "Encounter," find meaning only in what they signify. When fixed signs encounter signifiers that disrupt the ontological "problem of being"[1]—a problem that is always negotiated through and between the self and Other—a space emerges, a space of enunciation that "problems of meaning and being enter ... as the problematic of subjection and identification."[2] If this encounter is encountered, it has the potential to be the Third Space, the encounter within interstitiality that can re-make meaning beyond mimicry or metonymic banality.

FRIENDLY

ENCOUNTER

> "It is through self-consciousness and renunciation, through a permanent tension of his freedom, that [hu]man can create the ideal conditions of existence for a human world. Superiority? Inferiority? Why not simply try to touch the other, feel the other, discover each other? Was my freedom not given me to build the world of *you*, man?... My final prayer: O my body, always make me a [hu]man who questions!"
>
> Fanon, Frantz. *Black Skin, White Masks*. London, UK: Pluto Press, 1967, p. 206.

FRIENDLY
Hi!

ENCOUNTER
(*Looks up, smiles robotically, and looks away*)

FRIENDLY
(*Sits down beside Encounter*)
Nice to see you again. What brings you to this class?

ENCOUNTER
My car.

FRIENDLY
No, I mean why are you taking this class? (*Looking uncomfortable and a little panicked that this conversation is not following the usual repetitive social script.*)

ENCOUNTER
Academic attainment signifies a form of discursive legitimacy to which the post-colonial subject—when reaching the limits of signification—can depart from and return in mimetic forms as the Other. This "Strategy of Doubling" means that we are involved in a discursive strategy of the moment of interrogation of identity. This doubling is a frame of identity that opens into a space of potentiality where we may "elude the politics of polarity and emerge as the others of our selves."[3] Isn't that exciting?

"Fields belong to in-between; they are instrumental in the creation of sensitive, intelligible characteristics of language that steadily modify content. The spark that flashes between two words is what in mathematics is called an independent variable, a factor not fully explained by the words themselves. Not only is the spark unpredictable but it also has the power to burn away any cliché and in so doing illuminates the context, whose existence—like that of everyone whole—is dependent on how it is reflected in its parts."

Asenjo, F. G. *In-between: An Essay on Categories.* Center for Advanced Research in Phenomenology & University Press of America, 1988, pp. 62–63.

FRIENDLY

Umm ... no ... I mean, what is it about this specific class that interests you?

ENCOUNTER

The walls. I really like the walls in this class. The carpet is problematic, but the diffusion of light and lack of direct air vents, external sounds.

FRIENDLY

(*Interrupts, annoyed, emphasizes the words "classroom" and "subject" as if Encounter didn't hear.*)

No. Not the classroom, but the subject.

ENCOUNTER

(*Speaks very rapidly, intensely, and monotone.*)

The discursive field of subjective inquiry that we are entering into is being enacted in a spatial and temporal and ontological location. Juxtaposed, of course, to our sense of personal locatedness and subjectivity. This classroom lets me manipulate the spatial structure of the ideas that will be presented. The teacher's voice, tone, and emotion hold the conceptual structure very well refracted off the walls in this classroom. So I am interested in this occurrence called a classroom. I was not interested in the occurrence called my car, but it got me here now. Other occurrences also got me here now (but not before): my age, my marital status, my gender, my prior occurrences with school, and my desire—a desire that intersects with a mimicked colonial desire for legitimacy via institutions of knowledge production and officiation—to be something that I am not yet, through a space that receives a particular discursive legitimacy. But really … (pausing, smiling happily) it is the class that I like the most.

FRIENDLY
Ummm … I am confused.

IN-BETWEEN
She is puzzled by the mysterious moment where the expected interaction is not present or presented—a presentience. It is a perplexing moment whereas McGuire and Michalko (2011, p. 2) say, "The reasonable thing to do … is to find the missing pieces," to embark on a search to know. To fix, to place the Other in a certain position that can be known. What becomes interrogated now is not simply the "Other" but the position of that Other to the "discursive and disciplinary place from which questions of identity are strategically and institutionally posed."[4] The space of that inscription is in the enunciation that informs any cultural performance. It is dramatized in between the subject of a proposition and the subject of enunciation, which is not represented in the statement but which is the acknowledgement of its embeddedness, its cultural positionality, its reference to a present time and a specific space. The pact of interpretation is never simply an act of communication between the I and the You designated in the statement. The production of meaning requires that these two places be mobilized in the passage through a Third Space, which represents both the general conditions of language and the specific implication of the utterance in a performative and institutional strategy. This is where culture is located!

FRIENDLY pulls out a deck of cards, places them on the table and flips over a sign on the desk that says "Fishing for the Normative Social Interaction." She picks up a handful of cards from the pile and organizes them in her hand. She begins a game of Go Fish. Encounter has no cards in her hand and sits patiently observing the situation. She knows the game that is about to occur. This has been played many times in her life, and in fact ALL medical interventions in her life have required her to learn how to play the game or perish. She has never won at this game. This time, there is a refusal.

FRIENDLY
(Excited to be playing the game.)

Okay … Do you have a "smile and say hello"?

ENCOUNTER
No. Go fish.

FRIENDLY
(*Picks up another card from the pile.*)

Do you have a "talk about the weather"?

ENCOUNTER
No. There is an app for that. Go fish.

FRIENDLY
(*Picks up another card from the pile a little more panicked.*)

Do you have a "two professional adults greeting each other"?

ENCOUNTER
No. Go fish.

FRIENDLY
(*Picks up another card from the pile—very frustrated now.*)

Do you have a "we have been going to a number of classes together and so you should recognize me by now and say hello"?

ENCOUNTER
No.

FRIENDLY
(*Puts down her cards and is frustrated.*)

Do you have a normal response to anything at all? I am really fishing here, and this is getting a little awkward!

ENCOUNTER
(*Non-verbal response, stimming by braiding and unbraiding her hair.*)

FRIENDLY and ENCOUNTER look at one another while the awkward silence between them becomes tension. FRIENDLY observes ENCOUNTER in an expression of question-ing incomprehension; ENCOUNTER just stares blankly while braiding and unbraiding her hair. IN-BETWEEN becomes the mediator of the interaction, quickly interposing-interpolating possible meaning in between each utterance.

IN-BETWEEN
Wait. McGuire and Michalko[5] explain that, instead of making autism the problem, we can "treat it as an example of the fundamental human features of uncertainty, of the incompleteness and partiality of communication, of the constant risk presented by the potential undoing of the tie that makes you and I a 'we' … not simply as a problem requiring a solution, but as a reminder that we live in the risk of incompleteness."

ENCOUNTER
So, what exactly is it that you want? Like in Fanon's play on the question "What does man want," he asks, "What does the black man want."

IN-BETWEEN
McGuire and Michalko explain that autism can teach us something about some of the ways we find ourselves bound and tied up with one another in a spoken and unspoken language.

FRIENDLY
What do I want? I was just trying to be friendly; you could at least show some manners.

IN-BETWEEN
They go on to say that We (you and I) are tied to each other by way of our communication, a mode of relation that is, also and always, coming undone, incomplete, partial, due to a fundamental excess inherent in every moment of contact.[6]

ENCOUNTER
Why does your version of a friendly exchange take precedence over my encounter? What you mean by friendly comes from this set of cards here … and that is the only actionable range of options you can use to identify with me. And in order for you not to lose at this game … if you can't identify *with* me, then you have to *identify* me. As Difference.

IN-BETWEEN
Bhabha explains that "we need the response and recognition of others and of the Other to arrive at what we experience as our identity."

FRIENDLY
(*Getting angry.*)

You are being very rude. I wasn't trying to start a fight with you.

ENCOUNTER
Why is my Difference then problematized by your set of social expectations?

IN-BETWEEN
Encounters with signifiers of identity that exceed the assumed mimetic sign or mirrored frame of reference "[evacuate] the self as site of identity and autonomy."

FRIENDLY
I wasn't expecting anything from you, except common courtesy.

ENCOUNTER
What is common courtesy?

IN-BETWEEN
This lack of complete control over language stands for a form of destabilization.

FRIENDLY
That you'd at least recognize me and say hello.

ENCOUNTER
I have no facial recognition or way to connect you to a name. *(Points at cards.)* Your expectation comes from that set of possible interactions, and I become problematized and labelled when I don't meet them. Even worse, the problematization launches an industrial complex of solutions in order to either make me a normal player of the game or make me disappear.

IN-BETWEEN
It is from this position of in-betweenness that the most interrogative forms of culture are produced, situated as they are at the disjunctions, cleavages, and fissures.

FRIENDLY
Well, that is none of my business. All I wanted was that you'd answer my questions politely. I WAS JUST BEING FRIENDLY!

ENCOUNTER

And you made no effort to negotiate what polite might be. It was assumed that I would play your social interaction game. It was imposed.

Your friendliness was inscribed on me. My lack of *your* friendliness then becomes a problem.

But it is not a problem with me. It is a problem with your failed attempt at identifying yourself with me via Sameness, which leads you to now only be able to identify yourself through me as Difference.

IN-BETWEEN

If we enter into and hold this irresolvable borderline, this interstitial culture organized within this temporal and spatial dislocation, which is at once "the time of cultural displacement, and the space of the 'untranslatable,'"[7] we can resist totalization and cultural hegemony.

FRIENDLY

Why won't you just act friendly!? That is all I am asking.

ENCOUNTER

You are asking me to mimic a set of behaviours that are required by a particular culture, created externally to us (*pointing at the cards*), in order to affirm your sense of self.

This is the only permissible way that I can have an interaction with you that does not problematize my difference. This is a violation of MY selfness in order to affirm YOURS.

Even if I mimic your friendliness, there is a limit. There is a threshold at the boundary of what I can do.

These cards are not mine, and so even by mimicry I will change the meaning of the enactment, and by doing so we risk a re-inscription through the discourse of Other, separating me from the interaction in order to affirm your identity, or (*getting hopeful and excited*) we together can change the meanings inscribed in the parameters of the interaction thereby changing the expected interactions! (*smiling, happy now*)

FRIENDLY

Fine, whatever. I was just being nice. (*Walks away.*)

ENCOUNTER

But wait ... isn't this exciting? (*And then a little forlorn as FRIENDLY walks away ... saying sadly*) But ... but ... don't you want to be my Homi?

THE END

> "*I was pulled this way and that for longer than I can remember. And my problem was that I always tried to go in everyone's way but my own. I have also been called one thing and then another while no one really wished to hear what I called myself. So after years of trying to adopt the opinions of others I finally rebelled. I am an* invisible *man.*"
>   —Ralph Ellison, *Invisible Man*

NOTES

1. Quoted from Bhabha, 1994, p. 71.
2. Also quoted from Bhabha, 1994, p. 71.
3. Quoted from Bhabha, 1994, p. 56.
4. Quoted from Bhabha, 1994, p. 68.
5. See McGuire & Michalko, 2011, p. 3.
6. See Gay, Evans, and Redman, 2013.
7. Quoted from Bhabha, 1994, p. 225.

REFERENCES

Bhabha, H. K. (1994). *The location of culture*. Routledge.

Gay, P. D., Evans, J., & Redman, P. (2013). *Identity: A reader*. SAGE.

McGuire, A. E., & Michalko, R. (2011). Minds between us: Autism, mindblindness and the uncertainty of communication. *Educational Philosophy and Theory*, *43*(2), 162–177. https://doi.org/10.1111/j.1469-5812.2009.00537.x

CHAPTER 23

The Magic Wand

Lynn Manning

Quick-change artist extraordinaire,
I whip out my folded cane
and change from Black Man to 'blind man'
with a flick of my wrist.
It is a profound metamorphosis –
From God-gifted wizard of round ball
Dominating backboards across America
To God-gifted idiot savant
Pounding out chart busters on a cocked-eyed whim;
From sociopathic gangbanger with death for eyes
To all-seeing soul with saintly spirit;
From rape deranged misogynist
To poor motherless child;
From welfare rich pimp
To disability rich gimp;
And from White Man's burden
To every man's burden.

It is always a profound metamorphosis –
Whether from cursed by man to cursed by God,
Or from scripture condemned to God ordained.
My final form is never of my choosing;
I only wield the wand;
You are the magician.

Contributor Biographies

Sarah Beck is currently enrolled in the Masters of Education at York University. Her research interests focus on the inclusion of culturally deaf students, those whose primary language is American Sign Language, within Canadian post-secondary institutions. Culturally deaf students have unique needs and challenges because of their cultural and linguistic differences that often get overlooked. Her interest is in focusing on these areas in the hopes of uncovering ways to improve access and inclusion for students with hearing loss.

Elaine Cagulada is a teacher, poet, and PhD candidate studying disability studies within the Department of Social Justice Education at the Ontario Institute for Studies in Education (OISE) at the University of Toronto. Influenced by interpretive disability studies, Black studies, and critical race theory, her research engages the meanings made of deafness, disability, race, and policing in the media and in educational texts through storytelling. Elaine feels very lucky to be a co-editor of *DisAppearing: Encounters in Disability Studies*.

Maya Chacaby (Odehamik) is Anishinaabe (Ojibwe) from the Kaministiqua region. Her family comes from Red Rock First Nation. Maya is a lecturer in sociology and linguistics at Glendon Campus, York University, where she works in the field of Anishinaabe futurities—a multidisciplinary field that includes critical disability studies, social justice, Indigenous language and culture reclamation, and Indigenous liberal arts. Maya is an autistic Anishinaabe survivance philosopher (survivance, not survival).

Madeleine (Maddy) DeWelles (she/her) is a PhD candidate in the Department of Social Justice Education at OISE at the University of Toronto. Maddy studies disability and childhood studies. Her dissertation research is about how Down syndrome is represented to children and adults before, at, and following the birth of a baby with Down syndrome. Maddy's interest in and commitment to disability and disability studies flows throughout her life and work. She believes in living with and through disability in ways that position disability as integral to our lives, relationships, and ways of being. Maddy is very happy to be a co-editor of *DisAppearing: Encounters in Disability Studies*.

Dr. Diane Driedger is a poet, visual artist, scholar, and educator. She has published 11 books. Her latest book is *Still Living the Edges: A Disabled Women's Reader* (2021). Diane has been involved in the disability rights movement at the local, national, and international levels for 40 years. Her latest poetry book is *Red with Living: Poems and Art* (2016). Diane is an assistant professor in the Interdisciplinary Master's Programme in Disability Studies at the University of Manitoba.

Dr. Tracey Edelist obtained her PhD from OISE at the University of Toronto in the Department of Social Justice Education. The interdisciplinary theories and methods of disability studies provided a much-needed critical perspective of health professional practices that Tracey found missing from her prior professional training as a speech-language pathologist. In her research, Tracey questions societal norms and assumptions about speech, language, and hearing, while examining the lived consequences these norms and assumptions have for deaf children and their families. She has an interest in bringing critical perspectives into health professional education, in particular speech-language pathology and audiology training programs. She teaches disability studies and social justice–related courses at various universities.

Jose Miguel (Miggy) Esteban is a Filipino-Canadian dance/movement artist and educator based in Tkaronto/Toronto. Miggy is a PhD student in the Department of Social Justice Education at OISE at the University of Toronto. His research engages with disability studies, dance/performance studies, and embodied practices of research-creation to encounter the interpretations of gesture as sites for inspiring a return to our bodies, to our (un)belonging within space, and to our movement in relation to one another.

Sid Ghosh is a 14-year-old non-speaking Autistic teen with Down syndrome. He is a poet and rebel in pursuit of other similar souls. He is interested in rescuing poets from the quiet clutches of rhyme. One of Sid's essays has been published in the book *Leaders Around Me* (2019). Sid's poetry chapbook *Give a Book* was published in 2021.

Efrat Gold is defending her PhD dissertation on June 15, 2022 at the University of Toronto. She engages in mad and disability studies, challenging dominant views of mental health and illness, moving toward contextualized and relational understandings of suffering, crisis, and distress. Gold critiques psychiatry, focusing on those most vulnerable and marginalized by psychiatric power, discourse, and treatments. Her work is staunchly feminist, anti-racist, and anti-oppressive. Through explorations of norms, meaning-making, and constructions of legitimacy, Gold unsettles psychiatric hegemony by returning to the sites where psychiatric certainty has been produced.

Lindsay Gravelle is an artist and arts educator working at Inspirations Studio in Toronto, Ontario. Her work involves art making as a social practice, using creative materials to invoke a sensory language that unites diverse ways of being, knowing, and understanding the world. The arts—wonderfully disobedient and generative by nature—are integral to Lindsay's research methods and pedagogy. A desire to explore the ways that creativity can encourage otherwise unfamiliar imaginings and understandings informed her research in critical disability studies while completing an MEd in Adult Education and Community Development at OISE.

Josh Guberman is an autistic, multiply-disabled National Science Foundation Graduate Research Fellow and PhD student at the University of Michigan School of Information. Through his research and advocacy, he works to dismantle sources of systemic ableism within higher education that bar disabled participation. Broadly, his research draws on and translates insights from critical disability studies, feminist science and technology studies, and lived experience to interrogate forms of pervasive ableism within academia and, in particular, within human-computer interaction (a multidisciplinary field focused on the design and human usage of computer technologies). Adjacent to his research, Josh works to address disability-related issues at the University of Michigan through his involvement with and/or leadership of various disability-related boards, committees, and initiatives.

Dr. Nancy Hansen, PhD, is a professor and director of the Interdisciplinary Master's Program in Disability Studies at the University of Manitoba. Nancy obtained a PhD in Human Geography from the University of Glasgow, and her research interests in disability studies are varied, including disability in spaces of culture education, literacy social policy, employment health care access, and experiences of disabled and LGBTQ communities in post-conflict areas. She is co-editor of the *Routledge History of Disability* (2018) and *Untold Stories: A Canadian Disability History Reader* (2018). In addition, Nancy has written numerous book chapters and contributed to various international academic journals.

Dr. Devon Healey is an assistant professor of Disability Studies at OISE at the University of Toronto. Her work is grounded in her experience as a blind woman guided by a desire to show how blindness specifically and disability more broadly can be understood as offering an alternate form of perception to all of us, and is thus a valuable and creative way of experiencing and knowing the world. She is the author of *Dramatizing Blindness: Disability Studies as Critical Creative Narrative* (2021). Devon is an award-winning actor and the co-founder of Peripheral Theatre. In 2020 she was awarded a commission by Outside the March (a Dora award-winning Toronto theatre company) to both write and perform in *Rainbow on Mars*, a sensory reclamation of blindness. Her work has been published in *The Metanarratives of Disability: Culture and the Normative Social Order* (Bolt, 2021), the *Canadian Journal of Disability Studies*, and the *Journal of Literary and Cultural Disability Studies*.

Hanna Herdegen is a PhD student in the Department of Science, Technology, and Society at Virginia Tech. She holds an MS from Georgia Tech in the History and Sociology of Science and Technology and an MS from Virginia Tech in Science, Technology, and Society. Her academic interests have recently led her in the direction of disability studies, a field that has broadened her scholarship and influenced the development of her PhD work. Her current research looks at diagnostic technology, disability storytelling, and the persistence of vision in the making of medical ontologies.

Sammy Jo Johnson is a Child of deaf adults (Coda) currently in the Critical Disability Studies PhD program at York University. She has a Master's degree from the same program and a Bachelor's degree in Women's and Gender Studies from the University of Alberta. Her research interests include and are influenced by deaf studies, disability studies, and critical animal studies.

Dr. Chelsea Temple Jones is an assistant professor in the Department of Child and Youth Studies at Brock University in St. Catharines. Jones completed her PhD in Communication and Culture (Ryerson/York universities) in 2016 with a research focus on intellectual disability and non-normative writing. In 2018 she was the Mitacs Postdoctoral Fellow at the University of Regina, and later she was a research associate at Re•Vision: Centre for Art and Social Justice at the University of Guelph. Her writings on disability and methodology appear in *Disability Studies Quarterly*, *Journalism & Mass Communication Educator*, and *Canadian Journal of Disability Studies*, among other publications.

Dr. Maria Karmiris currently teaches in elementary schools for the Toronto District School Board. She is also a part-time contract lecturer for X University and for OISE at the University of Toronto in their Master of Teaching Program. Her research interests include inclusion and how conceptions of normalcy shape teaching and learning processes. Her work foregrounds concepts from disability studies, post-colonial studies, decolonial studies, post-structural feminisms, and their intersections. One of her recent publications in the *Canadian Journal of Disability Studies* foregrounds concepts from disability studies and decolonial studies: "The Myth of Independence as Better: Transforming Curriculum Through Disability Studies and Decoloniality" (2020).

Dr. Satsuki Kawano is a professor of anthropology in the Department of Sociology and Anthropology in the College of Social and Applied Human Sciences at the University of Guelph. After receiving a PhD from the University of Pittsburgh, she held positions at Harvard University (senior fellow, Center for the Study of World Religions) and the University of Notre Dame (assistant professor) before joining the University of Guelph in 2004. Her research interests include learning disability, ritual, aging and death, family, childrearing, and Japan. Kawano initially turned to disability studies due to her personal experience of living with a family member with a mobility impairment and her research interest in making sense of Japan through life-history narratives. She has since received grants and fellowships from the Japan Foundation, the Japan Society for the Promotion of Science, the Social Science Research Council of the United States, and the Social Sciences and Humanities Research Council of Canada (SSHRC). Kawano's major publications include *Ritual Practice in Modern Japan* (2005), *Nature's Embrace: Japan's Aging Urbanites and New Death Rites* (2010), and *Capturing Contemporary Japan* (with Glenda S. Roberts and Susan Orpett Long, 2014).

Lynn Manning (1955–2015) was a Blind poet, athlete, and Watts theater group founder. In his plays, Lynn Manning often riffed on the themes of discrimination and violence. After a stranger blinded him with a gunshot to the face at a Hollywood bar, Lynn Manning wrote funny, angry, poignant poems and read them at poetry slams. To grapple with stage fright, he studied acting. To find his voice on a tangle of profound issues that were wrapped up in having a disability and being an African American, he wrote acclaimed one-act plays and co-founded a theatre company in Watts (Los Angeles). Manning's best-known piece is the autobiographical "Weights," which traces his life from a tortured childhood up to the shooting. In addition to his Los Angeles performances, Manning played himself in productions off-Broadway as well as in Edinburgh; Adelaide, Australia; and Hart House at the University of Toronto. Manning also appeared in commercials and had small roles on several TV shows, including *Seinfeld*, and attended a White House celebration on the 25th anniversary of the Americans With Disabilities Act. He died in 2015 at the age of 60. [Adapted from Chawkins, S. (2015, August 5). Lynn Manning dies at 60; blind poet, athlete, Watts theater group founder. *Los Angeles Times.* https://www.latimes.com/local/obituaries/la-me-lynn-manning-20150806-story.html]

Dr. Rod Michalko has taught sociology and disability studies in several Canadian universities including, most recently, the University of Toronto. Since his retirement a few years ago, though he continues to publish scholarly work, his main focus has been on writing fiction, with all of his work featuring characters who are blind. He is the author of numerous articles and books, including *The Mystery of the Eye and the Shadow of Blindness* (1998), *The Two in One: Walking with Smokie, Walking with Blindness* (1999), and *The Difference that Disability Makes* (2002). He is co-editor with Tanya Titchkosky of *Rethinking Normalcy: A Disability Studies Reader* (2009). Rod's first collection of short stories, *Things Are Different Here*, was published in 2017. He has completed manuscripts for two novels and is working on a third. All of his work, scholarly and fiction, begins in his experience of blindness, revealing how blindness may be understood as framing the scenes and activities of everyday life. He lives in Toronto with his partner and colleague, Tanya Titchkosky.

Ben Pfingston is an autistic first-year PhD student in the University of Oregon's Department of Psychology. Using concepts such as anti-ableism, neurodiversity, and the social model of disability, he bridges the fields of psychology and disability studies in his research. Currently, his work focuses on autistic identity and self-acceptance, cross-neurotype theory of mind, and individual differences in social cognition, but he hopes to expand his work to include the cognitive basis of autistic masking in the future. By bringing together concepts of disability studies and psychology, Ben aims to improve acceptance of neurodiverse people in the field of psychology.

Thomas Reid is a freelance audio producer working on several projects with an emphasis on disability and social justice. He is especially interested in using stories to challenge myths and misconceptions about disability. As a voice talent and audio description narrator, Thomas has appeared on several Netflix projects, and he has served as a moderator or panelist for several discussions on audio description, diversity, adjusting to blindness, and more. Shortly after becoming blind in 2004, Thomas decided to reignite a dormant interest in audio production, after years of pairing his interest in audio with advocacy. In 2014 he was selected as a recipient of the Association of Independence in Radio New Voices scholarship. During that same year he began his podcast, *Reid My Mind Radio*, which pairs narrative storytelling with music and sound design to address various topics from a pro-disability, social model perspective. Thomas lives in the Pocono Mountains in Northeastern Pennsylvania with his wife and two daughters.

Helen Rottier is a PhD candidate in Disability Studies at the University of Illinois at Chicago. She is a graduate research assistant at the Institute on Disability and Human Development and the student coordinator of the Chicago Coalition of Autistic and Neurodivergent Students. Her research investigates academic ableism, access, student mentorship, and autistic knowledge production within and outside of academia within a disability studies framework.

Leanne Toshiko Simpson is a mixed-race Yonsei writer and educator living with bipolar disorder. Her scholarly work is grounded in disability arts and race and citizenship studies, focusing on the intergenerational impact of the Japanese Canadian internment. She holds a SSHRC Doctoral Scholarship and is currently completing an EdD in Social Justice Education at the University of Toronto. Her debut novel, *Never Been Better,* will be published in 2023 by HarperCollins.

Dr. Steve Singer lived an adult life marked by extreme poverty, acute "brain weather" (his preferred term for mental illness), and frequent hospitalizations. At age 28, he became Deaf and found a Deaf identity that reflected this facet of his existence, the Deaf community, and his new language, American Sign Language (ASL). While struggling to develop strategies to mitigate the effects of his learning disabilities and align with institutional standards, he conducted graduate work at the National Technical Institute for the Deaf in Deaf Education and earned a PhD in Cultural Foundations of Education and Disability Studies from Syracuse University. Now an assistant professor and coordinator in the Education of the Deaf and Hard of Hearing program at The College of New Jersey, his scholarship straddles deaf studies and disability studies. He negotiates his disability and Deaf identities in new ways as his relative social stratum has shifted from that of a supposed social liability to a supposed social contributor—or perhaps not.

Joey Tavares is a father, grandfather, brother, uncle, and friend to friends one and all. He enjoys his genetic diversity as much as his neurodiversity and shares these experiences with love. He is an avid adult educator, having volunteered at his alma mater, the Transitional Year Programme at the University of Toronto, for well over a decade. He is a practising intuitive empath, and he takes joy in volunteering with his Elders (who he feels take more care of him than he does them). He also enjoys reading, writing, la saveur de la lecture et de l'écriture de la poésie, la belle langue, feeding strays, and making friends with trees. He holds an HBA with a Specialist in Indigenous Studies, a Major in Sociology, and une Mineur en Français comme Langue Secondaire from the University of Toronto, as well as a Masters of Education in Adult Education and Community Development from OISE.

Sharry Taylor is a high school guidance counsellor and PhD candidate at OISE at the University of Toronto. Her doctoral work is a critical realist exploration of the use of psychiatric language and labels in secondary school environments. She seeks to understand how educators evoke "mental health" narratives in their classrooms, how these narratives are understood by young people, and how the use of psychiatric language and labels shape young people's sense of self and identity.

Dr. Tanya Titchkosky is a professor of disability studies in the Department of Social Justice Education at OISE, University of Toronto. Her disability studies teaching and writing is committed to an interpretive approach informed by phenomenologically oriented Black studies, critical Indigenous studies, queer and feminist studies, and disability studies. Her own experience with dyslexia makes the questions of words, word order, and meaning-making intense points of engagement with daily life. Tanya's partner, blind scholar and storyteller Dr. Rod Michalko—as well as her relations with other blind scholars and artists, and disabled students, faculty, and staff—has also been a vibrant source of provocation for rethinking the meaning and movement of disability in daily life. These provocative disability experiences have led to her interest in how institutions codify the meaning of disability in order to use disability categories to sustain the status quo. Her books include *The Question of Access: Disability, Space, Meaning* (2011), *Reading and Writing Disability Differently: The Textured Life of Embodiment* (2007), and *Disability, Self and Society* (2003). Her next book, *Humanities Edge: Disability Understandings*, as well as her work toward this *DisAppearing* collection, is supported by an Insight SSHRC grant. Tanya is a proud dyslexic, an award-winning teacher, and the 2014 recipient of the Tanis Doe Award for Canadian Disability Study and Culture.

Index